Navigating the Maze of Health Insurance Choices

Other books by Stephen J. Stellhorn

Brokers, Financial Advisors & Insurance Agents
An Investigative Process – the Book that **Some** *May Not Want Their Clients to Read*

Available in digital format only on Kindle, Apple and Nook platforms

Navigating the Maze of Medicare
2013 Edition and 2014 Edition
A Comprehensive Look at your Coverage Choices

Available in softcover at Amazon.com
2014 Edition also available in digital format on Kindle, Apple and Nook platforms

Coming Soon on Amazon.com

Navigating the Maze of Social Security
Claiming Strategies for Fifty Shades of Grey

Navigating the Maze of Health Insurance Choices

A Comprehensive Look at Individual & Small Business Options

STEPHEN J. STELLHORN, RMA[SM]

CALMSEASMEDIA
Tampa, Florida

Published by **CALMSEAS**MEDIA, Tampa, Florida

Cover design: Don Saunders
Photos: iStockphoto® and Photography by Robin.
Quotations: Courtesy *BrainyQuote*® unless otherwise noted.

Library of Congress Cataloging-in-Publication Data

Stellhorn, Stephen, 1954
    Navigating the Maze of Health Insurance Choices: a comprehensive look at group and individual options / Stephen Stellhorn.

        p. cm.
    Includes index.
    ISBN: 978-0-9894265-2-7
    CIP:

First Edition

Printed in the United States of America

Table of Contents

Request for Feedback

I am very respectful of your time and privacy. I will not share any information you provide without your expressed consent to do so. I also want to thank you in advance for your consideration.

I invite readers to share their feedback with me on this subject matter. What topics did I cover too much and what should I have covered more? Did I not cover a topic that should have been covered? Should I have completely deleted a topic?

*Your comments are very valuable in helping to make future editions better. I've established an email address for receiving your feedback: readercommunity@msmcapital.net. Please insert the name of the book, "**Navigating the Maze of Health Insurance Choices**" in the subject line of your email.*

Dedication

It is my honor to dedicate this book to my family; especially to my mother Mildred, my sister Sue, my niece Carolyn and most especially to my lovely wife Linda. All of whom have known cancer. All of whom have had different forms of it.

They all fought with courage and fortitude. Though some won and some lost, they remain an inspiration and constantly remind me to never take good health for granted. Circumstances of life can change, quite suddenly and unexpectedly, with dire consequences.

For those that lost, I miss them immensely but know they are in a better place. For those still here, may God bless them all with his love each day, every day; especially my daughter Marissa.

"Live your life and forget your age!"

Dr. Norman Vincent Peale
Minister, Author and Professional Speaker

Setting the Context

As the month of November 2013 nears an end, health care is a subject which has been front and center in the media and in the minds of many Americans. Two pieces of legislation which became the cornerstone of President Obama's health care reform, the *Patient Protection and Affordable Care Act* (PPACA) signed March 23, 2010 and the *Health Care and Education Reconciliation Act of 2010* which amended the PPACA, became law on March 30, 2010 and are now in various stages of enactment. This legislation, referred to as Obamacare or just the *Affordable Care Act* (ACA) are terms which will be used interchangeably throughout the book.

Elements of the ACA began being implemented in 2010. One of the critical components of the new health care laws, the creation of the health insurance exchanges or marketplaces, went live on October 1, 2013. The significant technological problems plaguing the systems are now well known in terms of consumers being able to access the online portals. The latest reports indicate it may not be until late November or December before the online portals are properly functioning. Kathleen Sebelius, Secretary of the Department of Health and Human Resources (HHS), and Marilyn Tavenner, Administrator of the Centers for Medicare and Medicaid Services (CMS), an agency within HHS, are now on the hot seat with Congress as are others. Calls to push back deadlines and even alter the health care laws are growing within the ranks of Congress. The desire to meet the October 1st deadline appears to have been more important than whether or not all the software components were integrated properly and tested. It appears HHS opted to act as their own "general contractor" for the project and may have been way in over their heads. A strategic course of action of ready-shoot-aim seems like it was now pursued.

There is a lot of misinformation and misunderstanding about the ACA by the general public. Depending on whose shoes you walk in, there are some very good inclusions regarding preventative health care and access to health care by some who truly need it. On the other hand, are the costs really affordable and who funds these programs long-term remains a hotly debated topic among the state's various elected officials.

Current events are compounding the confusion when trying to understand health insurance and what might be your best options. This can be a daunting process for many individuals and families. What type of coverage should I get? Can I afford that coverage? What if I can't afford health insurance? What public assistance programs are there? The list of questions can go on and on. Figuring out your health insurance options and what's most cost effective can be a frustrating and time consuming experience for many.

If you're covered by an employer-sponsored health plan, October is when you should have received your benefits package for the upcoming plan year. Each fall there is an Open Enrollment Period, when you get the opportunity to make changes to your health care benefits for the coming year. How many actually take the time to look back at what they spent on health care during the year to determine whether or not the plan they have will still be the best plan for them in the coming year?

This book provides you with a solid understanding of the options available to you for your personal health insurance; whether your need for coverage is for an individual, small business group or you just want to understand your corporate health benefits better. Included in the book are the following topics which will be covered:

- The Affordable Care Act (ACA)
- Health Insurance Marketplace
- Marketplace for Individuals & Families
- Small Business Health Options Program (SHOP)
- Medical and Dental Insurance
- Flexible Spending Accounts (FSA)
- Healthcare Savings Accounts (HSA)
- Health Insurance Continuation - COBRA
- HIPPA
- Medical Insurance Bureau (MIB)
- Disability Income (DI) Insurance
- Long-Term Care (LTC)
- Original Medicare Part A & Part B
- Medicare Advantage Part C Plans
- Medicare Supplement/Medigap Plans
- Medicare Prescription Drug Part D Plans
- Medicaid
- Concierge Medicine

Where you fall on the age continuum of life is also very significant. If your single and starting out you're probably thrill to be covered under your employers' group health insurance plan, even if you hardly get sick (you just never know). If you're married and have children you already know about what happens during the winter months and the visits to the pediatrician and all those copays. If you're a budding entrepreneur and have started your own company and your spouse isn't employed, you know the challenges of getting reasonable cost effective health insurance for you and your family. If you're getting ready to retire, health care takes on an entirely new perspective. Are you an employee or self-employed? What health insurance options do you have and what is available to you when you finally retire from an employer-sponsored health plan.

Like investment choices, health insurance also has numerous choices available. What your coverage needs are, your marital status, number of dependents, your age and your income level will probably be the key drivers in your decision making. Up through your 40s you're probably most concerned with having medical/dental insurance, possibly disability income coverage and maybe some life insurance. As you get into your late 50s you might start thinking about long-term care and then when you get to 64 you begin investigating your Medicare options for the coming year as you turn that youthful age 65.

Health care is not a topic most individual want to discuss. It makes them contemplate their own mortality; a scary subject for most people. Nobody wants to think about the possibility of their own incapacitation due to an unforeseen accident or medical event and all the expenses that go with it. I get it! If you're 35 or 45 and reading this book, how much of your monthly thought process goes to thinking about what your health care needs will be 20-30 years from now or what the costs might be? Your answer is probably very little to none at all at this stage in your life. You have more pressing issues which consume your time and thought. Even in their mid-fifties, I have a hard time getting clients to have a conversation on this topic. The fear is more health care coverage means more expenses they will have to deal with; possibly for something they may or may not ever need.

Health care premiums are an expense and in the current economic environment individuals, couples, as well as small business owners are trying to keep a tight control over their monthly expenses. With millions of jobs lost since the Great Financial Crisis, more individuals are deciding to go the entrepreneur route and are starting small businesses as a means to re-establish their income source. What this means is they are now responsible for paying their entire benefits package, whatever they want it to be, *themselves*. Many times health care is one item that is passed on, in the short run, simply because of its cost. I also run my own small business so I understand all the challenges you face each and every day as an entrepreneur.

Usually a major medical event occurs before someone starts the conversation or begins investigating what their best options may be. At that point, one of three things usually happens; (1) they can't get health care coverage because they no longer qualify. They are now uninsurable, (2) what they really need it for is now classified as a pre-existing condition that won't be covered immediately or (3) it has become so expensive they can't afford to get it any longer. Beginning January 1, 2014, many of these worries disappear as no one can be denied health insurance coverage for their current health status or pre-existing conditions. Addressing these issues is a significant piece of the ACA legislation. However, this does not apply to disability income, long-term care or life insurance.

Advances in biomedical science, an integrated process of employing the principles of biology, biochemistry, physiology and other basic sciences along with engineering principles are solving problems in clinical medicine which clearly have helped in extending our life spans. Through biomedical engineering, advances in the design and functionality of artificial limbs have greatly improved quality of life issues for those in need of limb replacement. Look no further than to Oscar Pistorius, the 2012 Olympic runner from South Africa who is a double amputee and was 25 years old at the time. Pistorius was born without fibulas and both his legs were amputated below the knees before he was a year old. His nickname is "The Blade." Who would have thought someone with these physical limitations could compete at the Olympic level. It is truly an amazing and inspirational story for those who watched him compete during the London Olympics despite the tragic events which surrounded the death of his girlfriend in 2013, circumstances, which have now implicated him in the murder investigation as a suspect.

These advances are now starting to extend to organ replacement. What's beginning to happen is just amazing compared to what existed in this field just ten years ago. Americans will most likely continue to have the capacity to live longer than their forbearers. Today in fact, healthy 65-year-olds have at least a 40% chance of living into their 90s. That's the good news. However, the bad news is, many will likely live their lives with some sort of chronic illness such as obesity, some form of cardiovascular disease or neurological degenerative process, skeletal issues involving orthopedics or Type-2 diabetes, which will require ongoing medical care. Expanding longevity plus chronic illness will place many at risk of outliving their savings as they age.

By the time you get to your early 50s you should, at a minimum, begin exploring what options you have and developing an understanding of what you might need, its cost and how health care fits into your overall financial plan for successful and enjoyable longevity. You can have all the wealth in the world but if you don't have your health, your quality of life can be an agonizing ordeal to live with each day, every day.

Most individuals have no idea as to the changes which are coming to health care, what it costs, who provides it and how they access it. If steps aren't taken soon to control both the escalating costs of funding government entitlement programs and the premiums worker's pay for health insurance, this country may well face a health care crisis as it enters the third decade of the 21st century. The cost of health care has the potential to torpedo many future retirement plans, if individuals don't do some thoughtful planning ahead of time to ensure they are adequately protected against the rising risks to their health as they age. Life is good.

Cheers! Here's to a healthy and full-filled life!

Stephen

Stephen J. Stellhorn
December 2013
Tampa, Florida

CHAPTER ONE

THE CHANGING FACE OF HEALTH CARE
IN THE UNITED STATES

The entire spectrum of health care issues which face us today and in the near future cannot be thoroughly covered in just one chapter. The complexities are too great and diverse. It bears repeating again, if steps aren't taken soon to control both the escalating costs of funding government entitlement programs and health care premiums worker's pay, this country may face a health care crisis as we enter the third decade of the 21st century. Health care costs do have the potential to torpedo many future retirement plans if individuals don't engage in some thoughtful planning, in advance, to ensure they are adequately protected against the risks that will rise as they age and their health changes, which for some could be rapid and unforeseen. Those who have a family medical history of cardiovascular issues and/or more importantly, neurological or cognitive impairment should definite do planning in advance.

The concept of national health insurance began in the early 20th century in the United States and came to prominence during the Harry Truman administration. From Wikipedia, is a summary of key health care reform legislative achievements which have been implemented at the national level in the United States.

- **1965** - The *Social Security Amendments of 1965* was legislation whose most important provisions resulted in creation of two programs: Medicare and Medicaid. The signing of the act, as part of President Lyndon Johnson's Great Society, began an era with a greater emphasis on public health issues. The bill was introduced in Congress in March 1965 and President Johnson signed the bill into law on July 30, 1965. Medicare was designed to cover both hospital and general medical insurance for senior citizens, paid for by a Federal employment tax over the working life of the retiree. Medicaid permitted the Federal government to partially fund a program for the poor, with the program managed and co-financed by the individual states. This legislation was vigorously opposed by the American Medical Association (AMA) until it had been enacted, following which the AMA cooperated in its implementation.

- **1985** - The *Consolidated Omnibus Budget Reconciliation Act of 1985* (COBRA) amended the *Employee Retirement Income Security Act of 1974* (ERISA) to give some employees the ability to continue health insurance coverage after leaving employment. COBRA was a law passed by the Congress, on a reconciliation basis, and signed by President Ronald Reagan. The statute became law on April 7, 1986.

- **1996** - The *Health Insurance Portability and Accountability Act* (HIPAA) not only protects health insurance coverage for workers and their families when they change or lose their jobs, it also made health insurance companies cover pre-existing conditions. If such condition had been diagnosed before purchasing insurance, insurance companies were required to cover it after patient had one year of continuous coverage. If the condition was already covered on their current policy, any new insurance policies due to changing jobs, etc. would have to cover the condition immediately. HIPPA was enacted by Congress and signed by President Bill Clinton in 1996. It has been known as the *Kennedy-Kassebaum Act* after two of its leading sponsors.

- **1997** - The State Children's Health Insurance Program, or SCHIP, was established by the federal government in 1997 to provide health insurance to children in families at or below 200 percent of the federal poverty line. Now known more simply as the Children's Health Insurance Program (CHIP), it is a program administered by the U.S. Department of Health and Human Services (HHS) that provides matching funds to states for health insurance to families with children. The program was designed to cover uninsured children in families with incomes that are modest but too high to qualify for Medicaid. It was sponsored by Senator Edward Kennedy in a partnership with Senator Orrin Hatch with support coming from First Lady Hillary Rodham Clinton during the Clinton administration.

- **2003** - The *Medicare Prescription Drug, Improvement, and Modernization Act*, also called the Medicare Modernization Act (MMA) is a federal law enacted in 2003. It produced the largest overhaul of Medicare in the public health program's 38-year history. The MMA was signed by President George W. Bush on December 8, 2003, after passing in Congress by a close margin. Initially, the net cost of the program was projected at $400 billion for the

3

ten-year period between 2004 and 2013. As of February 2009, the projected net cost of the program over the 2006 to 2015 period was $549.2 billion.

- **2009** - *The Health Information Technology for Economic and Clinical Health Act*, abbreviated HITECH Act, was enacted under Title XIII of the American Recovery and Reinvestment Act of 2009. Under the HITECH Act, the U.S. Department of Health and Human Services is spending $25.9 billion to promote and expand the adoption of health information technology. The HITECH Act set meaningful use of interoperable electronic health records (HER) adoption in the health care system as a critical national goal and incentivized EHR adoption. The Act also requires HIPAA covered entities to report data breaches affecting 500 or more individuals to Health and Human Services (HHS) and the media, in addition to notifying the affected individuals.

- **2010** - Landmark reform was passed through two federal statutes enacted in 2010: the *Patient Protection and Affordable Care Act* (PPACA), signed March 23, 2010 and the *Health Care and Education Reconciliation Act of 2010*, which amended the PPACA. President Barack Obama signed both pieces of legislation which became law on March 30, 2010. *The Patient Protection and Affordable Care Act*, also known as the *Affordable Care Act* (ACA) and Obamacare, provides for the introduction over four years of a comprehensive system of mandated health insurance with reforms designed to eliminate what is perceived as some of the worst practices of health insurance companies — pre-condition screening, premium loadings, policies which rescind on technicalities when illness seems imminent and annual and lifetime coverage caps. It also sets a minimum ratio of direct health care spending to premium income and creates price competition bolstered by the creation of three standard insurance coverage levels to enable like-for-like comparisons by consumers and a web-based health insurance exchange where consumers can compare prices and purchase plans. The system preserves private insurance and private health care providers and provides more subsidies to enable the poor to buy insurance.

These legislative acts have changed the face of health care in this country for many individuals for the better. Though at the time they were being debated in Congress, it may not have seemed that way. With these legislative changes which have been implemented through the years and the innovative improvements occurring in health care products and medical services; where does that leaves us as we move further into the second decade of the 21st century?

According to the U.S. Census Bureau, in 2010 there were 49.9 million uninsured individuals in the United States; representing 16.3% of the population. In 2011, this figure dropped marginally to 48.6 million. Back in 1999, there were 37.7 million individuals uninsured, representing 13.6% of the population. The U.S. Census report found that state rates of uninsured residents under age 65 ranged from 4.9% in Massachusetts to 25.7% in Texas. More than one in four Texans under the age of 65 lacks health insurance, more than any other state in the nation. Florida is next then followed by Nevada, New Mexico and Oklahoma. In Figure 1.1, on the next page, the graph displays the percent uninsured under the age of 65 by state. The report also showed that uninsured rates from 2010 to 2011:

- Remained constant in 29 states and the District of Columbia.
- Decreased in 19 states.
- Increased in two states.

5

Figure 1.1 Percent Uninsured, Under Age 65, by State, 2011

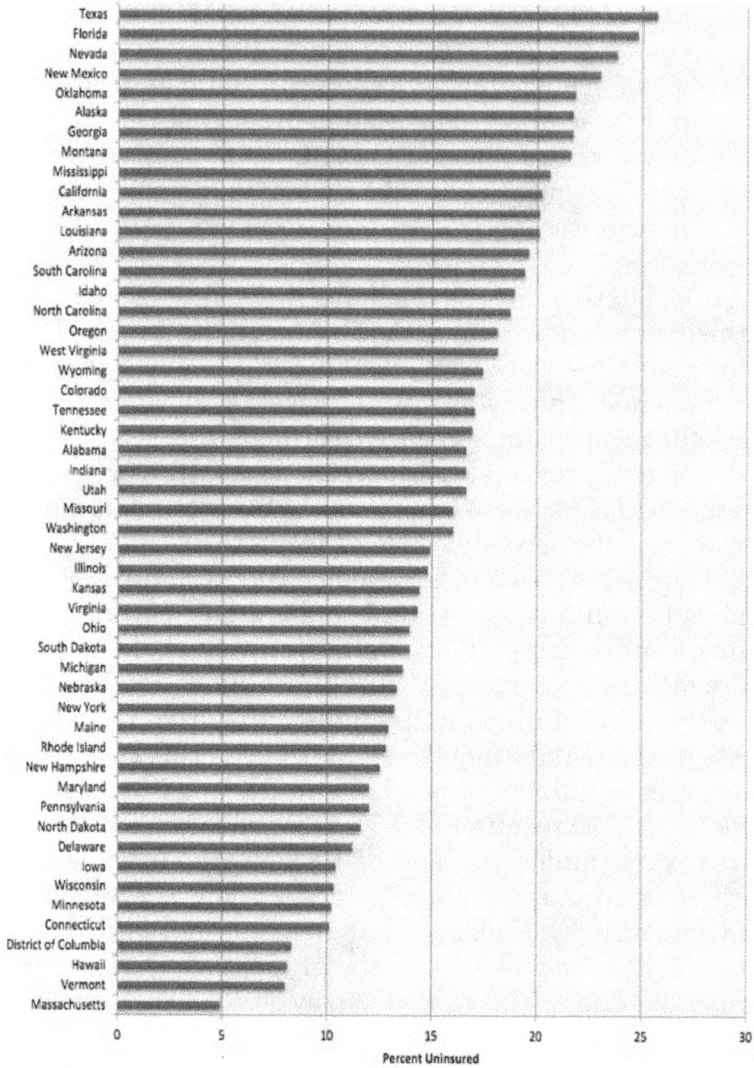

Notes: The percentages shown are estimates containing uncertainty. Apparent differences may not be statistically significant.
Source: U.S. Census Bureau, 2011 Small Area Health Insurance Estimates, August 2013

Source: U. S. Census Bureau

In the table below the uninsured are illustrated by age brackets based on the percentage of the population.

Table 1.1 Percentage of Uninsured - By Age Bracket

Age Brackets	2011	1999	% Change
Under 18 Years	9.4%	12.0%	-19.4%
18 to 24 Years	25.4%	26.1%	+11.3%
25 to 34 Years	28.0%	21.1%	+40.2%
35 to 44 Years	21.0%	14.8%	+27.8%
45 to 54 Years	17.9%	11.3%	+85.6%
55 to 64 Years	14.6%	11.7%	+97.2%
65 Years and Older	1.7%	1.1%	+91.7%

Source: U.S. Census Bureau

From the years 1999 to 2011, the number of uninsured individuals in this country grew by nearly 29%. Individuals age 25 to 34, total 11.5 million who are uninsured. The Census Bureau reports that in 2010, persons covered by private health insurance decreased to 64%. This was not a dramatic decrease from those being covered by private insurance companies in 2009, at 195.9 million. Private health coverage has continued to decline since 2001. For those covered by private health insurance, both as employment based and direct purchase, 63.9% of individuals receive their health coverage in this fashion. This is down from 73% in 1999.

Individuals who desire health insurance can obtain their coverage in two ways, as private health insurance or through a federal assistance program with a governmental agency. Beginning in January 2014, private health insurance will now be able to be obtained by individuals in the following ways.

- Health insurance inside the Marketplace.
- Health insurance outside the Marketplace.
- Job-based Insurance.
- Insurance for dependents under a parent's policy up to age 26.

We'll cover these options in more detail in subsequent chapters. Those eligible for public programs can obtain health insurance in the following ways.

- Medicare
- Medicaid
- Children's Health Insurance Program (CHIP)
- TRICARE
- Veterans Affairs (VA) health benefits

TRICARE is the Department of Defense health care program available to eligible members and their families of the seven uniformed services. This includes the U.S. Army, U.S. Navy, U.S. Air Force, U.S. Marines, U.S. Coast Guard, Commissioned Corps of the U.S. Public Health Service and the National Oceanic and Atmospheric Administration. The Department of Veterans Affairs administers a variety of benefits and services which provide financial and other forms of assistance to service members, veterans, their dependents and survivors. As part of these benefits and services, the VA provides health coverage for eligible veterans who served in the U.S. military.

In 2009, government programs covered 31.0% or 95.0 million. During 2010 individuals insured through government programs totaled 93.2 million, covering 30.6% of the population. By 2011, those receiving their health coverage through the government, including Medicaid, Medicare and military health care, totaled 32.2% of the population. This is up from 24.2% in 1999. When the three groups are looked at individually the numbers are quite startling. In 1999 there were 27.3 million individuals covered by Medicaid. By 2011, just twelve years later, this number had exploded to 50.8 million individuals, a nearly 86% increase. Those covered by Medicare totaled 37 million in 1999. By 2011 this group had increased by nearly 27% to 46.9 million individuals.

The start of the Great Financial Recession of 2008-2009 saw a significant jump in the number of uninsured individuals. From 2008 to 2009 the number of uninsured swelled by over 5 million. Since that jump, there has been some stabilization in the numbers. Beginning with 2014 and the next phase of the *Affordable Care Act*, the numbers of uninsured should see a trendline change with the numbers beginning to decline over the next few years. With the ACA implementation, a greater number will be getting their health coverage through the government as we should see the number on Medicaid swell quickly while the aging baby boomers will begin their ascent into Medicare. Unfortunately many consumers and small business still struggle to afford health insurance premiums.

In April 2013, the Washington National Institute for Wellness Solutions (IWS), a subsidiary of CNO Financial Group released a report, *Middle-Income America's Perspective on Critical Illness and Financial Security*. It is based on a survey of 1,001 Americans, between the ages of 30 to 66 with annual household incomes of $35,000 to $99,999. Only 10% of respondents indicated they have enough money saved to cover family emergencies and health care costs not covered by health insurance. The survey revealed 75% have less than $20,000 in savings; 50% have less than $2,000 and 25% have no savings. A significant number of Americans believe they would never get over the financial implications of a serious illness. In the survey 38% believe they would never recover from a battle with cancer and 45% believe they would never recover financially from a diagnosis of dementia or Alzheimer's disease.

"I think that age as a number is not nearly as important as health. You can be in poor health and be pretty miserable at 40 or 50. If you're in good health, you can enjoy things into your 80s."

Bob Barker – Age 90
Former Television Game Show Host
The Price is Right – 1972-2007
Truth or Consequences – 1956-1975

CHAPTER TWO

COST OF HEALTH CARE

According to the Centers for Medicare and Medicaid Services (CMS), in their National Health Expenditures Projections 2011-2021 report, total health care spending in the U.S. is expected to reach $4.8 trillion in 2021. This is up from $2.6 trillion in 2010 and $75 billion in 1970. From the Bureau of Labor Statistics, medical costs have risen, on average, 5.7% per year for the past twenty years. This is double the rate of inflation as measured by the CPI.

How does health care spending and life expectancy rates in the United States compare with those of other developed countries? The facts are not what you might expect. In 2009, health care spending per person was far higher in the United States than any other industrialized country, at nearly $8,000 per person. This probably isn't a surprise to most of you. Switzerland was second at roughly $5,000 per person while New Zealand was the lowest at just under $3,000 per person. Figure 1.1, on the next page, illustrates a number of industrialized countries and their health care expense per person along with their estimated life expectancy rates for 2009.

Figure 1.1 Health Care Spending Per Person and Life Expectancy Rates in Years

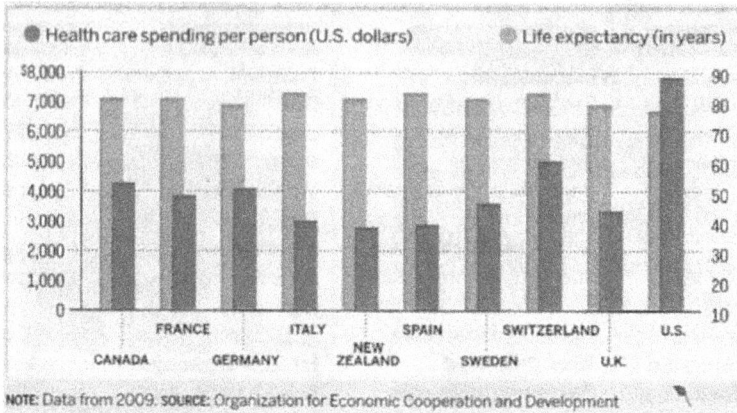

Courtesy: *MONEY magazine, October 2011*
Source: *OECD*

What you might not expect from the chart above is Americans aren't necessarily healthier as evidenced by our life expectancy rate which is the lowest.

As measured by GDP, the overall costs for health care have been expanding at a rate of two percentage points faster than the economy. This problem will only get worse in the coming decade as aging baby boomers flood the Medicare system and longer life spans add more years of medical care. Americans age 65, in 2012, have an average life expectancy of 18 additional years.

Under the current law most Americans collect far more from the Medicare system than they pay in. According to calculations by the Urban Institute, a married couple who retired in 2011 can expect to receive $350,000 in lifetime benefits. To receive this benefit they only paid in about $150,000 in Medicare taxes. A couple who are 46 today can expect to receive $525,000 in benefits when they retire at 65. Their cost in Medicare taxes; just over $200,000. This example assumes a two-earner couple; one with $69,600 income and the other with $43,500 in income during 2011.

In 1880 there were only 1.7 million individuals 65 and older. Even by 1940; 60 years later, there were still less than 10 million individuals 65 and older.

Figure 1.2 U.S. Population By Age 65+ - 1900-2050

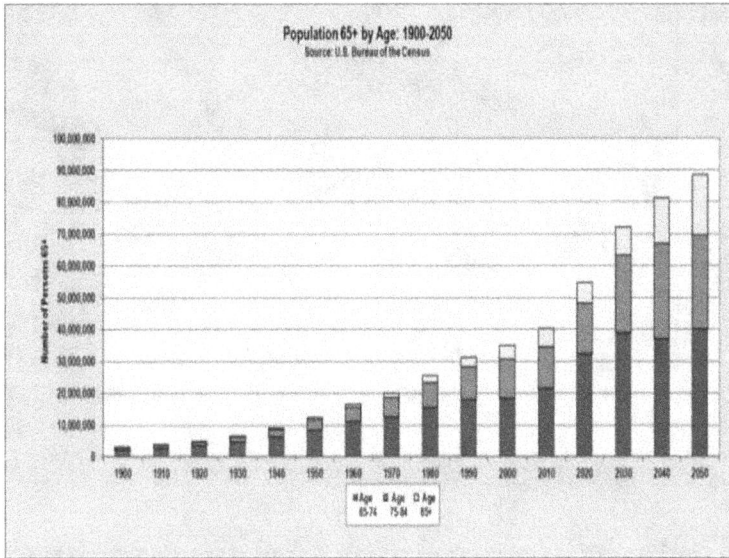

Courtesy: U.S. Administration on Aging
Source: U.S. Census Bureau

However by 1970, just 30 years later, the figured had double and by 2010 the figure had doubled again to just over 40 million. Between 2000 and 2010, the population age 65 and over, increased at a faster rate (15.1%) than the total U.S. population (9.7%). According to the U.S. Administration on Aging, by 2050 there will be an estimated 88.5 million individuals 65 and older as illustrated in Figure 1.2 above.

Figure 1.3, on the next page, the future percentage makeup of GDP is illustrated. The large area at the bottom of the graph labeled "Everything Else" includes Social Security.

Figure 1.3 Estimation of Future Percentage Makeup of GDP: 2011-2051

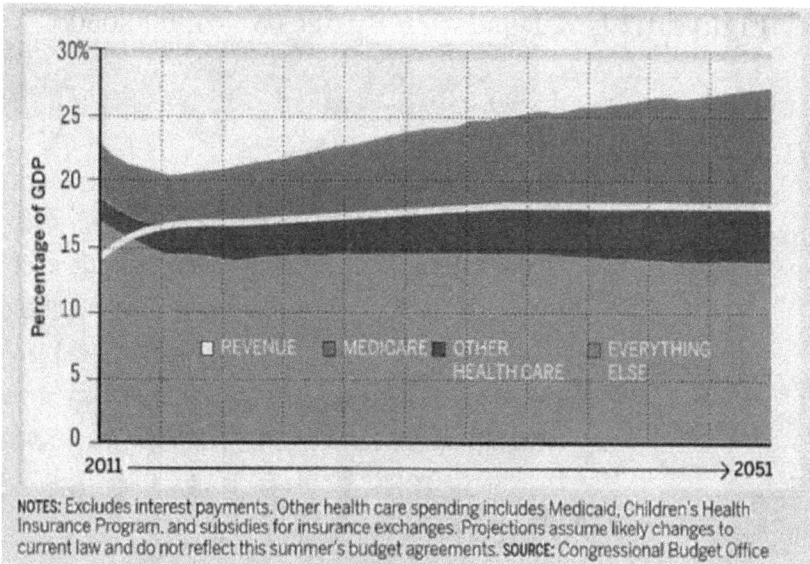

NOTES: Excludes interest payments. Other health care spending includes Medicaid, Children's Health Insurance Program, and subsidies for insurance exchanges. Projections assume likely changes to current law and do not reflect this summer's budget agreements. SOURCE: Congressional Budget Office

Courtesy: MONEY magazine, October 2011
Source: Congressional Budget Office (CBO)

While Social Security is an important issue, it pales in comparison to the rising costs for entitlements for Medicare. By 2030, maintaining benefits at current levels would push government spending to 24% of the economy; with even higher percentages as the years go on. Taxes on the other hand, are expected to generate revenues equal to only 18% of the economy. Clearly this is an unsustainable glide path in the long run.

There is a great deal of dissension in Washington on a variety of issues other than health care, both parties agree that controlling Medicare costs is critical to controlling the growing budget gap and future fiscal deficits. Even with reforms, fixing Medicare will be tough. In the end there will need to be some combination of premium/tax increases, increases in copays and coinsurance, higher deductibles, cap limits and possible changes in the eligibility age to receive these benefits. The bottom line; expect and plan for higher costs and less benefits.

Even when health insurance offered by employer-sponsored plans is examined, the trends are not good. Since 1999, inflation and workers' earnings have risen by cumulative percentages of 40% and 50%, respectively. During the same period, cumulative percentage increases for health insurance premiums and worker' contributions to premiums have seen a three-fold increase since 1999. Figure 1.4 below, plots the *cumulative* increases in health insurance premiums, workers' contributions to premiums, inflation and workers' earnings over a fourteen year period.

Figure 1.4 Cumulative Increases in Health Insurance Premiums, 2013

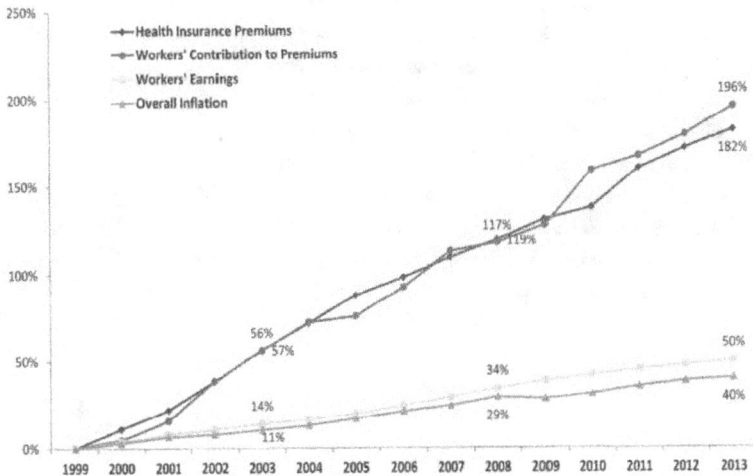

SOURCE: Kaiser/HRET Survey of Employer-Sponsored Health Benefits, 1999-2013. Bureau of Labor Statistics, Consumer Price Index, U.S. City Average of Annual Inflation (April to April), 1999-2013; Bureau of Labor Statistics, Seasonally Adjusted Data from the Current Employment Statistics Survey, 1999-2013 (April to April).

Courtesy: The Kaiser Foundation; 2013 Employer Health Benefit Survey

When we examine average annual health care premiums for single and family coverage over the same time horizon we see an equally disturbing picture in cost trends. These are the total of both the employee and employer contribution.

As illustrated in Figure 1.5 in the graph below, in 1999 the average premium for single and family health insurance coverage was $2,196 and $5,791, respectively. Fourteen years later, in 2013, these average annual premiums for single and family coverage had risen to $5,884 and $16,351 per year, respectively.

Figure 1.5 Average Annual Health Insurance Premiums for Single and Family, 2013

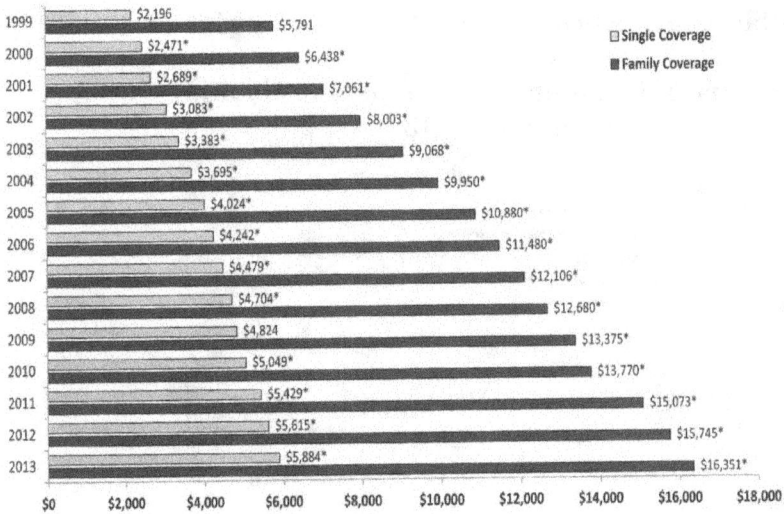

* Estimate is statistically different from estimate for the previous year shown (p<.05).

SOURCE: Kaiser/HRET Survey of Employer-Sponsored Health Benefits, 1999-2013.

Courtesy: The Kaiser Foundation; 2013 Employer Health Benefit Survey

Where does all the money go? Figure 1.6, on the following page, graphically displays health care spending for 2010.

Figure 1.6 U.S. Health Care Spending Breakdown, 2010

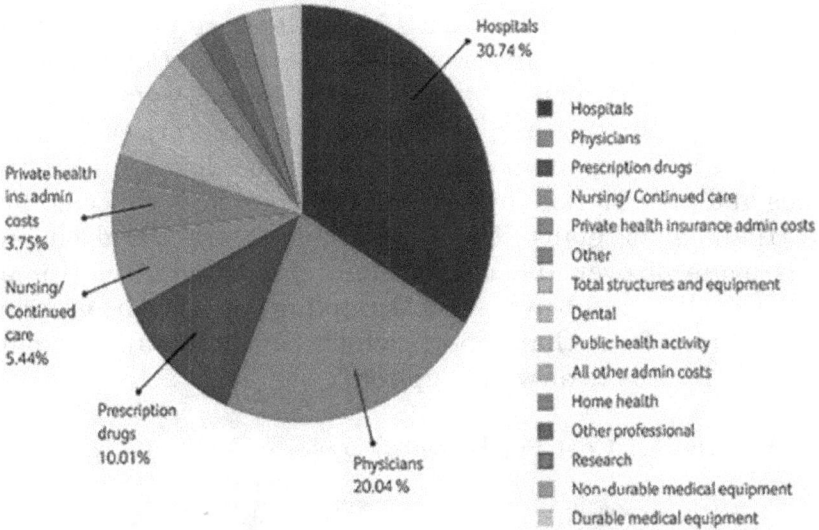

Source: Centers for Medicare and Medicaid Services (CMS)

From the pie-chart above, the top three spending categories were hospitals at nearly 31%, followed by physicians at 20% and prescription drugs at 10%. These three categories account for 61% of all health care spending in 2010.

Recently at the 2014 World Economic Forum in Davos, Switzerland, the CEO of Aetna, Mark Bertolini characterization that "medical expenses remain out of control in the U.S., where Americans have an unsustainable attitude that ignores the increasing cost of health care." The health care system needs to shift to a system which pays for the quality of care rather than the quantity.

The *International Federation of Health Plans (iFHP)* was founded in 1968 by a group of health insurance industry leaders and is now the leading global network for the industry. The federation is based in London, England. Through its diverse membership of over one hundred health insurers, in twenty-five countries, the iFHP is in a unique position to observe cost trends in health care products and services. They recently released their *2012 Comparative Price Report*, which is their fourth annual survey. This report contains 28 graphs which display the prices for the cost of specific hospital costs, medical procedures, physician fees and prescription drugs, compiled from data collected by iFHP member plans. The U.S. numbers are based on an aggregate of over 100 million paid claims across multiple payers. What follows is a sampling of eleven graphs reproduced from that report, which can be obtained from the iFHP website at www.ifhp.com.

Figure 1.7 Cost Per Hospital <u>Day</u>

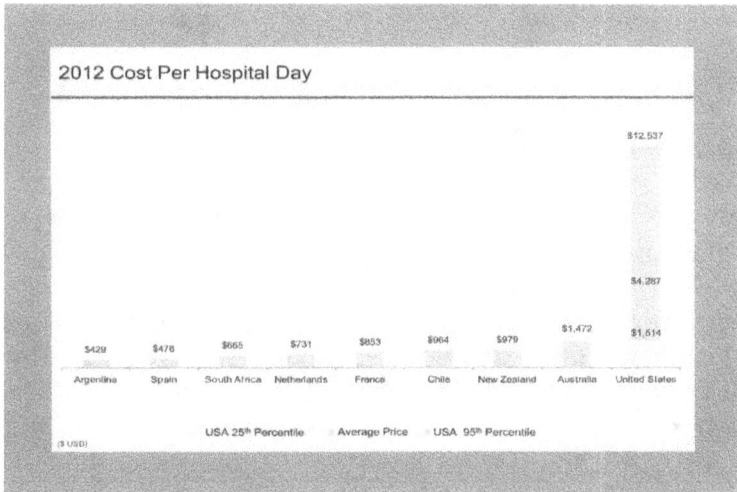

Courtesy: The International Federation of Health Plans;
2012 Comparative Price Report

Figure 1.8 Angiogram Imaging Cost

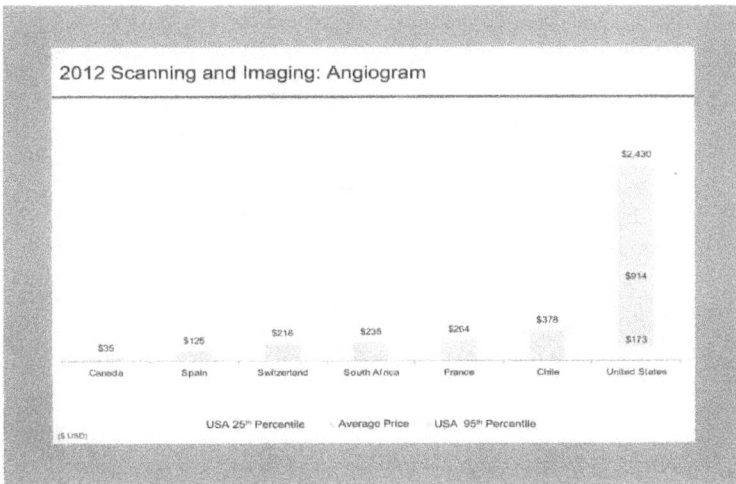

2012 Scanning and Imaging: Angiogram

						$2,430	
						$914	
				$378			
$35	$125	$216	$238	$264		$173	
Canada	Spain	Switzerland	South Africa	France	Chile	United States	

USA 25th Percentile   Average Price   USA 95th Percentile

($ USD)

Courtesy: The International Federation of Health Plans;
2012 Comparative Price Report

Figure 1.9 Routine Office Visit Cost

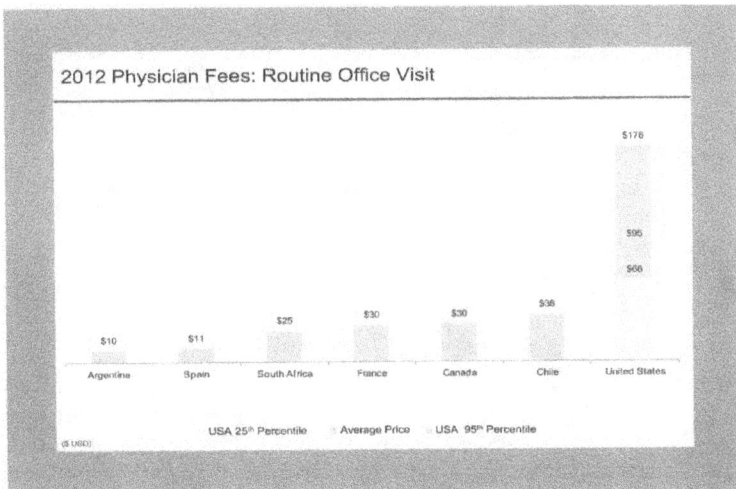

2012 Physician Fees: Routine Office Visit

						$178	
						$95	
						$68	
					$38		
		$25	$30	$30			
$10	$11						
Argentina	Spain	South Africa	France	Canada	Chile	United States	

USA 25th Percentile   Average Price   USA 95th Percentile

($ USD)

Courtesy: The International Federation of Health Plans;
2012 Comparative Price Report

Figure 1.10 Coronary Artery Bypass Cost

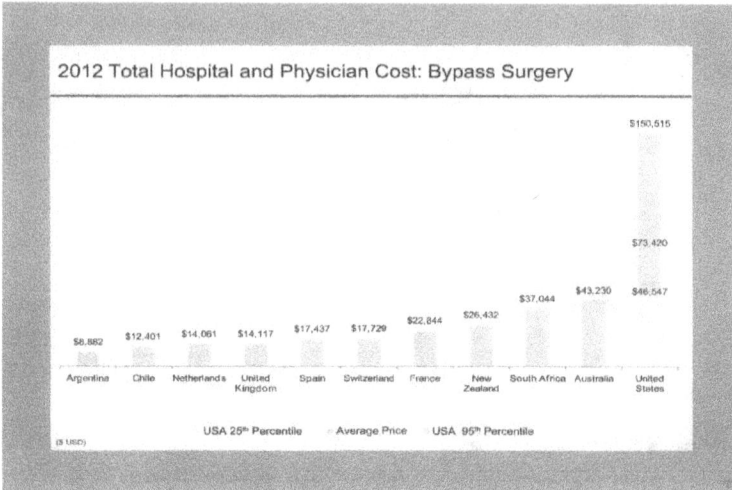

Courtesy: The International Federation of Health Plans;
2012 Comparative Price Report

Figure 1.11 MRI Imaging Cost

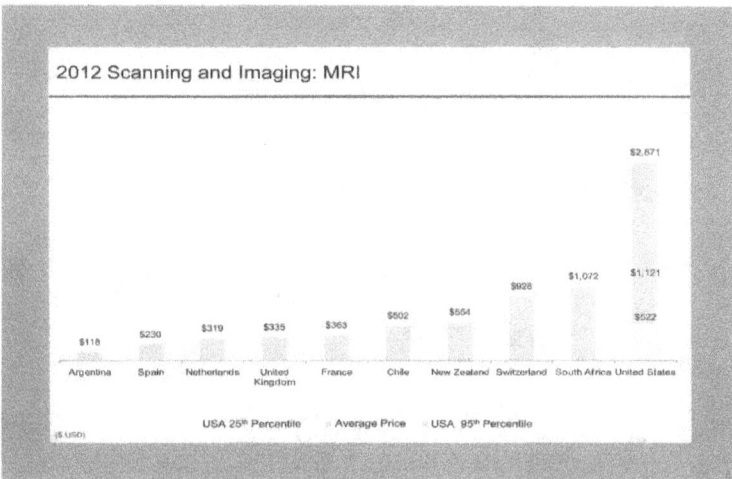

Courtesy: The International Federation of Health Plans;
2012 Comparative Price Report

Figure 1.12 Hip Replacement Cost

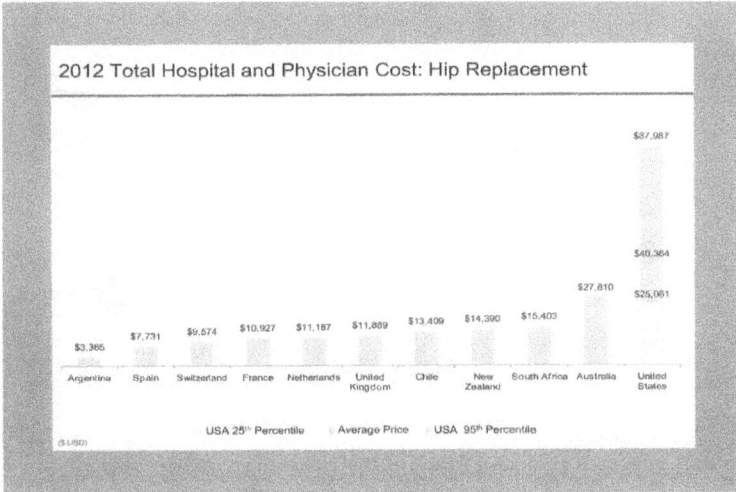

Courtesy: The International Federation of Health Plans;
2012 Comparative Price Report

Figure 1.13 Cataract Surgery Cost

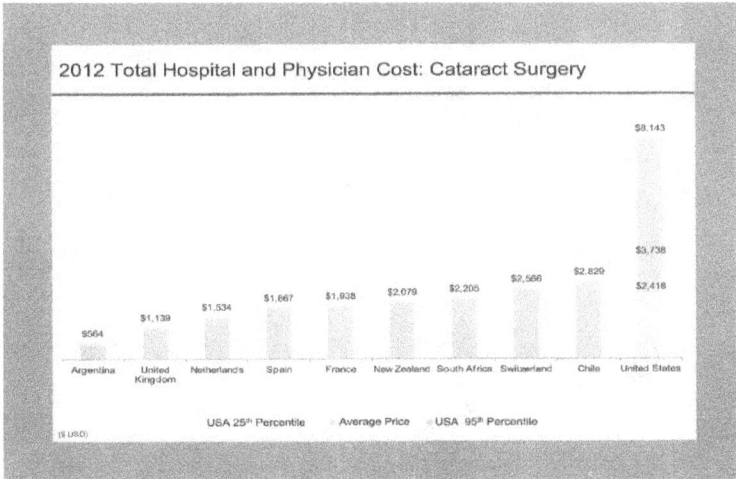

Courtesy: The International Federation of Health Plans;
2012 Comparative Price Report

Figure 1.14 Colonoscopy Cost

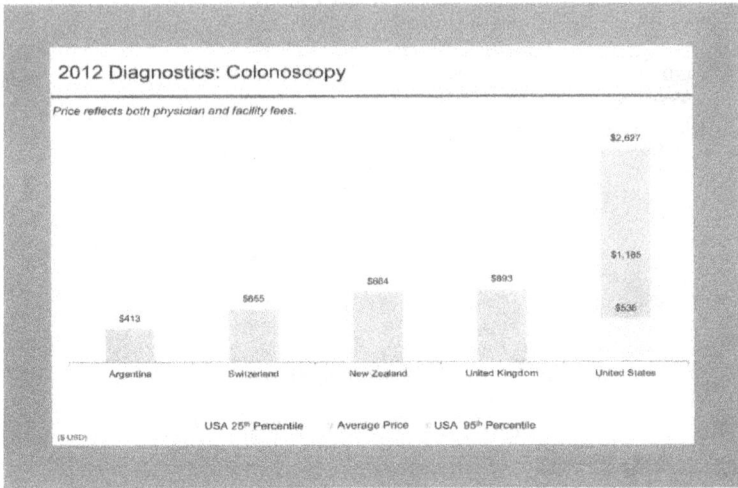

Courtesy: The International Federation of Health Plans;
2012 Comparative Price Report

Figure 1.15 Nexium Drug Cost

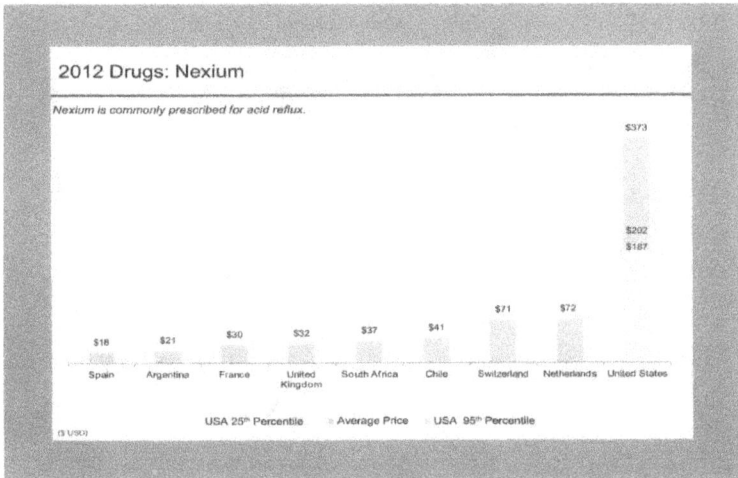

Courtesy: The International Federation of Health Plans;
2012 Comparative Price Report

Figure 1.16 Lipitor Drug Cost

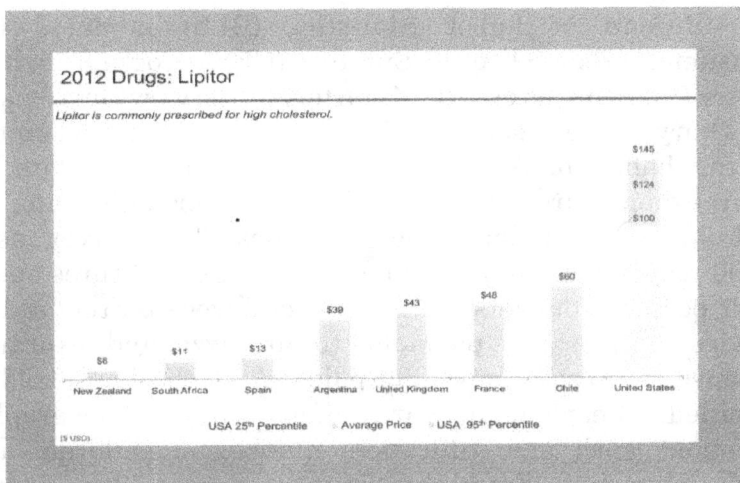

Courtesy: The International Federation of Health Plans;
2012 Comparative Price Report

Figure 1.17 Cymbalta Drug Cost

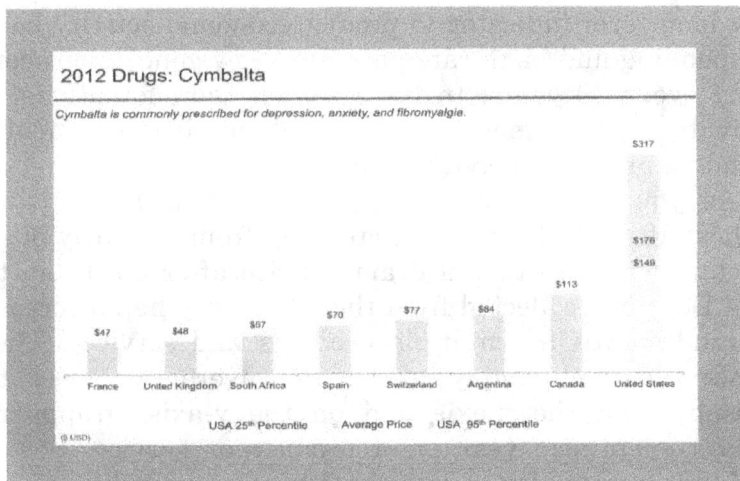

Courtesy: The International Federation of Health Plans;
2012 Comparative Price Report

HEALTH CARE DEMAND CURVES

The Bureau of Labor Statistics (BLS) produces the Consumer Expenditure Survey (CE) program which consists of two surveys, the Quarterly Interview Survey and the Diary Survey. These surveys provide information on the buying habits of American consumers including data on their expenditures, income, and consumer unit (families and single consumers) characteristics. The survey asks 5,000 respondents to list all income and expenditures out of their personal budgets for a period of 6 weeks. From sodas, movies and mortgage payments to car, pizza, and insurance expenses - literally anything paid out of the household is recorded. Respondents are then asked demographic questions such age, education, number of children, and where they live. From this data we can see how people spend money at different ages and on what products and services.

Harry Dent has done some of the best research and analysis I've seen regarding long-term consumer buying habits and demographic trends. In 1988, Dent developed a new long term indicator to predict economic activity based on spending and birth rate patterns. New generations come along every 40 years. In his research Dent found that as individual's age, they move through predictable earning, spending and productivity cycles.

As you might expect, demand for healthcare is the highest after 50. It begins to creep up from the early 30s to 40s but begins to take a dramatic rise after 50. From the data Dent has collected from the CE survey he has created demand curves for multiple products and services. These demand curves simply graph the average age of the household on the x-axis and on the y-axis, graphs the dollars spent per year on a product or service. Several demand curves for select healthcare expenditures are presented next. I've organized them according to the age when a person may be in need of the specific product or service. We're not going to explain each one because they are pretty self-explanatory. What's important to think about is the age where peak demand occurs and when it finally begins to trend lower. The nine graphs are courtesy of H.S. Dent. If you're interested in more demand curves, you can view the PDF file at Dent's website at www.hsdent.com.

Eye exams, treatment or surgery, glass/lens service, glasses repaired

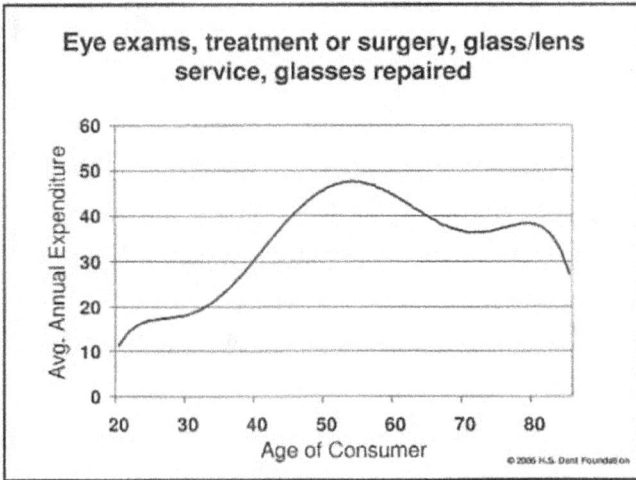

X-axis: Age of Consumer (20–80), Y-axis: Avg. Annual Expenditure (0–60)
© 2006 H.S. Dent Foundation

Dental services

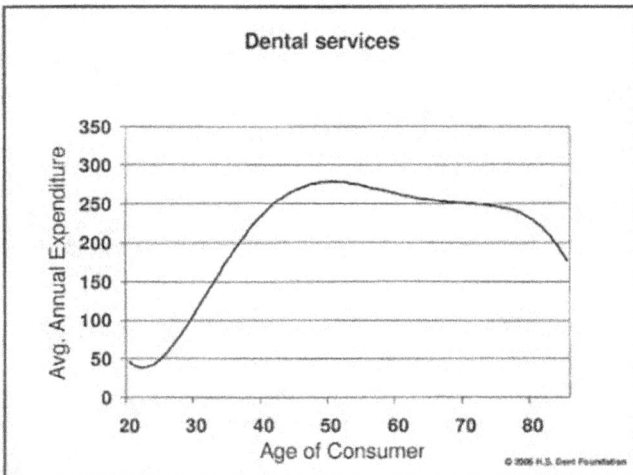

X-axis: Age of Consumer (20–80), Y-axis: Avg. Annual Expenditure (0–350)
© 2006 H.S. Dent Foundation

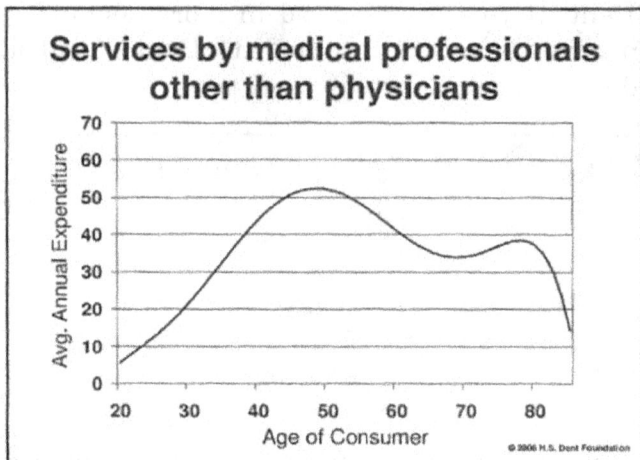

Services by medical professionals other than physicians

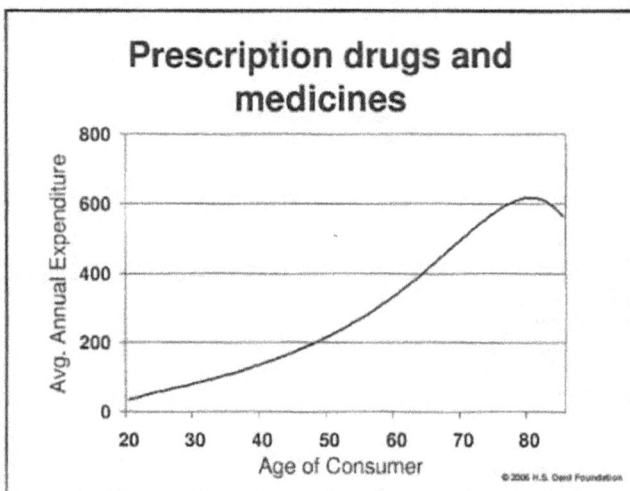

Prescription drugs and medicines

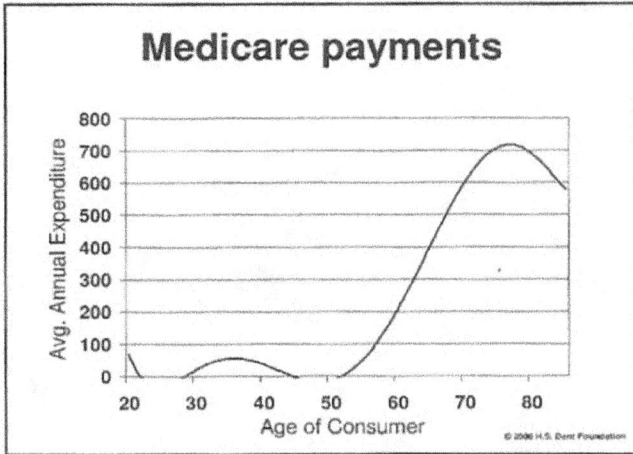

Medicare payments

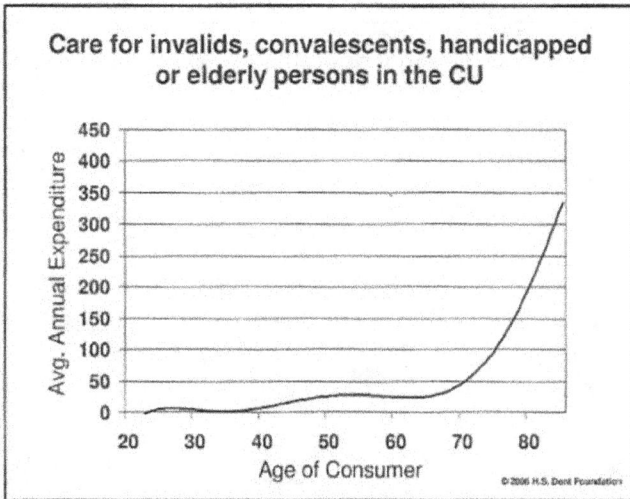

Care for invalids, convalescents, handicapped or elderly persons in the CU

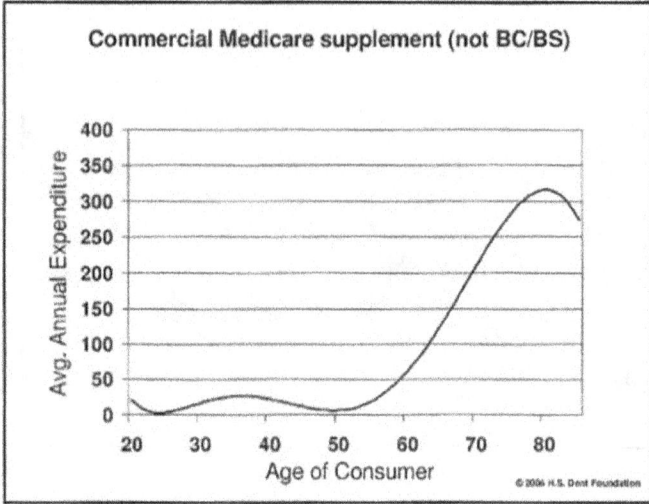

Commercial Medicare supplement (not BC/BS)

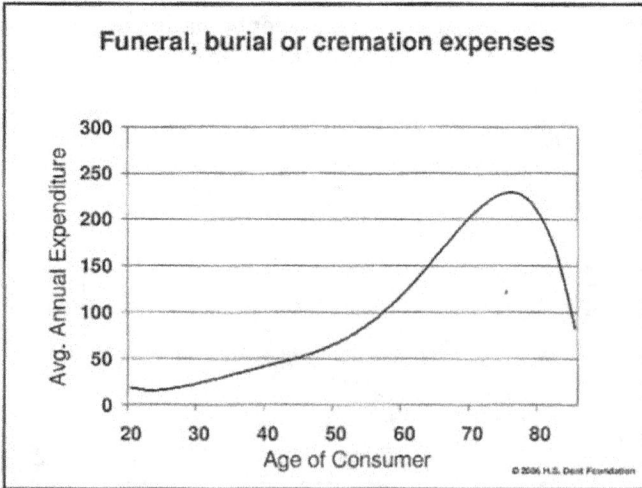

Funeral, burial or cremation expenses

CHAPTER THREE

THE AFFORDABLE CARE ACT

As of 2011, there were nearly 49 million uninsured Americans without health insurance. One of the goals of President Obama's presidency in reforming healthcare was to increase the affordability of it and reduce the number of uninsured in this country. After a hotly contested battle between Democrats and Republicans alike, a bill was finally placed on the President's desk. On March 23 & March 30, 2010 President Barack Obama signed into law two pieces of legislation, which had been passed by Congress. The *2010 Patient Protection and Affordable Care Act* included an individual mandate that all U.S. citizens would have to buy health insurance and the states would be required to expand Medicaid programs. This law, along with the *Health Care and Education Reconciliation Act of 2010*, comprises the principal health care reform legislation which is also called Obamacare or the *Affordable Care Act* (ACA). Known for its concentration of top hospitals and healthcare facilities, Massachusetts overhauled its healthcare programs in 2006 and was the model for the *Affordable Care Act*. The ACA did not incorporate all components of the Massachusetts program into the federal governments' model.

The battles didn't stop just because legislation had been signed into law. Many states subsequently sued the federal government on grounds the new law was unconstitutional. Legal arguments were made to the U.S. Supreme Court and on June 28, 2012, in a 5-4 vote, the high court rendered a final decision to uphold the health care reform laws. The high court upheld the individual mandate. However, in the case, *National Federation of Independent Business v. Sebelius*, the Supreme Court ruled the states do not have to agree to this expansion in order to continue to receive existing levels of Medicaid funding. The mandate for Medicaid expansion was left optional. Many states have chosen to continue with current funding levels and eligibility standards. The laws put in place comprehensive health care reforms which have been rolled out over the past four years and will continue into 2020, with most changes taking place in 2014. The primary goal of the ACA is to help millions of Americans obtain health insurance coverage utilizing federal subsidies such as premium tax credits and cost-sharing reductions.

The intent of this chapter is not to debate the politics of the *Affordable Care Act*. There are clearly aspects of this legislation which are both good and bad for individuals. The objective here is to present the facts to help you understand how this may impact you and your family or small business and how to best navigate the changing and dynamic health care insurance landscape.

An overview of the ACA will be covered while in the next chapter the new Health Insurance Marketplace and its early issues, since becoming "operational" on October 1, 2013, will be discussed. The ACA includes many provisions to make health insurance coverage more accessible and affordable though it comes at a cost. Key components of the ACA which will affect individuals include new health law changes and major consumer protection.

OVERVIEW OF THE AFFORDABLE CARE ACT

The *Affordable Care Act* requires consumers to have health care coverage which provides a minimum level of coverage called minimum essential coverage (MEC). Individuals can meet the MEC requirements by:

- Applying for coverage through the Marketplace and choose an available qualified health plan.
- Qualifying for and enrolling in Medicaid after submitting a Marketplace application.
- Enrolling in a job-based health care plan with appropriate coverage.

The ACA also implements numerous changes to both health care providers and the health insurance industry. It changes the way health insurance is regulated. Another change now requires many health benefits be offered as part of mandatory coverage by health insurers. This includes a number of preventive services which must be provided without copays or coinsurance charges. Existing policies which don't provide these essential health benefits can no longer be offered. Each state will be responsible for setting up and administering its own specific health care Exchange or Marketplace. As mandated by ACA, if a state makes an executive decision not to set up its own health exchange the federal government will set up and manage the exchange in that state. I live in Florida and Florida was one of the states which decided not to set up its own health exchange. One of the factors which played into Florida's decision was related to the funding of these programs after the federal government's incentives end in 2020.

Another key component of the ACA was to give Americans greater access to health care by creating a competitive private health insurance market through the creation of health insurance exchanges. According to the U.S. Census Bureau, in 2010 there were 49.9 million uninsured individuals in the United States; representing

31

16.3% of the population. For 2011, this figure dropped marginally to 48.6 million. For many it is simply a matter of cost in that health insurance is just too expensive. For others it is a case of being uninsurable or having pre-existing health conditions. The ACA will provide them with financial assistance so they can get essential health coverage, either through Medicaid or subsidized health insurance through these newly established health exchanges or what will be termed the Health Insurance Marketplace.

Under the new health care laws, Congress and its staffers, along with other federal employees will have to switch their health insurance coverage from the Federal Employees Health Benefits (FEBH) Program to the Health Insurance Marketplace. The FEBH is a group of private insurance plans that cover 8 million federal employees and retirees. By federal statute, the government contributions are the lesser of 72% of the weighted average of all FEBH plan premiums or 75% of the individual plan premiums. With the Health Insurance Marketplace, the contribution will be 75% of the total cost of the health plan premium. There are some in Congress who have decided not to accept the subsidy but most are. The option still exists to obtain health insurance off exchange, but the federal government will NOT make any contribution to the cost of premiums.

THE AFFORDABLE CARE ACT TIMELINE

While the ACA was passed in 2010, many of its reforms, mandates and subsidies have already been enacted. More will be phased in over the coming decade. The majority of these changes will take place in 2014, including the rollout of the health exchanges. Below is a timeline of the changes which have already been implemented and those which will be implemented in the future. Some of these topics will be explored in greater detail later in the chapter. This list may not be all inclusive.

2010

- Extends coverage to children, under the age of 19, with pre-existing conditions.
- Extends coverage to dependent children up to age 26.
- No more lifetime limits on coverage.
- No more arbitrary cancellations or rescissions.
- Right to appeal health plan decisions.
- Small business tax credit.
- One time rebate of $250 for Medicare beneficiaries who reach the donut hole.

2011

- Prescription drug discounts for seniors.
- Free Medicare preventive services for seniors.
- Minimum medical loss ratio (MLR) requirements.
- Rate review requirements.
- 10% Medicare bonus for primary care physicians and general surgeons in underserved areas.
- Increased funding for community health centers for care to low-income and uninsured.

2012

- New preventative services for women.
- Summary of benefits and coverage (SBC).
- MLR reporting requirements begin.
- Hospitals with high rates of preventable readmissions face reduced Medicare payments.

2013

- Open enrollment in the Health Insurance Marketplace begins.

- Employers must report cost of employees' health coverage in 2012 on their 2012 W-2 form. Applies to employers issuing 250 or more W-2s.
- Contributions to health care FSAs limited to $2,500 a year for medical expenses.
- Individuals earning more than $200,000, $250,000 if married filing jointly or $125,000 if married filing separately, in income, face a higher FICA tax of 3.8%, a higher Medicare payroll tax of 2.35% and a Medicare surtax on unearned income of 3.8%.
- Threshold for deducting medical expenses on Schedule A, of federal tax returns, increases from 7.5% to 10.0% of adjusted gross income.
- There is a temporary exemption from Jan. 1, 2013 to Dec. 31, 2016 for individuals age 65 and older and their spouses. If you or your spouse is 65 years or older or turned 65 during the tax year you are allowed to deduct unreimbursed medical care expenses that exceed 7.5% of your adjusted gross income. The threshold remains at 7.5% of AGI for those taxpayers until Dec. 31, 2016.
- Medical device manufacturers face a 2.9% tax, with some exemptions.
- Deduction ends for Medicare Part D subsidies for employers who maintain retiree drug plans.
- Limits the tax deductibility of compensation to health insurance company executives.

2014

- Individuals are required to have health care coverage or face tax penalties.
- Tax credits and premium subsidies available on the new health insurance marketplace for eligible individuals.
- Eliminates annual dollar limits on coverage.

- Small business tax credits are expanded. The tax credit is worth up to 50% of contribution toward employees' premium costs (up to 35% for tax-exempt employers). The credit is available only if you get coverage through the SHOP Marketplace.
- Eliminates discrimination due to pre-existing conditions or gender.
- Employer groups may not impose waiting periods longer than 90 days.
- New uniform insurance rating rules apply limiting rate bands to a 3:1 ratio.
- Employer group health plans may not impose annual dollar limits on essential health benefits.
- Minimum MLR of 85% for Medicare Advantage plans becomes effective.
- Medicaid expands to everyone at or below 138% of the federal poverty level (FPL).
- Health insurers pay an annual fee to offset exchange subsidies and tax credits. $8 billion in fees in 2014 then increasing to $14.3 billion in 2018.

2015

- The Employer Shared Responsibility Payment is a new requirement which applies to some larger employers. May have to make this payment if they have 50 or more full-time equivalent employees and at least 1 of their full-time employees gets lower costs on their monthly premiums through the Marketplace.

2016

- States which previously defined the small group market as 50 or fewer employees must expand that definition to 100 or fewer.

2017

- States may opt to open the health insurance marketplaces to large employers.

2018

- Employers will be required to pay a 40% excise tax (Cadillac tax) if coverage under their group health plan exceeds annual premium costs of $10,200 for individuals or $27,500 for families, adjusted for inflation.

2020

- The donut hole or coverage gap in Medicare prescription benefits end. Seniors will continue to pay the standard 25% of their drug costs until they reach the Medicare catastrophic coverage threshold.

During the recent partial U.S. Government shut down there was debate that the ACA may not be funded. However, on October 17th, after a 285-144 vote in the House followed by an overwhelming vote in the Senate, an agreement negotiated by Senate Majority Leader Harry Reid (D-Nev.) and Minority Leader Mitch McConnell (R-Ky.) to end the tense political standoff that had shut down federal programs for 16 days was passed by Congress. President Barack Obama quickly signed the 11th-hour deal. This isn't the first time the federal government has shut down. During the Clinton administration there were 2 shutdowns. One lasted just 5 days in November 1995 while the second lasted 21 days during the period from December 1995 to early January 1996. Prior to that, was the government shutdown during the Jimmie Carter administration, which lasted 19 days during the fall of 1978.

MEDICARE

One of the more vocal groups opposing the ACA is individuals over age 65 and on Medicare. Budget cuts in the Medicare program would provide much of the funding for ACA. When the bill was signed into law in 2010, budget forecasters projected cuts would total $455 billion over the next decade. The Congressional Budget Office (CBO) has since updated their figures twice to reflect new realities. In 2011, the CBO revised their outlook that Medicare cuts would total $507 billion between 2012 and 2021. Then in July 2012, the CBO projected Medicare outlays would be reduced by $716 billion between 2013 and 2022. Medicare officials stress the spending changes will not reduce Medicare benefits. The cuts will be made by lowering reimbursements to nursing homes, hospitals, home health agencies and other health care providers. It also cuts payments to Medicare Advantage plans to bring those payments closer to what Medicare pays for care for beneficiaries enrolled in the traditional fee-for-service plan. Of the pluses coming from the ACA is the expansion of Medicare's prescription drug coverage, closure of the donut hole by 2020 and new coverage for certain preventive care services for beneficiaries.

PHYSICIANS

In a poll conducted for the Physicians Foundation, 40% of physicians who participated in the survey said they would retire, seek a non-clinical job or seek a job unrelated to healthcare during the next three years. Many physicians believe the ACA represents an ideological assault on their ability to maintain their current earnings and will ultimately reduce their earnings potential. A cornerstone of the healthcare delivery system, from a physician's perspective, has been the fee-for-service payment system which is the foundation of most physicians' earnings. As the tsunami of baby boomers continues to swell and enter the

Medicare system, many physicians see the ACA as another opportunity by the federal government to put new restraints on payment rates.

At a time when many believe there is an acute shortage of primary care physicians developing, the passage of the ACA may only exacerbate this situation. With medical student loan debts among the highest in the world, students could reassess their desire to attend medical school or enter family medicine with a significantly reduced earnings outlook.

EXISTING HEALTH INSURANCE POLICIES

What if you already have an individual health insurance policy, not through an employer-sponsored plan? How will that policy be affected by the implementation of the ACA? This has been an interesting question with even more intriguing answers, which many individuals came to realize during the summer and fall of 2013. Not that the Obama administration needs any more health care headaches but this may become more fuel for the fire for the opponents of health care reform. President Obama had repeatedly assured Americans, on many occasions, that if they liked their health insurance they would be able to keep it. He began saying this in 2009 and continued through 2012.

One of the provisions within the ACA states that health insurance policies in effect, as of March 23, 2010, will be "grandfathered" in. This implied that consumers could keep their policies even though they don't meet the requirements of the new health care law. Then Health and Human Services rewrote the regulations which narrowed that provision by saying if any part of a policy was significantly changed since that date, such as the deductible, copays or benefits for example the policy would not be grandfathered.

As a licensed insurance agent who offers both Medicare health plans and individual health insurance plans, one thing I know for certain; plans change from year to year. According to an NBC News report, buried in the ACA regulations from July 2010 is an estimate that because of normal turnover in the individual health insurance market, 40 to 67% of consumers would not be able to keep their policy. This was three years ago when the Obama administration knew what the impact would be to consumers. History may place this right up there with former President George H. Bush's line, *"Read my lips. No new taxes."* President Bush then went on to raise taxes. This could be the most disingenuous pledge that any president has made to get his legislation passed.

The report continues to say that between 50% and 75% of the 14 million Americans that have individual policies have already received or will soon receive a cancellation letter from their health insurance carrier that the plan they have is not in compliance with the new health care laws governing coverage. That puts the number forced to change to new policies at roughly 7 to 10.5 million policyholders. Many policyholders are experiencing sticker shock over the premiums which will be charged on their new policies. That doesn't means they will not be able to find lower cost policies though the marketplace.

RATE REVIEWS AND RATING VARIATIONS

An issue which consumers have been very vocal with over the last few years has been the significant increases in health insurance premiums with little to no explanation as to why they must be so large from the health insurers. The passage of the ACA brings an increased level of scrutiny and transparency to health insurance rate increases.

Rate Reviews

Moving forward the ACA ensures that any health insurance company seeking a rate increase will be evaluated by experts to ensure those proposed increases are based on reasonable cost assumptions and qualified evidence. The expectation is this enhanced level of financial analysis will help moderate premium increases and provide those who buy health insurance with a greater value for their premium dollars. In addition these health issuers must provide easy to understand information to their members regarding any reasons for rate increases. They must also publicly justify and post on their corporate websites any rate increases determined to be unreasonable. Rates for qualified health plans (QHPs) in the Individual and SHOP Marketplaces will be reviewed for reasonableness and compliance with market rating reforms under the ACA.

Rate reviews of premium increases are called effective rate reviews and will be conducted by independent state or federal experts. Many states have already established and been classified as having an *Effective Rate Review Program (ERRP)* for all or some markets. If a state lacks the resources or authority to conduct these effective rate review standards, the review will be accomplished by the CMS. This expanded level of monitoring along with review of premium rates as part of the qualification process for health insurance plans will enhance consumer protection through increased transparency.

Rating Variations

There are only four factors which can affect premium rates under the ACA. This applies to both the Individual Marketplace as well as the SHOP Marketplace for small business owners. Both of these Marketplaces will be discussed in greater detail in subsequent chapters. Premium rates can vary based on age, family composition, geographic area and tobacco usage. Let's look at each element in more detail.

1. **Age Rating Standards:** Health insurance companies are NOT allowed to charge an older adult more than 3x the rate of a 21 year old. States can establish an age curve or default to a federal age curve. There are three age bands – 0-20 years, then

one year bands between ages 21 and 63, followed by an age 64 and older band.

2. **Family Rating Standards:** This includes the number of family members within the family, including 1 or 2 parents and up to 3 family members under the age of 21. Family premiums are based on the premiums for each family member including each individual's age and tobacco usage. Only premiums for the first three children under 21 contribute towards the total family premium and family rates include per-member rates for dependent children ages 21 and older.

3. **Geographic Rating Standards:** Premium rates may reflect geographic rating areas in the state. A rating area is the home address for individual market coverage or the employer's primary place of business in the state for small business coverage.

4. **Tobacco rating standards:** Health insurance companies will NOT be able to charge an individual who uses tobacco products more than 1.5x the non-tobacco user's rate. The tobacco rating can vary based on age with individuals under age 35 paying no more than 1.2x the non-tobacco user's rate. The tobacco surcharge can only be applied to the portion of the premium attributed to the individual family member. For small business owners, covered individuals will be able to avoid the tobacco surcharge by participating in a wellness program.

QUALIFIED EXEMPTIONS

The health care law requires all individuals who can afford health care coverage to take responsibility for their own health insurance or pay a penalty beginning January 1, 2014. This fee is known as the *Individually Shared Responsibility Payment*. To avoid the fee you need health insurance that qualifies as minimum essential coverage (MEC). This includes:

- Individual health insurance policies
- Job-based coverage
- Medicare
- Medicaid
- Children's Health Insurance Program (CHIP)
- TRICARE
- Veterans health care programs
- Peace Corp Volunteer plans

Types of health plans that don't meet the minimum essential coverage include:

- Coverage for only vision care or dental care.
- Worker's compensation
- Coverage for only a specific disease or condition.
- Plans which offer only discounts on medical services.

If you only have these types of coverage you may have to pay the penalty fee.

PENALTY FEES AND THE IRS

Consumers will owe a penalty if they do not have coverage that meets MEC requirements and do not qualify for an exemption from the Individually Shared Responsibility Payment requirement. After March 31, 2014 the ACA imposes penalties on Americans without health insurance coverage. **For 2014, the fee is 1% of your yearly income or $95 per adult, whichever is higher, for the year.** The fee for uninsured children is half the adult amount or $47.50 per child. The most a family would have to pay in 2014 is $285. The fee is paid on the 2014 federal income tax form, which most individuals and families will file in 2015. **It's important to remember that someone who pays the fee will not get any health insurance coverage and will be responsible for 100% of the cost of their medical care.**

In 2015, the fee increases to 2% of yearly income or $325 per adult and $162.50 per child, whichever is greater, with a family maximum of $975. In 2016, the fee increases to 2.5% or $695 per adult and $347.50 per child, whichever is greater, with a family maximum of $2,085. The percent of the income fee is capped at the national average of cost for the Bronze coverage category for the individual and dependents. Beginning in 2016, the Internal Revenue Service (IRS) indicates the applicable dollar amount will be indexed by a cost-of-living adjustment.

Enforcement of the new health-care laws, to collect penalties, will be under the IRS. Of the 500 provisions in the ACA, 40 amend or add provisions to the U.S. Tax Code. In addition, the IRS is charged with carrying out nearly four dozen new tasks under the ACA, which is the biggest increase in its responsibilities in decades. The one year delay in applying the new health care laws to large corporations will hamper coverage information the IRS needs to enforce the health care mandate. This will be further complicated by the fact that when lawmakers drafted the ACA they intentionally barred the IRS from using its customary tools for collecting penalties. This could include liens, foreclosures and criminal prosecution. The only means of collecting the fines is to garnish tax refunds for individuals who overpaid their taxes.

When Massachusetts overhauled their program, it initially attracted individuals who were relatively unhealthy. As the state publicized possible penalties, enrollment in the program shot up very quickly and stabilized the demographics of the risk pool.

Exemptions from the Individual Responsibility Requirement

Exemptions can be granted from the Marketplace or the IRS through the tax filing process. Individuals only need to be eligible for and get one exemption per calendar year to avoid having to pay a penalty fee on their federal income tax return. The ACA exempts several categories of

43

individuals from the shared responsibility payment. Exemptions may be granted by the Marketplace for:

- Hardship: includes those who become homeless, were evicted from their home in the past six months or are facing eviction, experienced domestic violence or the death of a close family member.
- Lack of affordable coverage using projected income. Job-based coverage which meets the minimum value standard and is more than 8% of their projected annual household income.
- Membership in a health care sharing ministry.
- Incarceration status except for pending disposition of charges.
- Membership in a federally recognized tribe or eligibility for services through an Indian health care provider or Indian Health Services. Must indicate their tribal membership on the Marketplace application and submit documentation proving their membership or claim this exemption when they file their federal income tax returns with the IRS.
- Membership in a recognized religious sect objecting to health coverage.

The IRS may grant exemptions on a federal income tax return for:

- Lack of affordable coverage based on actual income. Cost of health coverage is more than 8% of household income.
- Having income below the federal income tax filing threshold. In 2012, the federal income tax filing threshold was $9,750 for a single individual and $19,500 for married individuals filing jointly.
- Unlawful presence in the U.S.
- Lack of health insurance coverage for less than three consecutive months between months of coverage.

- Hardships
- Incarceration status except for pending disposition of charges.
- Membership in a health care sharing ministry.
- Membership in a federally recognized tribe or eligibility for services through an Indian health care provider or Indian Health Services.

Exemption requests must be submitted by mail. Individuals have 90 days to provide the necessary documentation after submitting an application. If they receive an approval notice or exemption certificate they should keep this certificate, which includes a number that they'll need to provide on their federal income tax return. They should also keep copies of any documentation that was provided with their application in case follow-up is needed.

HEALTH LAW CHANGES

The health law changes include:

- The creation of Health Insurance Marketplaces for individuals and small businesses. Individuals who do not have access to public assistance programs or affordable employer-sponsored health coverage can compare and purchase plans. Some individuals will be eligible for financial assistance through premium tax credits and/or cost-sharing reductions.
- Medicaid will be expanded in some states to cover individuals between the ages of 19 and 65, whose household incomes are less than 138% of the Federal Poverty Level (FPL). In 2013, 138% FPL is $15,586 for an individual and $32,499 for a family of four.
- Requires individuals to maintain minimum essential health coverage, qualify for an exemption from that coverage or make a payment when filing their federal income tax returns.

Major Consumer Rights and Protections

ACA offers new rights and protections which make coverage fairer and easier to understand. Some of these new rights and protections apply to plans in the Marketplace or other individual insurance, some apply to job-based plans and some apply to all health coverage. The new health care law protects you by:

- Expansion of the "guaranteed issue" requirement to ensure that health insurance issuers offer group and individual market policies to any individual in a state, regardless of health status. The applicant must agree to the terms and conditions of the policy, including the payment of premiums.
- Requires "guaranteed renewability" on the part of health insurers. The companies must offer to renew or continue in force coverage at the option of the policyholder.
- Prohibition on coverage limitations or exclusions based on pre-existing conditions. A pre-existing condition is any health condition or illness that was present before the effective coverage date, regardless of whether medical advice or treatment was actually received or recommended.
- Prohibition on charging consumers a higher premium based on health status or gender.
- Helps you understand the coverage you're getting.
- Makes it illegal for health insurance companies to arbitrarily cancel your health insurance just because you get sick.
- Protects your choice of physicians.
- Extension of health insurance coverage to young adults under 26.
- Provides free preventive care.
- Ends lifetime and yearly dollar limits on coverage of essential health benefits (EHBs). Health insurance

companies can still put a lifetime dollar limit on spending for health care services which are not part of EHBs.

- Guarantees your right to appeal.
- Prohibition on precluding a qualified individual's participation in an approved clinical trial or discriminating against an individual based on such participation.
- Introduction of an 80/20 Medical Loss Ratio (MLR) rule ensure that at least 80% of the premium dollars paid to a health insurer are spent on providing health care. This will help hold health insurance companies accountable for rate increases.

Health insurers can only retroactively cancel a consumers' health insurance if their application are intentionally false or incomplete. Health issuers may terminate coverage for enrollees who knowingly submit false information on their applications and for those who have not paid their premiums before the end of the payment grace period.

Medical Loss Ratio

A goal of the ACA is to keep costs down by limiting the proportion of premiums that a health insurer can spend on expenses other than providing and improving the quality of the health care provided to its members. The medical loss ratio (MLR) is a financial measurement which shows how much of the premium dollars a health insurance issuer spends on health care expenses as opposed to profits or administrative costs.

As of 2012, a health insurance issuer who does not spend enough of its premium dollars on health care services must provide rebates to insured individuals or policyholders. MLR is not calculated at the individual level but at the state level for each health insurance issuer. This calculation is done separately for the small business group and individual markets. As of 2012, a health insurance

47

issuer is required to spend at least 80% of premium dollars on medical care. The ACA sets minimum MLRs for different markets, as do some state laws.

FINAL THOUGHTS ON OBAMACARE FOR 2013

Anecdotal evidence now is coming in with regards to costs and coverage for the various states. As these exchanges get up and running, real cost data from the exchanges, is beginning to emerge from the various states. While this is an oversimplification, the consensus seems to indicate the following points are most contentious regarding the ACA:

- Premium increase much higher than expected.
- More existing policies are being cancelled than expected.
- Grandfather status extremely confusing to most that have existing individual policies.
- Scope of the participating network physicians and medical centers is much more narrow and limited than previously anticipated by consumers in the state exchanges.

In November 2013, the Manhattan Institute for Policy Research released a comprehensive 49 state analysis (excludes Hawaii) of premiums individuals will pay who shop around for their own health insurance coverage. Their conclusion – in the average state, the ACA will increase underlying premiums by 41%. The steepest hikes will be on the healthy, the young and the male. The ACA funded subsidies will primarily benefit those nearing retirement. In the analysis they discovered that men will face the steepest increases.

- 27-year old – 77% increase.
- 40-year old – 37% increase.
- 64-year old – 47% increase.

Women will see increases but not as steep as with men.

- 27-year old – 18% increase
- 40-year old – 28% increase
- 64-year old – 37% increase

According to the analysis there are 41 states, plus Washington D.C., which will experience premium hikes.

Figure 3.1 below displays a map of the U.S., excluding Hawaii, which illustrates the average premium changes in each state after the implementation of the ACA.

Figure 3.1 Percent Change in Individual Market Premiums, Average of All Age Groups, Post- vs. Pre-ACA

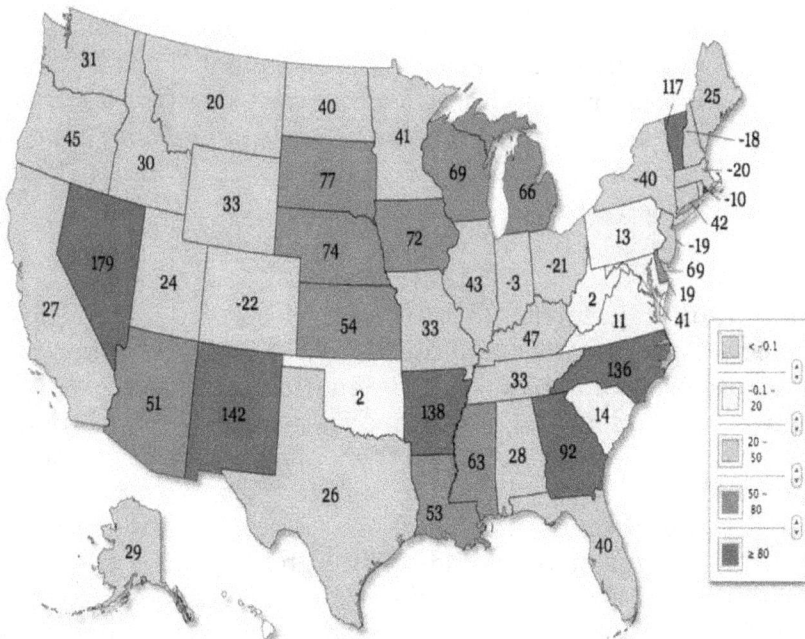

Source: Forbes – The Apothecary, With Avik Roy, 11-04-2013

Those states which will face the biggest underlying increase in premiums include:

- Nevada – 179% increase
- New Mexico – 142% increase
- Arkansas – 138% increase
- North Carolina – 136% increase
- Vermont – 117% increase
- Georgia – 92% increase
- South Dakota – 77% increase
- Nebraska – 75% increase

The states which will be the biggest winners and see average premium reductions under the ACA are:

- New York – 40% decline
- Colorado – 22% decline
- Ohio – 21% decline
- Massachusetts – 20% decline
- New Jersey – 19% decline
- New Hampshire – 18% decline
- Rhode Island – 10% decline
- Indiana – 3% decline

The Manhattan Institute has produced an interactive tool called, The Obamacare Rate Map at (www.manhattan-institute.org/html/obamacare_evaluation.htm), to assist individuals in learning about health insurance prices under the ACA. If you want a further understanding of their methodology used in developing these maps, visit www.manhattan-institute.org/knowyourrates/about.htm.

Many argue that individuals will be protected from the increases by federal subsidies. These subsidies are not "free". They are taxpayer-funded subsidies which are critical to getting the "affordable" part of the "A"CA realized in the new health insurance program. There's also another issue here, the subsidies increase in proportion to the percentage of your income that is tied up in health insurance. For those nearing retirement, their premiums are much higher but so are the subsidies they'll be entitled to. Older individuals will disproportionately benefit from the federal subsidies.

Their analysis also looked at the average of premiums paid, pre- and post-ACA unsubsidized and pre- and post-ACA including the median federal subsidy. It's important to remember these are averages. If you're young and healthy you'll most likely face steeper increases than the figures below illustrate. If you have had a pre-existing condition or serious health issues and haven't been able to get health coverage, you'll most likely do better than then average. For a 27-year old, the average premiums would be:

- Male pre-ACA (unsubsidized) - $133/month
- Male post-ACA (unsubsidized) - $201/month (+52%)
- Male post-ACA (median subsidy) - $188/month (+41%)

- Female pre-ACA (unsubsidized) - $165/month
- Female post-ACA (subsidized) - $201/month (+22%)
- Female post-ACA *(median subsidy) - $157 (-5%)*

Looking at a 64-year old, from their analysis, the average premiums would be:

- Male pre-ACA (unsubsidized) - $465/month
- Male post-ACA (unsubsidized) - $545/month (+17%)
- Male post-ACA *(median subsidy) - $377 (-19%)*

- Female pre-ACA (unsubsidized) - $430/month
- Female post-ACA (subsidized) - $545/month (+27%)
- Female post-ACA *(median subsidy) - $292 (-32%)*

A major factor driving premium rates higher is community ratings, which is used in the ACA. The ACA requires that health insurers can only charge 3x as much to their costliest beneficiaries as what they charge their least costly ones. Insurance industry data shows that, on average, a 64-year consumes 6x as much health care as does a 19-year old. As a result this is leading to the significant premium increases we're now seeing for young adults within the exchanges. According to the Manhattan Institute, their overall conclusion of the financial impact of Obamacare is that in the average state it is a massive transfer of wealth from the young to the old. It's ironic that in the 2012 presidential election, younger voters overwhelmingly support President Obama, while older voters supported Mitt Romney.

Follow the Bouncing Ball

In somewhat of a reversal of policy, on November 14, 2013, recognizing the frustration many individuals are having with their insurers which have cancelled their existing health care insurance policies, President Obama indicated he is giving those Americans a one-year reprieve before they have to get new policies under the new health care law. The administration is sending letters to the state's insurance commissioners to notify insurers they can continue the sale of cancelled policies for an additional year. The extension will is only available to those already enrolled in the policies which were cancelled because they didn't meet coverage standards. This would mean some individuals could remain on their existing health plan well in 2015. Those health insurance companies which extend policies must notify members that alternatives exist, under the new health care law, including tax credits and are also required to describe the ways their existing plan does not meet the consumer protections required under the new law.

However, the states are not mandated to abide by the president's request. Some state insurance commissioners are concerned this undermines the "risk pool" of consumers needed to make the law viable. If consumers have the option to renew existing plans, it may leave a disproportionately sick pool of consumers for plans operating in the Marketplaces. States which have already opted out include Washington, Massachusetts, New York, Minnesota, Vermont, Rhode Island and now California. There are twelve states which have agreed to extend existing policies. Florida's largest health insurer, Florida Blue, announced on Friday, November 15, 2013 it will give 300,000 members who earlier received cancellation notices the option to renew their existing plans for one more year.

On December 19, the CMS imposed another twist to the ACA. CMS indicated that consumers who have received cancellation notices from their insurers could purchase cheaper, catastrophic coverage if their out-of-pocket costs to get a new policy are higher than they have been. Under the original ACA rules these catastrophic policies were only available to individuals under the age of 30. Under the new rule imposed by CMS, individuals over that age will still need to apply for the same hardship exemption which younger individuals would need to do in order to avoid the penalty tax.

Concerns raised by health insurance companies are these constant changes to the ACA are adding instability and confusion in the Marketplace for consumers. Some of the concern regarding the risk pool is mitigated in part by a program within the ACA. Under the program, called a risk corridor, the federal government will cover as much as 80% of a health plan's losses by taking money from the plans which get a larger number of healthier consumers than expected. The program was envisioned to be budget-neutral for the federal government.

"If you look at the studies coming out of the Congressional Budget Office, the number one thing that's going to blow a hole in the federal deficit as we go forward 20, 30 years is government spending on healthcare."

Christina Romer
Professor of Economics – University of California at Berkeley
Former Chairperson – Council of Economic Advisors
President Barack Obama's Administration

CHAPTER FOUR

THE HEALTH INSURANCE MARKETPLACE

Original language in the ACA used the term health insurance exchanges but the terms seen will refer to them as Marketplaces, which is perceived to be more consumer friendly by the CMS. It is likely you will see exchange and marketplace used interchangeable by both the health insurance industry and the media. These Marketplaces can be operated by a state, the federal government or a combination of both. Those Marketplaces operated by the state are called State-Based Marketplaces (SBM), those operated by the federal government are called Federally-Facilitated Marketplaces (FFM) while those which are a combination are called a State Partnership Marketplace (SPM). In a FFM, the federal government manages all Marketplace functions. In an SPM, the federal government runs some but not all Marketplace functions. A state with an SPM can choose, for example, to be responsible for plan management activities, consumer assistance activities or a combination of both. There are two types of Marketplaces: the Individual Marketplace and the SHOP Marketplace for small business owners.

One pillar of the ACA is the Obama administration's creation of these Exchanges or Marketplaces to provide affordable health care coverage to millions of Americans. These new health insurance plans, available through the Marketplace, will be offered by private health care insurance companies. Marketplace enrollment began on October 1, 2013 for individuals and families. Small business owners will be able to buy health insurance coverage beginning November 1, 2013. Health care coverage for both will be effective January 1, 2014 for those individuals who enroll by December 24, 2013. With one Marketplace application, you can learn if you can get lower costs based on your income, compare your coverage options side-by-side, and enroll.

Technological Issues

Houston, we have a problem. That is the line spoken by James Lovell, Commander of Apollo 13 the seventh manned mission to the moon. An explosion in an onboard oxygen tank 2 days into the flight set into motion a heroic rescue process which may have been the finest hour(s) in NASA history. Gene Kranz, NASA Flight Director at the time, never actually spoke another specific line made famous in the Ron Howard directed film, *Apollo 13*; failure is not an option. As they analyzed the situation they faced in Houston, on the spacecraft and evaluated the options presented, Kranz indicated failure was never one of the options presented or considered by the team.

Washington, D.C., we have a problem. Since the launch of the federally-facilitated Health Insurance Marketplace, on the HealthCare.gov website, the technological problems inherit with the various applications and systems have been well documented and publicized. There are 36 states which are currently using the HealthCare.gov website while 14 states and the District of Columbia created their own websites.

Normally when a company develops a new software application or it integrates a new application into their existing programs, there is an alpha and/or beta testing period. The alpha test is usually conducted among the development team(s) to confirm the application works. This is the first phase of testing and can include unit testing, component testing, and system testing. Most known critical issues are fixed, some features may change or be added based on feedback. A good alpha test sets well-defined benchmarks and measures an application against those benchmarks. During the second phase, a beta test is conducted. This includes a sampling of the intended audience as it tries the new application out. Its purpose is to improve the quality of the application, integrate customer input on the complete application and ensure release readiness. Some bugs may still exist but there should be significantly fewer system crashes than what occurred during alpha testing. The alpha test can last 3x-5x longer than the beta test, which is usually only a few weeks, sometimes up to a couple of months at most with few new major iterations being incorporated. It's been documented the HealthCare.gov website wasn't significantly tested by a user group (about 200 individuals) until the last week before going live. The website crashed almost immediately. At some point this will all be "old news" as the issues will ultimately get resolved. However, at this specific point in time it may provide the reader with some interesting insight they haven't read about.

Before a House committee on November 14, the key Obama administration players; Todd Park, chief technology officer, Henry Chao, chief digital architect and Steven Van Roekel, chief information officer could not answer questions from the committee about the cost of repairing the website. On November 19th, Chao indicated in congressional testimony that unfinished work remains primarily in back-office payment systems needed to transfer tax subsidies to the health insurers and that these payment will not need to begin until January 2014.

Just recently, on November 26, Bloomberg News published an article based on interviews with administration officials and industry representative involved in the efforts to fix the website. They spoke on condition of anonymity to provide a first-hand account of the push to reboot the HealthCare.gov website during the last several weeks. Jeffrey Zients, a former acting budget director, management consultant and business entrepreneur and who is scheduled to start as Obama's top economic advisor on January 1, 2014, got his reentry to the public sector accelerated to October 18th by Denis McDonough, President Obama's White House Chief of Staff. Zients' role is to oversee the private contractors and government officials charged with fixing the flawed HealthCare.gov website.

For the next six days Zients focused on the complex, interlocking systems behind the malfunctioning HealthCare.gov website. Some of his initial findings were the software code underlying the website was riddled with errors while other portions contained placeholder language which programmers typically use in preliminary drafts. Only six individuals managed to enroll on the day HealthCare.gov went live. To accommodate the number of individuals working on various problems, some computer programmers sat on the floors, against the walls as they typed new coding into laptops. In mid-October, the average load time for the site's pages was 8 seconds. On October 24, Zients assessment presented to the Oval Office was this is fixable. As of November 22nd, the teams had made more than 300 software fixes and hardware upgrades, with another 50 more set as an upcoming priority. The average load time for the site's pages had now dropped to less than a second. An error rate now exists of below 1% compared with 6% when the Marketplace was launched. Since becoming the White House turnaround point man, each Thursday Zients has been meeting with President Obama, Vice President Joe Biden, HHS Secretary Kathleen

Sebelius, Denis McDonough and other senior officials in the Roosevelt Room for a progress report.

November 30, 2014

These problems have been serious and should not be minimized considering the taxpayer dollars which have gone into its development. The Obama administration has spent more than $600 million on the troubled website. The administration is trying to meet a self-imposed deadline to correct the deficiencies by November 30, 2013. Zients has warned publicly this date will not be a magic moment for the website. According to a recent briefing for reporters, traveling with the president on Air Force One, HealthCare.gov should be able to handle 50,000 concurrent users by the deadline date. A queuing system has been created so that if more than 50,000 individuals are trying to use the site, they will be able to choose to receive an e-mail from CMS when there's less traffic and can be place them at the front of the line. HealthCare.gov will be a work-in-progress project by the federal government.

Though there have been significant improvements in the HealthCare.gov website since the initial launch, issues remain with the back-end systems. While this is an oversimplification, once you set up an account and enter the required information, that information is cross-referenced with the associated databases used with HealthCare.gov to insure eligibility. If you meet the requirements you then select a health plan offered by an insurer. Once selected, a completed enrollment application is then set to that health insurer. It is here where consumer information being transmitted is sometimes inaccurate, incomplete or doesn't get transmitted at all. You are not enrolled in a plan until you receive notification from the health insurer.

These issues involving the health insurance marketplace initiative, probably the most critical component of the ACA is clearly impacting the president in surveys and polls. In a recent survey from the Kaiser

Family Foundation, it found that just 33% of Americans now support the health-care law, down from 38% a month earlier. It is the lowest support level measured by the foundation since the law's passage in March 2010. The president's own approval rate is down to 41%. It's the lowest level for that indicator according to a *CNN/ORC* poll released on November 21st.

Federal Data Services Hub

CMS uses a system called the Federal Data Services Hub (the Hub) to verify the information entered in the application is correct. The Hub provides a single secure connection between state and federal systems to trusted data sources to verify specific information in the consumers' application. The Hub pulls this information about individuals from other federal agencies, such as the IRS, SSA and the Department of Homeland Security (DHS). The Hub is not a database as it does not retain or store data. It is a routing tool to securely send information from various trusted government databases through secure networks. This data being shared with or received from the Hub is protected and isn't shared for any other purposes.

Risk Pools

A critical objective to ensuring the Health Insurance Marketplace is a success is getting a younger demographic to enroll in a qualified health plan through the Marketplace. By requiring everyone to maintain health coverage or pay a penalty, it is hoped that the Marketplace will be large enough to have a risk pool comprised of high-risk and low-risk consumers. A risk pool is a term used to describe a group of individuals whose estimated medical costs are combined in order to calculate health insurance premiums. A well-balanced risk pool consists of a large group of consumers who rarely use medical services and those who frequently use medical services.

Functions of the Marketplace

The major functions of the Marketplace include:

- Certifying health plans to participate in a Marketplace as Qualified Health Plans (QHPs).
- Determining individuals' eligibility for enrollment in a QHP.
- Determining individuals' eligibility for premium tax credits and/or cost-sharing reductions.
- Determining or assessing individuals' eligibility for enrollment in Medicaid and/or the Children's Health Insurance Program (CHIP).
- Facilitating individuals' enrollment in a QHP.
- Carrying out certain plan oversight functions, including monitoring QHP issuers for continuing compliance with certification requirements.
- Facilitating employer's applications and employee enrollments for health insurance coverage through SHOP.

Qualified Health Plans

A qualified health plan (QHP) is a health plan which is certified by the Marketplace. The Marketplace certifies each QHP that is sold in a state. It must provide a minimum coverage level of a comprehensive package of benefits known as essential health benefits (EHBs) and follow established limits on cost-sharing, such as deductibles, copays and out-of-pocket maximums. The Marketplace certifies each QHP based on criteria including:

- The health plan is sold by a health insurance company which is licensed and in good standing in the state where the plan is sold.

- The health plan is sold by a health insurance company which offers at least one Silver and one Gold plan inside the Marketplace.
- The health plan meets non-discrimination, transparency and network adequacy requirements.
- The health plan premium is the same whether the plan is sold inside or outside of the Marketplace.

Network adequacy standards consist of offering a network with a sufficient number of health care providers including mental health and substance abuse providers to ensure access to all services without reasonable delay. A QHP's network must include a sufficient number and geographic distribution of essential community providers to ensure reasonable and timely access to care for low-income and medically underserved populations in the QHP's service area.

Eligibility Requirements

Most individuals will be eligible for health care coverage through the Marketplace. Eligibility is based on four criteria:

1. You must live in the United States.
2. You must be a U.S. citizen or national.
3. You can't be currently incarcerated.
4. You must be lawfully present.

Lawfully present refers a list of immigration statuses which will qualify you for Marketplace coverage. For a complete list of statuses and required documentation needed, refer to https://www.healthcare.gov/immigration-status-and-the-marketplace/.

The two main federal agencies which help determine an individual's eligibility for health coverage through the Marketplace are the Department of Health & Human Services (HHS) and the Internal Revenue Service (IRS). In addition, the Social Security Administration (SSA) and the Department of Homeland Security (DHS) provide data which may be used in the eligibility determination process.

Essential Health Benefits

A core set of benefits called essential health benefits (EHBs) will be covered by every health insurance plan. EHBs must include the following 10 care and services.

1. Ambulatory patient services (outpatient care you obtain without being admitted to a hospital, physician visits and clinics).
2. Emergency services.
3. Hospitalization (such as surgery)
4. Maternity and newborn care (care before and after your baby is born).
5. Mental health and substance use disorder services, including behavioral health treatment (including counseling and psychotherapy).
6. Prescription drugs.
7. Rehabilitative and habilitative services and devices (services and devices to help individuals with injuries, disabilities or chronic conditions gain or recover mental and physical skills).
8. Laboratory services.
9. Preventive and wellness services and chronic disease management (blood pressure screenings and immunizations).
10. Pediatric services including dental and vision care.

Each state has a benchmark plan that is the basis for what services a QHP must cover as EHBs. If a state's benchmark plan lacks pediatric dental or vision coverage it must be supplemented with the Federal Employee Dental and Vision Insurance Program (FEDVIP), pediatric vision/dental plan or the state's separate CHIP plan benefit if one exists. Pediatric services are required for individuals under age 19 but states have the flexibility to require covered for older individuals.

All Medicaid plans must also offer these benefits and services listed above by 2014.

Preventive and Wellness Services

Preventive and wellness services and chronic disease management deserve further explanation as this is a very comprehensive list of medical services which both adults and parents should take full advantage of under the new health care law. The following is a list of preventive services which are **covered without charging you a copay or coinsurance, even if you haven't met your yearly deductible.** For complete details regarding these medical procedures and services, refer to https://www.healthcare.gov/what-are-my-preventive-care-benefits/.

For All Adults:

- One Time abdominal aortic aneurysm screening.
- Alcohol misuse screening and counseling.
- Aspirin use to prevent cardiovascular disease.
- Blood pressure screening for all adults.
- Cholesterol screening for adults of certain ages or at higher risk.
- Colorectal cancer screening for adults over 50.
- Depression screening for adults.
- Diabetes (Type 2) screening for adults with high blood pressure.
- Diet counseling for adults at higher risk for chronic disease.
- HIV screening for everyone ages 15 to 65 and other ages at increased risk.
- Immunization vaccines for adults.
- Obesity screening and counseling for all adults.

- Sexually transmitted infections (STI) prevention counseling for adults at higher risk.
- Syphilis screening for adults at higher risk.
- Tobacco use screening for all adults and cessation interventions for tobacco users.

For Women:

- Anemia screening on a routine basis for pregnant women.
- Breast cancer genetic test counseling (BRCA) for women at higher risk for breast cancer.
- Breast cancer mammography screenings every 1 to 2 years for women over 40.
- Breast cancer chemoprevention counseling for women at higher risk.
- Breastfeeding comprehensive support and counseling from trained providers and access to breastfeeding supplies for pregnant and nursing women.
- Cervical cancer screening for sexually active women.
- Chlamydia infection screening for younger women and other women at higher risk.
- Contraception
- Domestic and interpersonal violence screening and counseling for all women.
- Folic acid supplements for women who may become pregnant.
- Gestational diabetes screening foe women 24 to 28 weeks pregnant and those at high risk of developing gestational diabetes.
- Gonorrhea screening for all women at higher risk.
- Hepatitis B screening for pregnant women at their first prenatal visit.
- HIV screening and counseling for sexually active women.

- Human papillomavirus (HPV) DNA test every 3 years for women with normal cytology results who are age 30 and older.
- Osteoporosis screening for women over age 60 depending on risk factors.
- Rh incompatibility screening for all pregnant women and follow-up testing for women at higher risk.
- Sexually transmitted infections counseling for sexually active women.
- Syphilis screening for all pregnant women or other women at increased risk.
- Tobacco use screening and interventions for all women and expanded counseling for pregnant tobacco users.
- Urinary tract or other infection screening for pregnant women.
- Well-women visits to get recommended services for women under age 65.

For Children:

- Autism screening for children at 18 and 24 months.
- Behavioral assessments for children at the following ages: 0 to 11 months, 1 to 4 years, 5 to 10 years, 11 to 14 years and 15 to 17 years.
- Blood pressure screening for children at the following ages: 0 to 11 months, 1 to 4 years, 5 to 10 years, 11 to 14 years and 15 to 17 years.
- Cervical dysplasia screening for sexually active females.
- Depression screening for adolescents.
- Dyslipidemia screening for children at higher risk of lipid disorders at the following ages: 1 to 4 years, 5 to 10 years, 11 to 14 years and 15 to 17 years.
- Fluoride chemoprevention supplements for children without fluoride in their water source.

- Gonorrhea prevention medication for the eyes of all newborns.
- Hearing screening for all newborns.
- Height, weight and body mass index measurements for children at the following ages: 0 to 11 months. 1 to 4 years, 5 to 10 years, 11 to 14 years and 15 to 17 years.
- Hematocrit or hemoglobin screening for children.
- Hemoglobinopathies or sickle cell screening for newborns.
- HIV screening for adolescents at higher risk.
- Hypothyroidism screening for newborns.
- Immunization vaccines for children from birth to age 18.
- Iron supplements for children ages 6 to 12 months at risk for anemia.
- Lead screening for children at risk of exposure.
- Medical history for all children throughout development at the following ages: 0 to 11 months, 1 to 4 years and 5 to 10 years.
- Obesity screening and counseling.
- Oral health risk assessment for young children at ages: 0 to 11 months, 1 to 4 years and 5 to 10 years.
- Phenylketonuria (PKU) screening for this genetic disorder in newborns.
- Sexually transmitted infection (STI) prevention counseling and screening for adolescents at higher risk.
- Tuberculin testing for children at higher risk of tuberculosis at the following ages: 0 to 11 months, 1 to 4 years, 5 to 10 years, 11 to 14 years and 15 to 17.
- Vision screening for all children.

Key Enrollment Dates

There are three dates to remember regarding the initial rollout of the Health Insurance Marketplace.

- October 1, 2013: Marketplace open enrollment begins for individuals and families.
- October 1, 2013: Marketplace open enrollment for small businesses with 50 full-time employees or less, including part-time employees who work more than 30 hours a week begins for paper application only.
- January 1, 2014: Coverage becomes effective for both, if enrolled by December 24th.
- March 31, 2014: Open enrollment ends.

During the open enrollment period, eligible individuals can select QHPs through the Marketplace or change from one QHP to another. If you want to have health care coverage effective January 1, 2014, you must enroll in a Marketplace plan by December 24, 2013. After open enrollment ends on March 31, 2014, you will not be able to get health insurance coverage through the Marketplace until the next annual enrollment period, unless you have a qualifying event.

Though it's not official at the time of this writing, it appears the Obama administration will give health insurers an extra month to evaluate the results of the 2013-14 enrollments to set premium rates. Instead of October 15, 2014 as the next Open Enrollment Period, it will now be November 15, 2014. This will now be after the mid-term elections. If there are big premium hikes, individuals may not see them until after the elections now.

If you qualify for Medicaid or the Children's Health Insurance Program (CHIP), your coverage can begin immediately. You can apply for either of these programs at any time if you qualify. Small employers generally may start offering health insurance coverage to their employees through the Marketplace at any time during the year.

Qualifying Life Events

Qualifying life events (QLEs) are changes in your life which can make you eligible for a *Special Enrollment Period (SEP)*, much like the SEPs in Medicare. This SEP allows you to enroll for health insurance coverage through the Marketplace. The Marketplace application includes questions to see if consumers qualify for SEPs. Consumers' eligibility notices will indicate whether they are qualified. The SEP generally lasts for 60 days from the date of the qualifying event. For the small business group the SEP last for 30 days from the qualifying event. Examples of QLEs include:

- Loss of minimum essential coverage.
- Moving to a new state.
- Certain changes in your income.
- You marry or divorce.
- You become pregnant, have a baby or adopt.
- Enrollment error.
- Change in citizenship.
- Violation of a contract by a health plan.
- Change in job-based coverage.
- Gain or loss of eligibility for premium tax credits or cost-sharing reductions or change in level of cost-sharing reduction if already enrolled in a QHP through the Marketplace.
- Change in status as an American Indian or Alaska Native.

Types of Health Insurance Plans Available

Nearly all health insurance companies use managed care to deliver health care services. Managed care is a way for health insurance companies to manage the quality, cost and access to services. The health insurance companies develop contracts with providers to create networks that will deliver care to consumers. There may be limits on the benefits or additional costs to consumers if they use non-contracted providers who are also called out-of-network providers. There are six different types of health insurance plans available in the Marketplace.

69

1. Health Maintenance Organization (HMOs)
2. Exclusive Provider Organization (EPOs)
3. Preferred Provider Organizations (PPOs)
4. Point-of-Service Plans (POS)
5. High Deductible Health Plan (HDHP)
6. Catastrophic Health Insurance Plan

In addition, there are three other types of plans available within the Marketplace. These are:

- *Consumer Operated and Oriented Plans (CO-OPs):* The ACA creates a new type of private nonprofit health insurer called a CO-OP. These CO-OP health plans are directed by their customers and designed to offer individuals and small businesses more affordable, consumer-friendly and high quality health insurance options. CO-OPs will be able to offer health plans through the Individual Marketplaces and SHOP beginning January 1, 2014. CO-OPs may also offer health plans outside of the Marketplaces.
- *Multi-State Plans (MSPs):* The ACA directs the Office of Personnel Management to contract with private health insurers to provide MSPs in State-based Marketplaces and Federally-facilitated Marketplaces. Through the MSP program, plans from the same health insurance issuer will be available to families or small businesses which mat reside or operate in more than one state. Enrollment in an MSP will be open to all consumers in both the Individual Marketplace and SHOP. These MSPs will not be available in all states.
- *Stand-Alone Dental Plans:* While pediatric dental is an EHB which health issuers must offer in their QHPs, adult dental coverage is not. Adult consumers may separately purchase a stand-alone dental plan through the Marketplace. These stand-alone dental

plans will be certified as meeting many of the same standards as the QHPs.

Health Plan Categories

In addition to covering EHBs and limiting cost sharing (including out of pocket costs) QHPs must also provide coverage that meets one of five levels of generosity. These health plans are separated into 5 plan categories, based on the percentage the plan pays of the overall cost of providing essential health benefits to members. The choice of plan category affects the total amount you'll likely spend for essential health benefits during the year. This isn't to be confused with coinsurance in which you pay a specific percentage of the cost of a specific service. The higher category plans will require members to pay higher premiums, but require the health insurers to pay a greater amount of the cost.

QHP insurers do not have to offer plans in all five levels. However, **each QHP issuer must offer a silver and gold QHP in the Marketplace.** These requirements begin on January 1, 2014. The 5 categories of generosity are:

1. Catastrophic – no AV percentage
2. Bronze – 60% AV
3. Silver – 70% AV
4. Gold – 80% AV
5. Platinum – 90% AV

Bronze, silver, gold and platinum health care plans are based on an actuarial value (AV) of benefits over the cost sharing. The AV is a measure of EHB coverage estimated to be paid by the QHP issuer for a standard population. The higher the AV, the more the member will pay in monthly premium cost and the less they will pay in out-of-pocket costs. AV is an average measure of generosity – the percentage of medical costs the plan will cover after premium payments. For example, with the Bronze plan the QHP issuer would pay, on average, 60% of the cost for essential health benefits (EHBs) coverage with the individual being responsible for the remaining 40% of the cost of covered benefits. However, individuals could be responsible for a higher or lower percentage of the total costs of covered services for the year depending on their actual health needs. The catastrophic plan operates differently from the other plans which are based on actuarial value (AV). The catastrophic plan offers a level of coverage that does not meet a specific AV but must comply with the maximum out-of-pocket limit. Catastrophic plans are offered in the Individual Marketplace and cover EHBs. Eligibility is available only to individuals who are under age 30, those who otherwise do not have an affordable coverage option or who would qualify for a hardship exemption to the minimum essential coverage rule. These plans have higher deductibles than the other plans. Benefits include lower premiums than the other plans, protection against out-of-pocket costs above $6,350 for an individual and $12,700 for a family and coverage of recommended preventive services without cost sharing.

On California's state-run marketplace, the standard low-premium bronze plan carries a $5,000 deductible per person, $60 copay to see a physician and 30% coinsurance for hospitalization. Rhode Island has a $5,800 deductible bronze plan while Missouri federally-run site has the maximum-allowable $6,350 deductible.

Out-of-Pocket Limits

QHPs are required by the ACA to provide recommended preventative health services without cost sharing or deductible requirements. All QHPs must limit cost sharing for its members in the following ways:

- Deductibles and copays cannot be applied to preventive services.

- Annual cost-sharing limits cannot exceed the limits for certain high deductible health plans (HDHPs) including catastrophic plans. The limits for 2014 are $6,350 for an individual and $12,700 for families.
- Deductibles for small group plans cannot exceed $2,000 for self-coverage or $4,000 for any other coverage, except to the extent that a higher deductible is necessary to create a reasonable bronze or silver plan. Figures can be adjusted annually.

Beginning January 1, 2014, no annual or lifetime dollar limits are allowed on EHBs.

Healthcare Planning

Consumers need to do some math to figure out what their maximum expenses will be under a particular plan and how much they would have to spend at a minimum. Your total possible healthcare costs for the year will be whatever your annual health insurance premiums are (based on the plan you have chosen) plus your maximum out-of-pocket expenses (should you reach that amount), based on either an individual or family status. Individuals who know they are likely to visit physicians and specialists frequently, particularly if they have a chronic illness which requires them to visit physicians often or take several medications may do better with a higher level metal AV plan which has a lower deductible but higher monthly premium.

Initial Marketplace Results

Despite the early malfunctions of the HealthCare.gov website, individuals have been filing applications and enrolling in qualified health plans through the Marketplace. By the end of the first week of operations California, one of 14 states running its own marketplace, reported that 28,699 individuals had signed up through their marketplace while New York indicated more than

40,000 had signed up. As the end of October drew to a close the Internal Revenue Service reported the federal healthcare website had delivered 330,000 premium subsidy calculations to individuals that have gotten deep enough into the system to find out whether they qualify for financial help.

On January 13, 2014, the Department of Health and Human Services released enrollment data statistics for the three month period from October 1st to December 28, 2013.

- The total number of individuals who applied for coverage through a federal or state marketplace portal – 4,348,224.
- The total number of individuals who have selected a Marketplace plan – 2,153,421.
- The number of individuals selecting a plan through the federal-run FFM Marketplace – 1,196,430.
- The number of individuals selecting a plan through the 15 state-run SBM Marketplaces, including the District of Columbia – 956,991.
- The number of individual told, during the application process, they were eligible for Medicaid or the Children's Health Insurance Fund (CHIP) – 1.6 million.
- Approximately 79% of the 4.3 million individuals who have gone through the Marketplace eligibility process qualify for the premium subsidies.

In addition, plan selection by metal level for the first three months has been as follows:

- Bronze – 20%
- Silver – 60%
- Gold – 13%
- Platinum – 7%
- Catastrophic – 1%

(Totals do not add up to 100% due to rounding.)

A comparison of the age distribution of Marketplace plan selections, both SBM and FFM combined, revealed the following:

- Age<18 – 6%
- Age 18-25 – 9%
- Age 26-34 – 15%
- Age 35-44 – 15%
- Age 45-54 – 22%
- Age 55-64 – 33%
- Age 65 or older – 0%

The goal of the Obama administration is to get about 7 million individuals to buy health insurance policies through the Marketplace during the initial 6-month open enrollment period ending March 31, 2014. As the program moves further in time one reporting difference should be noted regarding enrollments. The Obama administration includes anyone who has selected a Marketplace plan as enrolling. However, the health insurers do not count them as enrollee's until they begin to pay premiums, which may not begin for some until 2014.

In Florida, where I live, there are an estimated 3.8 million uninsured residents under the age of 65. This is nearly one-fourth of the state's residents who have no health care insurance. This is the second highest in the U.S. In October only 3,571 Floridians selected a federally-run Marketplace plan. In Texas, 2,991 selected a plan while in Alaska, which was at the bottom, only 53 individuals enrolled.

"We see healthcare shifting from a procedure reimbursement, where in this country doctors are reimbursed for how many procedures they conduct, to a world where people will be reimbursed for the outcomes - did the patient actually get better, and what was the total cost of the cycle of care."

John Sculley
Partner Sculley Brothers, LLC
Former CEO – Apple
Former CEO – PepsiCo

CHAPTER FIVE

MARKETPLACE FOR INDIVIDUALS AND FAMILIES

While all health insurance plans are offered by private companies, the Marketplace is run by either your specific state or the federal government. If your state runs its Marketplace, you'll need to use your state's website. No matter what state you live in, you'll be able to use the Marketplace to apply for coverage, compare your options, and enroll. Find out about your specific state, use this link at https://www.healthcare.gov/what-is-the-marketplace-in-my-state/.

The 36 states working with the federal government to run their Marketplace include Alaska, Arkansas, Arizona, Delaware, Florida, Georgia, Iowa, Idaho, Illinois, Indiana, Kansas, Louisiana, Maine, Michigan, Missouri, Mississippi, Montana, North Carolina, North Dakota, Nebraska, New Hampshire, New Jersey, New Mexico, Ohio, Oklahoma, Pennsylvania, South Carolina, South Dakota, Tennessee, Texas, Utah, Virginia, Wisconsin, West Virginia and Wyoming.

In late September 2013, The Office of the Assistant Secretary for Planning and Evaluation, along with the Department of Health and Human Services (HHS), released a report giving examples of the cost of health care purchased in the 36 previously listed states. Close to 95% of consumers will be able to choose between at least two health insurance plans. The weighted average lowest monthly premiums for a 27 year old in the 36 states will be $129 per month for a low-end catastrophic plan, $163 per month for a bronze plan and $203 per month for a silver plan. This is before tax credits are taken into account which are applicable to individuals and families with household incomes which are between 100% and 400% of the federal poverty level (FPL).

Individuals and families can apply for Marketplace coverage four ways:

1. By mail. Complete a paper application and return it. Downloadable on October 1, 2013.
2. In-person assister who is trained and certified to help you. Known as Navigators, Application Assisters, Certified Application Counselors or government agencies such as state Medicaid and CHIP offices.
3. By telephone. Use the National Marketplace Toll-Free Call Center, 1-800-318-2596 (TTY 1-855-889-4325) 24 hours a day, seven days a week. Assistance available in both English and Spanish.
4. Online using the federal government's website, HealthCare.gov.

The online application process begins at HealthCare.gov; https://www.healthcare.gov/marketplace/individual/. We'll review the online process in more detail at the end of the chapter.

The Individual Marketplace collects and verifies eligibility information from an individual then determines their eligibility for a QHP and facilitates their enrollment process into a QHP if desired. The application process has been streamlined and will assist in determining an individual's eligibility to enroll in Medicaid and CHIP. This process also helps in determining whether an individual is eligible for advance payments of premium tax credits and/or cost-sharing reductions. The applicant will need to provide information as to citizenship, incarceration, household income and residency status. The Marketplace process will verify the applicant's information through the Social Security Administration, the Internal Revenue Service and the Department of Homeland Security.

There are two types of individuals who may need to buy health insurance from the new health insurance marketplace. They are (1) those with no health insurance now because they were either uninsurable because of current health or pre-existing conditions or could not afford the premiums and (2) those that have costly coverage through their employer or an individual policy. New terminology may be confusing when you first begin speaking with individuals in the health insurance industry now. A key theme to understand is the concept of on exchange and off exchange. Simply put, on exchange refers to those health insurance policies which are offered through the Health Insurance Marketplace. Off exchange refers to those policies which are offered through the health insurance carriers. As individuals navigate this process there are three steps you need to be aware of when comparing health insurance policies on exchange and off exchange:

- Look at the premiums and compare the two.
- Look at the coverage and compare the two.
- Compare copays and deductibles.

There will be no easy way around this, you're just going to have to devote some time to this process to ensure you can find the most cost effective and benefits rich plan which will meet you and/or your family's needs.

Estimating your Income

If you plan to apply for lower costs, such as premium tax credits and/or cost-sharing reductions, in the Marketplace, you'll need to estimate your household income for 2014. For each of the following sources, estimate what your income will be in 2014:

- Wages
- Salaries
- Tips
- Net income from any self-employment or business (generally the amount of money you take in from your business minus your business expenses)
- Unemployment compensation
- Social Security payments, including disability payments but not Supplemental Security Income (SSI)
- Alimony
- Other items to include when estimating your 2014 income are: retirement income, investment income, pension income, rental income, and other taxable income such as prizes, awards, and gambling winnings.

DON'T include the following:

- Child support
- Gifts
- Supplemental Security Income (SSI)
- Veterans' disability payments
- Workers' compensation
- Proceeds from loans (like student loans, home equity loans, or bank loans)

Then add up these income items for:

- You and your spouse, if you are married and will file a joint tax return.
- Any dependents who make enough money to be required to file a tax return.

Your household income is your modified adjusted gross income (MAGI) (joint MAGI if you're married), plus the MAGI of your dependents who make enough money to have to file a tax return. MAGI is your adjusted gross income plus any **tax-exempt** Social Security benefits (except for Supplemental Security Income (SSI), which is not counted), tax-exempt interest, and tax-exempt foreign income. You don't have to figure out your household income or MAGI yourself when you fill out your application. It will be done for you with the income information you include on the application.

Premium Tax Credits

Premium tax credits can be used to reduce the cost of premiums for themselves and for any tax dependent. There are two options in using the premium tax credits.

1. **Choose to apply the tax credit towards QHP premium costs on an advanced basis.** Advance payments are paid directly to the QHP issuer on a monthly basis. The individual is required to file a federal tax return for the coverage year to reconcile any advance payments of the premium tax credit with the premium tax credit allowed on the return. If the premium tax credit allowed on their federal tax return is more than the amount of the advance payments of the credit advanced, they can receive difference as a tax return. However, if the premium tax credit allowed on their federal tax return is less than the amount of the credit advance, they will need to repay the difference on their federal tax return, subject to statutory caps.

2. **Choose to receive the credit on their federal tax return filed for the coverage year.** If you're married at the end of the coverage year, you are required to file a joint return to receive the premium tax credit.

Both Marketplaces will provide documentation to the tax filer and to the IRS that will support the reconciliation process just as it is done when an employer or bank provides a Form W-2 or 1099.

An individuals' eligibility to receive the premium tax credit is based on household income and access to minimum essential coverage. Individuals must meet the following criteria to be eligible.

- Is not eligible for minimum essential coverage (MEC). This would include employer-sponsored coverage, Medicaid, CHIP and Medicare. This includes employer-sponsored coverage which is not affordable or does not provide minimum value.
- Has an annual household income which is between 100% and 400% of the Federal Poverty Level (FPL) or below 100% of FPL for lawfully present non-citizens who are ineligible for Medicaid by reason of immigration status.
- Need to be part of a tax household which will file a federal tax return for the coverage year. If the tax household includes a married couple they will need to file a joint return.
- Enroll in a QHP through the Marketplace.

Table 5.1, on the next page, displays the FPL level for each family size and the percentage columns which represent income levels which are commonly used as guidelines for the Health Insurance Marketplace. Incomes in the table below are based on 2013 numbers.

Table 5.1 2014 Federal Poverty Levels Percentage Based on Household Size

Percent of Poverty Guidelines (in dollars rounded up)								
Family Size	1	2	3	4	5	6	7	8
100%	11,670	15,730	19,790	23,850	27,910	31,970	36,030	40,090
120%	14.004	18,876	23,748	28,620	33,492	38,364	43,236	48,108
133%	15,521	20,921	26,321	31,721	37,121	42,521	47,920	53,320
135%	15,755	21,236	26,717	32,198	37,679	43,160	48,641	54,122
150%	17,505	23,595	29,685	35,775	41,865	47,955	54,045	60,135
175%	20,423	27,528	34,633	41,738	48,843	55,948	63,053	70,158
185%	21,590	29,101	36,612	44,123	51,634	59,145	66,656	74,167
200%	23,340	31,460	39,580	47,700	55,820	63,940	72,060	80,180
250%	29,175	39,325	49,475	59,625	69,775	79,925	90,075	100,225

Courtesy: Medicaid

For example, from the previous table for 2013 this would include an individual with an income up to $45,960, for a family of two would include incomes up to $62,040 and for a family of four means those with incomes of less than about $94,200 will qualify for the premium tax credits.

Calculating the premium tax credit is based on annual household income, family size and the cost of a Silver level (70% AV) essential health benefit (EHB) benchmark plan for that individual or family. The amount of the premium tax credit also depends on the plan which the individual or family selects. If the premium for the plan selected is greater than the maximum premium tax credit allowed, the individual or family may elect to receive the maximum premium tax credit in advanced, which will be paid directly to the QHP, and pay the difference as a monthly premium to the QHP. If the premium for the plan selected is less than the maximum premium tax credit, they could elect to receive the premium tax credit in advanced, again paid directly to the QHP, and have no additional monthly premium payment. They may also be able to get the excess returned when they file their federal tax return.

A couple of examples may help to clarify this. In the first example, when calculated, family A is eligible for a maximum premium tax credit of $700/month. They choose to select a QHP from the Marketplace which costs $1,000/month. They also elect to have the full amount of their premium tax credit advanced. Thus, the Marketplace will pay the QHP the $700/month while family A will pay a monthly premium to the QHP for the balance of $300/month. In the second example, when calculated, an individual is eligible for a maximum premium tax credit of $500/month. They choose to select a QHP from the Marketplace which costs $400/month. They also elect to have their premium tax credit advanced. The Marketplace will pay the QHP $500/month. Thus, since the cost of the plan selected is less than their premium tax credit they will have no monthly premium. They may also be eligible for a return of that excess (up to $1,200; $100 difference x 12 months) on their federal tax return when they file.

Cost-Sharing Reductions

Cost-sharing reductions limit the out-of-pocket costs for essential health benefits covered by the QHP. To be eligible the individual must:

- Meet the eligibility requirements for enrollment in a QHP.
- Meet the eligibility criteria and receive the premium tax credit.
- Have annual household income less than or equal to 250% of FPL. This does not apply for members of federally-recognized Indian tribes which have special standards.

- Be enrolled in a Silver level QHP. Once again does not apply for members of federally-recognized Indian tribes, which have special standards.

For 2013, eligibility for cost-sharing reductions is based on whether the individual's household incomes are below the amounts shown below which are equivalent to 250% FPL.

- Individual – up to $28,725
- Family of Two – up to $38,775
- Family of Three - $48,825
- Family of Four - $58,875
- Family of Five - $68,925
- Family of Six - $78,975
- Family of Seven - $89,025
- Family of Eight - $99,075

QHPs may implement these differently based on their specific plan design. If an individual or family is eligible for a category of cost-sharing reductions, the plan comparison pages will reflect adjusted cost-sharing requirements of each plan available to them.

Qualifying for Lower Costs on Health Care

The following graphic, Table 5.2 on the next page, provides a summary of the household income levels needed to qualify for lower premiums, lower out-of-pocket costs and whether or not you may qualify for Medicaid coverage, depending upon whether your state is expanding Medicaid or not. If you're state is not expanding Medicaid and you have limited income and you don't qualify for Medicaid under your state's current rules, learn about how you can get low-cost health care at a Community Health Center near you. Community health centers are located in both urban and rural areas and provide:

- prenatal care
- baby shots
- general primary care
- referrals to specialized care, including mental health, substance abuse, and HIV/AIDS

For more information on reporting income, see IRS Publication 525. For further information as to who qualifies as a dependent, see IRS Publication 501.

Table 5.2 Summary of Qualifying Household Incomes

| | | Number of people in your household | | | | | |
		1	2	3	4	5	6
Private Marketplace health plans	You may qualify for **lower premiums on a Marketplace insurance plan** if your yearly income is between... *See next row if your income is at the lower end of this range.*	$11,490 - $45,960	$15,510 - $62,040	$19,530 - $78,120	$23,550 - $94,200	$27,570 - $110,280	$31,590 - $126,360
	You may qualify for **lower premiums AND lower out-of-pocket costs for Marketplace insurance** if your yearly income is between...	$11,490 - $28,725	$15,510 - $38,775	$19,530 - $48,825	$23,550 - $58,875	$27,570 - $68,925	$31,590 - $78,975
Medicaid coverage	If your state **is** expanding Medicaid in 2014: You may qualify for **Medicaid coverage** if your yearly income is below...	$15,857	$21,404	$26,951	$32,499	$38,047	$43,594
	If your state **isn't** expanding Medicaid: **You may not qualify for any Marketplace savings programs** if your yearly income is below...	$11,490	$15,510	$19,530	$23,550	$27,570	$31,590

Courtesy: Department of Health and Human Services (HHS); Health Insurance Marketplace

Household incomes in the table above are based on 2013 numbers. They are likely to be slightly higher in 2014.

Determining Eligibility

The Marketplace determines eligibility through a 4-step process.

1. Application: This can be accomplished either by mail, online, in-person or via a call center. Individuals provide their personal information to the Marketplace through the eligibility application.
2. Eligibility Determination: The applicant may request eligibility determination in a QHP and for insurance affordability programs, including Medicaid, CHIP, advance payment of premium tax credits and cost-sharing reductions. Depending upon the state in which the applicant resides in, the Marketplace may make an assessment of eligibility for Medicaid and CHIP instead of a determination for a QHP. If the applicant is potentially eligible the Marketplace will transfer the applicant to the state Medicaid or CHIP agency for final determination.
3. Verification: Assurance of correct data is done utilizing the applicant's Social Security Number, being a U.S. citizen or having lawful presence, incarceration status and American Indian/Alaska Native status, if applicable. If the applicant is seeking eligibility for an insurance affordability program their current monthly household income and annual household income will be verified for Medicaid/CHIP programs and/or advancement of premium tax credits or cost-sharing reductions. This would also apply to accessing minimum essential coverage.
4. Notification: Must provide the applicant timely written notice of eligibility determination. If application was submitted electronically, notification occurs immediately and will indicate if any further information is required. These notices will also include information regarding appeal rights. If the

applicant is assessed or determined eligible for Medicaid or CHIP, the Marketplace must transfer the applicant to the applicable state Medicaid or CHIP agency, which will follow up for plan/delivery system selection.

In states where the Marketplace assesses Medicaid and CHIP eligibility, consumers will have their account transferred to the Medicaid/CHIP agency for final eligibility determination. States then will notify the Marketplace of the final eligibility determination. In states where the Marketplace is authorized to make Medicaid and CHIP program eligibility determinations, no account transfer will take place. The Marketplace will issue a notice to those individuals containing their Medicaid or CHIP eligibility.

Effective Coverage Dates

The date which individuals can begin receiving benefits from their selected QHP depends on when they enrolled in the QHP. Once enrolled, individuals must first pay any premium which they owe to the health insurer before they can receive plan benefits. Coverage begins on the following dates for the individual:

- Selects a QHP during the open enrollment period (October 1st through December 15th) and submits the first premium payment by the date specified by the health insurer, coverage will start on January 1st.
- Selects a QHP during the open enrollment period (December 16th through March 31st), the start of coverage will begin based on either of the following:

  o If the QHP is selected between the 1st and 15th of the month and the premium is paid by the date specified by the health insurer, coverage will begin on the first day of the following month. For example, if selected on

88

February 7th and payment is due by February 15th and the premium is paid on February 12th, coverage begins on March 1st.

o If the QHP is selected between the 16th through the last day of the month and the premium is paid by the date specified by the health insurer, coverage will begin on the first day of the second following month. For example, if selected on January 20th and payment is due by February 15th and the premium is paid on February 12th, coverage begins on March 1st.

Effective dates of coverage for special enrollment periods generally follow the same timeline as the dates listed above. The exceptions are in the case of marriage or if a qualified individual losses minimum essential coverage, coverage becomes effective on the first day of the following month. In the case of birth or adoption, coverage is effective on the date of the event.

Annual Redetermination

Beginning September 2014, the Marketplace will automatically reassess the eligibility of all qualified individuals determined eligible for enrollment in a QHP in the previous year. Any changes in coverage or eligibility will be effective on January 1st of the following year.

When an individual completed the initial application and requested help paying for health coverage and agreed to allow the Marketplace to re-check data on an annual basis, the Marketplace will check income data from the IRS and SSA and use this data to re-determine eligibility. If an individual doesn't agree to a re-check of their data on an annual basis, the Marketplace will send a notice indicating they are unable to determine if they will remain eligible for programs to help lower their costs. The individual will need to contact the Marketplace directly to see if they still qualify for assistance such as premium tax credits or cost-sharing reductions.

Privacy and Security Standards

The Marketplace places a high value on privacy. It seeks to maintain consumer trust in its ability to protect a consumer's sensitive and personal information. The Marketplace has standards for privacy and security of personally identifiable information (PII) and federal tax information (FTI). These privacy guidelines provide consumers with information on how their personal information is used or shared and provide protections to prevent consumers from having their personal information used or shared in a harmful way. Marketplace requirements regarding consumer privacy include:

- Letting consumers know, in writing, what personal information is collected, why it's collected, how it will be used and maintained and when that collected information can be shared.
- Collecting only the information that's necessary to accomplish an authorized purpose.
- Obtain consumer consent by using a consent form approved by the CMS. Consent forms should be stored and protected as described in the privacy and security requirements.
- Having policies and procedures for protecting and securing all personal information.
- Complying with all applicable privacy and security requirements and IRS rules.

PII is a type of information that can be used to distinguish or trace a consumer's identity. Examples of PII you may be asked to provide include:

- Name
- Social Security number (SSN)

- Date and place of birth
- Mother's maiden name
- Biometric records (e.g., fingerprints)
- Medical, educational, financial, and/or employment information
- Phone number
- Home address
- Driver's license number

FTI is defined as information disclosed by the IRS or re-disclosed by an authorized recipient who got the information from the IRS. FTI is classified as confidential and may not be used or disclosed except as expressly authorized by the IRS. Examples of FTI include:

- Electronic or paper tax returns or forms such as 1040, 941, 1099, 1120, and W-2.
- Tax return information, which includes a taxpayer's name, mailing address and identification number such as SSN or Employer Identification Number (EIN).
- Information pulled from a tax return including names of dependents or the location of a business.
- Information on whether a tax return was, is being or will be examined or subject to other investigation or processing.
- Information about the consumer's income, personal finances, debts, deductions and exemptions.
- Any action taken by the IRS against the individual such as an investigation or a penalty.
- Any private written agreements between the individual and the IRS (pricing agreements) and any background information about these agreements.

There are Marketplace standards for protecting PII and FTI. These policies and procedures include, but aren't limited to:

91

- Consumers have a right to access their records in the Marketplace.
- The Marketplace, including individuals and organizations approved to provide assistance to consumers in the Marketplace, must ensure openness and transparency about policies and procedures that directly affect consumers.
- Consumers are provided a reasonable opportunity and capability to make informed decisions about the creation, collection, disclosure access, maintenance and storage and use of their PII.
- Information collected can only be used for Marketplace functions. It can never be used to discriminate against a consumer.
- The Marketplace and Marketplace entities approved to provide assistance to consumers in the Marketplace are responsible for data quality and integrity and must have procedures in place to assure that data is not altered or lost.
- The Marketplace and Marketplace entities approved to provide assistance to consumers in the Marketplace are accountable for appropriate monitoring and other means to identify and report incidents or breaches of security such as lost records and emailing PII or FTI.

The Marketplace, and Marketplace entities approved to provide assistance to consumers in the Marketplace, should have written procedures in place for addressing security issues. Issues which should be reported include:

- Lost, stolen, or misplaced records.
- Unauthorized personnel seeing or possessing PII or FTI information.
- Emailing PII or FTI between staff members.
- Instances you recognize as opportunities for compromising consumer information.

If an individual's FTI is breached, it may be required to report the incident to the Agent-in-Charge, Treasury Inspector General for Tax Administration (TIGTA) and the IRS Office of Safeguards.

Online Enrollment Process

The following flowchart on the next page provides an overview of the steps involved for the online enrollment process.

Figure 5.1 Overview of the Individual Enrollment Process

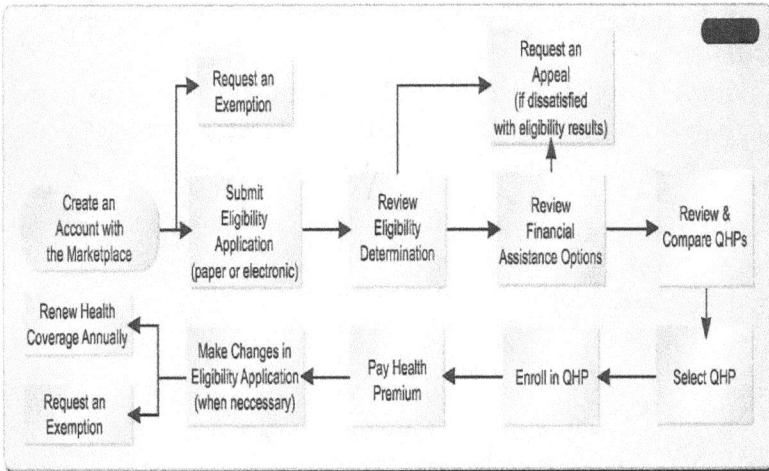

Courtesy: Department of Health and Human Services; Health Insurance Marketplace

Individuals may view and compare general health plan information at any time but complete health plan details including cost-sharing requirements and provider networks are only available after an individual creates an account. The basic online enrollment steps include:

1. Create an online account.
2. Fill out an online application

3. Review and compare QHPs
4. Enroll in a QHP.

Each step will be discussed in further detail.

Account Creation

Account creation is a two-step process. First, the individual will need to provide their name and email address to create a basic login which will enable them to begin an application or view QHP options and services. Second, individuals who want to submit an application or select and enroll in a plan need to provide additional information and complete an identity validation process to ensure the application process is secure.

Information which individuals will be asked to provide is considered personally identifiable information (PII). This includes:

- Username (required)
- Password (required)
- Four security questions (required)
- First name
- Middle name
- Last name
- Suffix (Jr., III, etc.)
- Physical address (required)
- Mailing address
- Social Security number or other document number for legal immigrants
- Date of birth (required)
- Telephone number (required)

Once the PII is entered the system will conduct the identity validation process. The system will present a series of real-time questions related to their personal information. These questions are the same types of questions that are used when individuals apply for a loan, request a copy of their credit report, or create an account to view their Social Security statement. If individuals successfully answer the questions, the process will be complete and individuals can move on to the application. If the validation process is unsuccessful, the system will direct the individual to contact the Call Center where they will be asked additional questions.

Application Process

Individuals need to fill out the application based on how they file their federal income tax return. For example, a couple who is married and filing jointly would complete one application. Individuals will need to provide the following information on each application:

- Basic contact information.
- Financial assistance (opt in or opt out).
- Names of individual(s) seeking health coverage.
- Personal information for each applicant (e.g., name, date of birth, relationship to the person filing the application).
- Family and household structure.
- Income information.
- Information regarding access to other health coverage.

Verification Process

An individual's application information must match the information from the trusted data sources before they are determined eligible for health coverage or the premium tax credit and/or cost-sharing reductions. The verification process occurs in real-time if applicant's information can be verified. If not, the individual will need to submit the required information and the verification process may take longer. You usually have 90 days to provide the needed documents or the Marketplace will make a decision based on the information which it has.

Additional Documentation Required

If the information provide can't be confirmed against the trusted data sources, individuals may be asked to submit documentation supporting the statements that they made about their citizenship or income. This could include a birth certificate, proof of income, passport number, etc. The online application will provide individuals with a notice that lists all documents they need to submit along with their application. The notice will also explain how long they have to provide the requested documentation. These documents can be immediately uploaded. This may require you to scan the needed documents, create a pdf file then upload those files. If they choose, this can be done later as long as they provide the information within the timeframe specified by the Marketplace. If a document is required which the individual no longer has they can request an extension. For example, the document needed is a birth certificate (to verify citizenship), which has been lost. The individual will need state the type of document for which they need an extension (birth certificate), the original deadline to provide the document, the reason why they're requesting an extension and how long is needed to supply the documentation. You don't need to state how and when the documentation was lost.

Account Profile Updates

Updating basic account profile information is different from updating application data, which could affect consumers' eligibility for health coverage. Updating an account profile could include changing a password, e-mail address or changing an authorized representative. To update their application information after it has been submitted, consumers need to revisit the online application to make real-time changes. For example, if consumers change their e-mail address in the account profile and update their communication preferences to receive application notices electronically, they will have to change the application data.

Eligibility Determination

When the Marketplace makes a decision about an individual's eligibility, it will send the individual a notice. If the individual is eligible, the notice will explain how the Marketplace made its decision and provide details about the programs in which the individual may enroll. If they're not eligible, the notice will explain how the Marketplace made its decision. All eligibility notices, regardless of whether individuals are determined eligible or ineligible, will explain to them how they can appeal the decision if they are dissatisfied with the outcome.

If they applied using a paper application, they will receive a notification in the mail. If you have an online account you can review the eligibility notice online. This notice will let the individual know if they're eligible for the Marketplace, premium tax credits and cost-sharing reductions, Medicaid, or CHIP. It will also show them QHPs that they're eligible to enroll in, and amounts of their premium tax credit and cost-sharing reductions.

Plan Selection and Enrollment

The online tool displays all QHPs available to consumers through the Marketplace and their associated costs and benefits. The amount of information you see depends on the stage you're at in the application process.

For those individuals that have not applied through the Marketplace, you will be able to see all plans available in their area, the associated premium cost without any financial assistance reflected and estimates for financial assistance they may qualify for. An important note, the final cost may change once you enter and submit your personal information and circumstances.

For those individuals that have created an online account and received an eligibility determination, they will be able to compare plans and save their plan comparisons to refer to in the future. They will also be able to see plan costs which are customized to reflect their premium tax credits and cost-sharing reductions.

There is the ability to compare plans by using the filtering and sorting tools. These tools help customize the QHPs that are displayed based on what factors are important to the individual. QHPs can be filtered based on many factors including:

- Premium price range
- Out-of-pocket maximum
- Cost-sharing reduction
- Annual deductible
- Availability of coverage across several states (this option might be important for families with children attending college in another state)
- Plan type (e.g., Health Maintenance Organization (HMO), Preferred Provider Organization (PPO))
- Category of coverage (e.g., Bronze, Silver, Gold, Platinum, Catastrophic)
- Dental coverage

You can also compare plans using the side-by-side comparison tool to explore different QHP features and see how plans differ in categories like costs for medical care, prescription drug coverage, and the availability of medical management programs such as pain management, diabetes and depression. You can also compare health plans based on the amount of advance premium tax credit you may be eligible for. The amount you choose at this point won't be permanent, it can be changed later. However, when you view and compare the QHPs, the premium amounts shown in the tool that compares plans will be discounted by the amount you selected. Choosing to use more or less of your available premium tax credit may impact the amount of taxes owed or returned when you file your family's federal income tax return for the year. You also need to ensure the importance of reporting changes in income and other eligibility factors if your circumstances change. Individuals may also be eligible for cost-sharing reductions. If individuals receive an eligibility determination and are eligible for cost-sharing reductions, they'll need to select a Silver level plan to receive the reductions.

When you make your final selection, the Marketplace is going to give you two options: 1) take you to the QHP's website to make a premium payment or 2) wait for the insurance company to send you a bill for the premium. You won't be enrolled in the plan until the QHP receives your first premium payment. **If you don't make your premium payment by the deadline, your coverage will be canceled.**

Requesting an Appeal

Individuals may request an appeal when they are dissatisfied with an eligibility determination. If you forgot to submit supporting documentation within the specified time period you may not be able to appeal. Reasons for an appeal could include:

- Consumers who were found not eligible for enrollment in a QHP.
- Consumers who disagree with the eligibility determination for premium tax credits or cost-sharing reductions.
- Consumers who were found not eligible for an exemption.
- Consumers who didn't receive their eligibility determination notice within a certain number of days (to be specified by the Marketplace).

Individuals must submit specific information to complete the requests. At a minimum, they should provide the following information:

- First Name
- Last Name
- Address
- Appeal Reason

Individuals can submit documents to the Marketplace which support their eligibility along with their initial appeal request any time during the appeals process leading up to the hearing. Supporting documents can be submitted to the Marketplace by mail. An individual can be granted eligibility while the appeal is pending, as long as they meet certain qualifications specified by the Marketplace. They may accept or waive the benefits while the appeal is pending. If they accept the health coverage benefits during the appeals process, they may need to pay a fee if the appeal decision states that they weren't eligible for the benefits that they accepted.

An informal resolution is attempted. The consumer decides whether or not to accept the informal resolution. If they accept the appeal is closed and the decision is communicated through a notice. If they don't accept, a hearing is requested and then conducted. After the hearing, the appeal is closed and the decision is communicated through a notice.

Fraud Referral Process

Fraud happens when an individual or an entity such as a business deliberately misrepresents important information for personal or inappropriate benefit. Individuals, representatives of health insurance companies, health insurance companies themselves and agents/brokers may intentionally submit or provide false or misleading information to the Marketplace and/or other individuals. In addition, others may falsely claim to be certified to offer consumer assistance in the Marketplace to gain access to individual's personal information. Examples of fraud could include:

- An individual uses another person's information to get health coverage through the Marketplace.
- An agent, broker or other type of individual assister uses false information to steer a consumer to a particular health insurance company's health plan.
- An agent, broker or other type of individual assister makes an unsolicited request for an individual's personal information to enroll them in a qualified health plan (QHP).
- An individual provides false identifying information such as a false name or Social Security number (SSN) or intentionally misrepresents their household income.
- An agent, broker or other type of individual assister requests payment to enroll a consumer in health coverage through the Marketplace.
- An agent, broker or other type of individual assister offers payment in exchange for a consumer's personally identifiable information (PII).
- An individual receives an e-mail from someone claiming to be an agent, broker or other type of individual assister asking for personal information to enroll the consumer in a QHP through the Marketplace.

To protect themselves against fraud, you should encourage consumers to follow a few basic guidelines related to the Marketplace:

- Look for official government seals, logos, or .gov web addresses given that official information about the Marketplace will have logos for the Department of

Health & Human Services and the Health Insurance Marketplace.

- Don't respond to unsolicited advertisements.
- Never sign blank insurance forms or applications.
- Be an informed consumer and take time to compare coverage options before making a decision.
- Be aware of product promotions, so-called "special deals," or other offers that seem too good to be true because these offers may be related to fraud or identity theft.
- Don't be pressured into making purchases, signing contracts or committing funds.
- Don't be afraid to ask questions and verify the answers.

If an individual feels they have experienced fraud or have been the victim of identity theft, you should report this to the appropriate authorities. It's important to collect as much information as possible so that you can accurately report it when you contact the proper authorities. The type on information an individual should collect includes:

- The name of the individual or entity suspected of fraud.
- Contact information for the individual or entity suspected of fraud.
- A summary of the suspected fraud.
- The date for when the suspected fraud occurred.
- Whether you suspected the fraud or heard about it from a third party.
- If that third party was an individual, then you should include contact information for that individual as well.

An individual can submit a report of suspected fraud by contacting the HHS OIG Fraud Hotline:

- Online by visiting: http://oig.hhs.gov/fraud/report-fraud/report-fraud-form.asp.
- By phone at: 1-800-HHS-TIPS (1-800-447-8477).
- By fax at: 1-800-223-8164.
- By mail at:

Department of Health and Human Services
Office of Inspector General
ATTN: OIG HOTLINE OPERATIONS
PO Box 23489
Washington, DC 20026

While the majority of individuals and entities are committed to providing accurate information and unbiased Marketplace enrollment assistance, some may have the intention to commit fraud against consumers, the government or both.

Older Individuals

Individuals who do not qualify for premium-free Medicare Part A may choose to enroll in coverage through the Marketplace rather than purchase premium Part A Medicare coverage. **Individuals who are eligible for premium-free Part A Medicare are ineligible to enroll in QHPs through the Marketplace regardless of their income.** Additional factors to consider include:

- Individuals may be eligible for premium tax credits and cost-sharing reductions. If elected must voluntarily end their premium Part A Medicare coverage.
- Individual may also be eligible to access programs available to help pay for Medicare costs including Medicare Savings Programs and the Low-income Subsidy (LIS) or Extra Help for Medicare Part D costs for prescription drugs.

Older individuals, who have incomes lower than 138% of the federal poverty level or $21,404 for a family of two in 2013, may qualify them for Medicaid. For more information see the chapters on Medicare and Medicaid.

Referrals to Medicaid and CHIP Assistance Programs

The following types of individuals could be referred to a Medicaid or CHIP agency in your state:

- Consumers who live in states where the Marketplace assesses Medicaid or CHIP eligibility are assessed as potentially eligible for these programs and referred to the state Medicaid or CHIP agency for the final eligibility determination.
- Consumers who live in states where the Marketplace makes Medicaid or CHIP eligibility determinations are referred to the state Medicaid or CHIP agency to enroll in coverage.
- Consumers who are either already enrolled in Medicaid or CHIP and aren't aware of their enrollment status or are already enrolled in Medicaid or CHIP and are seeking assistance regarding their existing coverage are referred to the state Medicaid or CHIP agency.

Some states have chosen not to expand Medicaid and your state may be one of them. In this case, individuals apply through the Marketplace for an exemption from the individual responsibility requirement.

Vulnerable and Underserved Populations

Individuals who are considered vulnerable and/or underserved may face barriers which make it difficult to get health coverage and basic health services. In Figure 5.2 below, the diagram illustrates the differences between vulnerable and underserved populations. Many individuals can fall into both categories.

Figure 5.2 Vulnerable and Underserved Populations

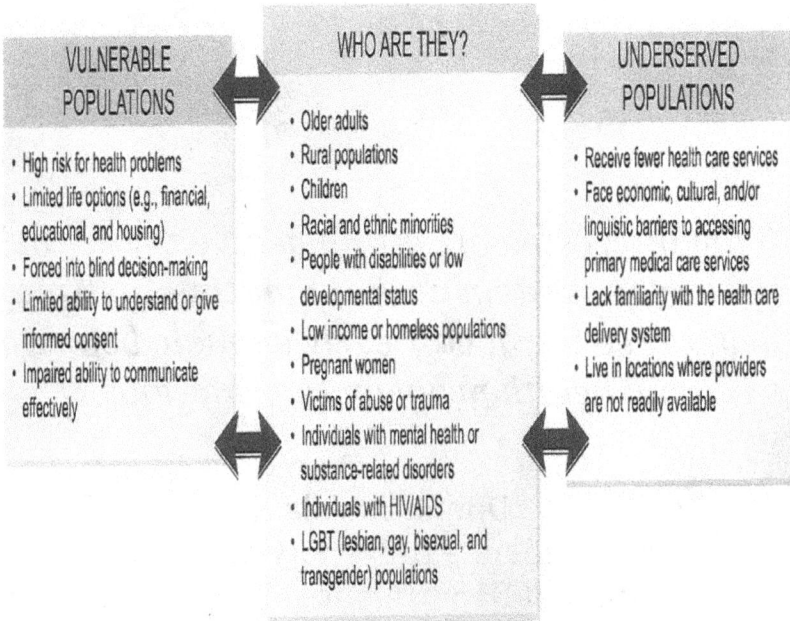

Courtesy: Department of Health and Human Services; Health Insurance Marketplace

Underserved individuals may have limited access to health care services while vulnerable individuals tend to experience additional issues with getting care. These segments of the population tend to have poorer health than the average individual and gets less or second-rate health care. Individuals from vulnerable and underserved populations may have to make health care decisions they do not agree with, do not understand or that don't meet their needs.

"I am interested in getting people to use the healthcare system at the right time, getting them to see the doctor early enough, before a small health problem turns serious."

Donna Shalala
5th President – University of Miami
18th Secretary of Department of Health & Human Services
Chancellor of the University of Wisconsin – Madison

CHAPTER SIX

MARKETPLACE FOR SMALL BUSINESS GROUPS

The Marketplace for small business groups is called the Small Business Health Options Program (SHOP). Under the ACA, during the first year of operation, small businesses which qualify for coverage through a Federally-facilitated SHOP (FF-SHOP) will be able to offer their employees a single QHP option. SHOPs will offer qualified small groups access to QHPs in each state and provide flexibility in the amount which members of the small business group contribute towards the total premium. Premiums for the employers and employees will not be based on their health or medical history. Like the Individual Marketplace, premiums can only vary based on age, family composition, geographic area and tobacco use.

On November 27th, the Obama administration announced a delay for its online small business insurance program. The SHOP marketplace will not offer online enrollment until November 2014, a one-year delay from a launch that was initially planned for October 1st, 2013.

Small businesses will still have the option to purchase SHOP health insurance plans through a broker, agent or health insurance company who can assist the employer with filing a paper application. The federal government expects to process those filings for eligibility within three to five days. With this new delay, small businesses will likely see little change in the way they purchase health insurance until 2015. This delay only affects the 36 states where the federal government is running the health insurance exchange. It does not change the small business options in the 14 states and the District of Columbia which are running their own exchanges.

For questions which may not be answered here you can contact the SHOP Marketplace for businesses with 50 or fewer employees at 1-800-706-7893 (TTY users: 1-800-706-7915), Monday through Friday, 9 AM to 7 PM EST.

SHOP Advantages for Small Business Owners

A few of the advantages which are available to small business owners as a result of the ACA include:

- Qualified small business owners will be able to offer a qualified health insurance plan (QHP) to all employees.
- Qualified small business owners decide on a percentage to contribute toward the health insurance premium of each employee.
- Qualified small business owners and their employees will no longer face premium rate increases or be ineligible to enroll in health insurance plans due to an employee's health status or medical history.
- The SHOP Marketplace may bring less financial uncertainty to qualified owners and employees at plan renewal time.

- The FF-SHOP has an online plan comparison tool which allows users to compare several plans on an apple-to apple basis.
- Qualified employers will be eligible to receive small business tax credits.

In 2014, employers can select one QHP to offer to their employees. Beginning in 2015 employers may offer their employees multiple health plan options. The SHOP Marketplace provides 4 plan categories based on how employees and the plan expect to share the costs for health care:

- Bronze – covers 60% of the total average costs of care
- Silver – covers 70% of the total costs of care
- Gold – covers 80% of the total costs of care.
- Platinum – covers 90% of the total costs of care

In addition, the SHOP Marketplace may also offer qualified dental plans. High coverage levels cover 85% of the total average costs of care while a low coverage level covers 70% of the total average costs of care.

One aspect of the new health care law came under fire for its confusing guidance and projected cost overruns. In July 2013, the Obama administration announced the provision known as the employer mandate would be delayed an additional year. This provision requires employers with more than 50 full-time equivalent (FTE) employees to provide health benefits or face penalties and fines. The issue for large employers dealt with the information reporting requirements of the ACA. This element will now become effective beginning January 1, 2015. Employers with 50 or fewer employees are still required to provide coverage for full-time workers beginning January 1, 2014.

Employees cannot purchase coverage through the Marketplace and get premium tax credits and/or cost-sharing reductions if the health plans offered by their employers are affordable and meet MEC requirements.

SHOP Eligibility

At least 70% of the total full-time employees must participate for the employer to be able to offer SHOP coverage. This excludes employees and dependents of employees who have other creditable health insurance coverage such as another group plan or public health insurance, including Medicare, Medicaid, Veteran's Affairs (VA), Indian Health Services or TRICARE. They are not included in the employer's minimum participation rate calculation. If more than 30% of employees deny the coverage the employer is offering; the employer will be unable to offer health coverage through the SHOP Marketplace. The following states require employers to meet a minimum participation rate other than 70%:

- Arkansas – 75%
- Iowa – 75%
- New Hampshire – 75%
- New Jersey – 75%
- South Dakota – 75%
- Tennessee – 50%
- Texas – 75%

If the employer doesn't reach the minimum participation rate for the SHOP Marketplace they have three options:

1. The employer can change their offer of coverage and increase the employer contribution towards premiums to encourage more eligible employees to participate. If the offer is changed, the employer's current offer will be cancelled.
2. An exception to the 70% rule applies in most states. From November 15 – December 15 each year, an

employer can get SHOP coverage without having to meet the 70% participation requirement.
3. Completely withdraw the offer of coverage.

The SHOP Marketplace collects and verifies eligibility information from employer's and their employees, determines their eligibility for enrollment in a QHP and facilitates enrollment. To qualify for coverage a small business owner must provide attestation to the following:

- Be located within the SHOP's service area. This is typically the entire state.
- Offer coverage to all full-time employees who are working an average of 30 hours or more each week.
- Must have at least one eligible common-law employee on payroll. This generally **excludes** owners including sole proprietors, owners' spouses and dependents on payroll. For a complete definition of a common-law employee, visit the IRS link at www.irs.gov/Businesses/Small-Businesses-&-Self-Employed/Employee-(Common-Law-Employee).
- Must have 50 or fewer FTEs on payroll in 2014. In 2016, the limit will automatically rise to 100 FTEs or less.

To calculate the number of full-time equivalent employees when you apply for SHOP, do the following:

- Use the most recent year.
- Exclude seasonal employees, those working fewer than 120 days a year, from the calculation.
- Count the number of employees who work an average of 30 or more hours a week.
- Add to the above the number of non-full time equivalent employees (total hours worked each week divided by 30).

For example, if an employer has 12 individuals working more than 30 hours each week and 4 individuals, each working 15, 20, 25 and 18 hours per week, the employer has 14 FTEs. The following calculation is made: 12 FTEs + (15+20+25+18=60; 60/30=2.6) + 2 non-full time FTEs = 14 FTEs. Always round down when calculating FTEs.

While Federally-facilitated SHOPs must use the above definition to determine eligibility, State-based SHOPs have flexibility in their counting approaches in 2014. Additional employer qualification requirement include:

- Employers who are part of the same control group must count all employees at the combined entities when answering eligibility questions.
- Employers must have at least one common-law employee. According to the IRS definition, under common-law rules, anyone who performs services for you is your employee **if you can control what will be done and how it will be done.** This is so even when you give the employee freedom of action. What matters is you have the right to control the details of how the services are performed.
- Sole proprietors reporting on Schedule C cannot form a group health insurance plan without having a common-law employee.
- A group cannot consist solely of S corporation shareholders or spouses.

Once all required information is submitted, the employer will receive an eligibility determination. This eligibility determination notice will list:

- The name of the qualified business owner.
- The names of all eligible employees.
- The start and end dates of eligibility for employees.

If the employer expands beyond 50 FTE employees after 2014, this does not disqualify the employer for the SHOP.

Multi-state employers may establish one SHOP plan in the state/SHOP service area of the corporate headquarters or they can establish one SHOP plan in each state in which they operate in. When separate accounts are established, information will not be shared across SHOPs. Employers will not be reassessed for eligibility in SHOP until their annual renewal.

Small Business Tax Credits

Premium tax credits and cost-sharing reductions discussed in the previous chapter are not available to employers and families covered through a SHOP. Employers meeting certain size and average wage requirements may receive a small business tax credit on their federal tax return of up to 50% of the employer's contribution to the premium for up to two years. For tax-exempt employers, generally non-profits, the small business tax credit is up to 35%. To qualify for the Small Business Health Care Tax Credit employers must:

- Have an average of fewer than 25 FTE employees (based on a 40-hour work week). This **excludes** owners, owners' family members and seasonal employees.
- Pay employees an average annual wage rate BELOW $50,000 (augmented to reflect cost-of-living adjustments (COLA) beginning in 2014.
- Pay at least 50% of their full-time employees' premium costs. Do not need to offer coverage to part-time employees or to dependents.
- Purchase health care coverage through a SHOP beginning in 2014.

There are two phases to receiving the small business tax credit.

1. *Phase 1 (2010-2013):* Eligible employers receive a small business tax credit of up to 35% of the

employer's contribution toward health insurance premiums. This is calculated on a sliding scale basis tied to average wages and the number of FTE employees. Those small businesses who have a tax-exempt status can receive 25% of the employer's contribution. For tax-exempt employers this credit is refundable. However, it is limited to the amount of the tax-exempt employer's payroll tax liability. Employers already receiving this credit must purchase health insurance coverage through a SHOP beginning on January 1, 2014 to qualify for this small business tax credit for 2014 and forward.

2. *Phase 2 (2014 and onward):* Eligible employers may receive a small business tax credit of up to 50% of the employer's contribution toward health insurance premiums when they purchase health insurance through a SHOP. Employers can take the credit for up to two consecutive taxable years. If the employer has no tax liability for their business, and meet all the eligibility requirements they may receive 35% of their contribution in the form of a refundable tax credit. The amount of the credit will also depend on the number of employees and average wages.

Additional guidance and a list of FAQs are available on the Internal Revenue Service website, www.irs.gov. In the keyword search area, type in ACA and hit enter.

Premiums in the SHOP Marketplace

As with the Individual Marketplace premium rates for the SHOP Marketplace will not vary based on health status, gender or claims experience. Premium rates can only vary due to:

- Age: The ratio of the premium for someone age 64 and older to the premium for someone who is 21 cannot be more than 3x that.

- Family Composition: There is a limit of 3 children under age 21.
- Geographic Area: Primary location of the employer.
- Tobacco Use: A surcharge may be applied to individual enrollees, which cannot equal more than 1.5x the non-tobacco user's rate. It must be offered with a wellness program which enrollees can participate in to remove the surcharge.

Individual premiums reflect age, family composition, geographic location and tobacco use. The family premium is the sum of premiums attributable to each family member. Group premiums are built up from members of that group. Each group's rates will be based on the individual rates of its members.

During the first plan year in 2014, the QHP issuer will be responsible for all billing and the employer will pay premiums directly to the QHP issuer.

Calculation of Employee Contributions

Starting in 2014, employers will decide on a QHP to offer their employees, what percentage of the cost of the QHP to contribute towards employee premiums and how employees will pay a share of the premium. In most states, employers will have a choice as to how employees will contribute towards their health insurance coverage. Employers can choose one of two methods in having employees contribute.

- Each employee's premium can vary by age which is referred to as list billing. Here the employer sets the employee contribution as a percentage of the underlying cost of the employee's coverage.
- Charging the same amount for all employees for the same coverage. This is referred to as a calculated composite premium. Here every employee pays a fixed amount for employee coverage.

115

An advantage to list billing is younger employees are able to afford coverage because both the premium and the employee's percentage contribution toward the premium are lower than it would have been if all employees contribute the same amount. This can encourage participation by younger employees, making it easier for employers to meet SHOP's minimum participation requirement. List billing means older employees will contribute a larger amount for their insurance coverage. If the employer contributes, for example, 80% towards the employee's premium, the employer's 80% will vary for each individual employee.

If an employer decides all employees will contribute the same amount toward the cost of the plan, the FF-SHOP website will automatically calculate an average premium for employees. Each employee will pay a uniform amount of those average premiums. For example, if the youngest employee has a premium of $100 and the oldest employee has a premium of $120, the average premium for everyone would be $110. If the employer contributes 80% ($88) towards premium payments, each employee will pay $22.

With either method premiums for adult dependents and children will always reflect a per-member calculated rate, not an average rate. Participation in wellness programs can reduce premiums for enrollees. If an employee is a smoker the health insurance companies will be able to apply a surcharge to that employees' premium. However, that surcharge may be eliminated if the employee participates in a wellness program.

EMPLOYER PROCESS

For 2014, an employer enrolls in SHOP coverage directly through an agent, broker or insurance company who can help them apply for SHOP eligibility and find and compare available SHOP plans. An employer can also use the premium estimation tool on HealthCare.gov to browse and compare plans and pricing information.

Employer Process Overview

The following graphic provides an overview of the entire eligibility and enrollment process.

Figure 6.1 Overview of Employer Enrollment Process

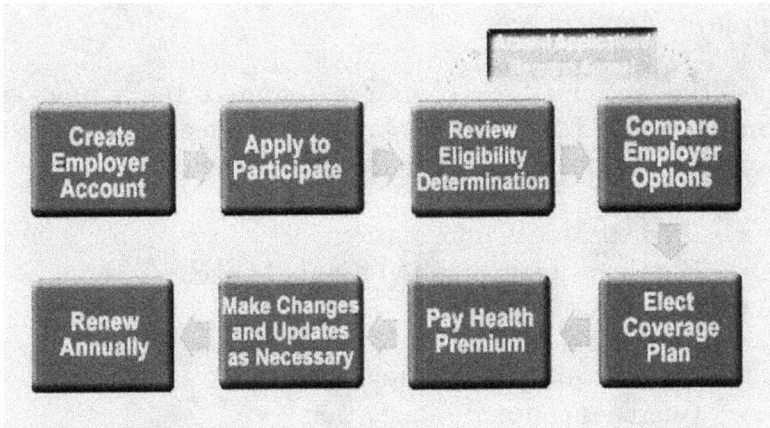

Courtesy: Department of Health and Human Services; Health Insurance Marketplace

Some of the following steps may not be available online until 2015.

Creating an Employer Account

The first step is to create an online account with the SHOP Marketplace. In states with a Marketplace operated by the federal government there is not a paper application for small business owners applying to participate in the SHOP Marketplace. To create an employer account the following information is needed:

- First name
- Last name
- Email

117

- Create a username
- Password
- Answer four security questions

This information should not be and shared with anyone. This becomes the employer's "My Account."

Employer Application

Once the account has been created and the employer's identity verified the SHOP Marketplace needs information about the business. This includes the following:

- Basic business information
- Employer identification number (EIN)
- Employer type
- Address
- Number of full-time equivalent FTE
- Business contact information
- Primary contact
- Secondary contact (optional)
- Preferred spoken or written language (optional)

The employer then needs to provide information about its employees, regardless of whether or not they enroll. The information needed includes:

- Employee name (first, middle, last and suffix, if any)
- Date of birth
- Social Security number (SSN) or Tax Identification number (TIN)
- Email address
- Employment status (full-time or part-time)
- Date of hire

Employer Enrollment Process

There are 12 enrollment cycles per year; one each month and a 9-step application and enrollment process.

1. Input basic information about their business. The employer can purchase health insurance coverage through one State-based Marketplace or apply separately in multiply SHOP's where they have more than one location such as in multiple states.
2. Input an employee roster with basic information about each employee. This roster must include all full-time employees on payroll. Each employee on the roster is then assigned a unique identification code. These are the only employees who will be eligible in SHOP coverage. If the employer offers affordable coverage to an employee, that employee is ineligible for premium tax credits in the individual Marketplace.
3. Once the above information is inputted into their account, SHOP will generate information about the range of premiums for all QHPs. The employer can also get detailed descriptions of the specific plans at different price points.
4. In 2014, the employer selects one QHP which will be the default reference plan. After the employer chooses a QHP, employees on the employee roster are eligible to enroll
5. The employer chooses a defined percentage of the reference plan to contribute for each employee. At this step the employer can also decide if and at what percentages they will contribute towards dependent and dental coverage. This can range from 0% to 100% contribution. If the employer doesn't set a contribution amount the default percentage is set to 0%. In 2014, employers are not required to offer dependent coverage. Dependents covered through a SHOP are also ineligible for premium tax credits

and cost-sharing reductions. Employers will review average plan premiums based on the ages of employees who are likely to participate and decide on a percentage contribution.

6. The employer then decides whether all employees will contribute the same amount for coverage or will pay a premium based on age. The option to charge younger employees lower premiums for a given level of coverage may help to attract enough into the risk pool, helping the employer meet any minimum participation rate. This methodology may result in higher premium contributions by older employees.

7. The employer views a summary of choices and has an opportunity to explore "what if" scenarios. Here they can consider the effect on each of their employees if they choose a different plan, a different employer contribution percentage or a different employee contribution method.

8. Enroll each eligible employee in the SHOP. An employee can choose to decline health coverage.

9. The employer reviews the completed application. Verify all required information has been provided and the minimum participation rate has been met. Here the employer can also establish a waiting period policy for newly-eligible or newly-hired employees. The length of the waiting period can be changed during an employer's annual renewal but cannot exceed 90 days.

An employer must submit the initial application by the 15th of the month for health insurance coverage to take effect by the 1st of the following month.

If an employee declines the health coverage offered by the employer and it's both affordable and meets minimum value, the employee will not qualify for programs to lower health care costs such as premium tax credits and cost-sharing reductions. If coverage offered is unaffordable the employee may qualify for the programs to help lower health care costs.

Employer-sponsored health insurance coverage is considered **unaffordable to an employee if an employee's share of the self-only coverage premium is more than 9.5% of the employees' household income**. How can an employer know what they can't know? How will the employer know what the wages are for an employee's entire household? This may cause many companies to elect the safe harbor of basing the cost on 9.5% of just an employee's wages. This could have significant repercussions for the cost and value of plans offered. Small businesses may find they need an integrated technology solution which brings together payroll, time and attendance, human resources and other systems, then can tie it all back with an audit trail.

Employer Plan Selection

Once an employer has entered basic information about their business and employees, the SHOP Marketplace will generate information on the range of premiums for all plans which are available to the employer. If coverage is offered by the employer to employee's dependents, the SHOP Marketplace also facilitates that enrollment. A small business owner can filter QHPs based on many factors:

- Premium price range.
- Geographic availability.
- Plan type.
- Health plan category (Bronze, Silver, Gold or Platinum).
- Availability of dental and vision benefits.

Employers can use their SHOP Marketplace account to save their plan comparisons to refer back to at a later date.

Enrollment is complete when the health insurance company receives the employer's premium payment.

Employers can make their initial premium payment through the SHOP Marketplace. All subsequent payments which follow must be made directly to the health insurer.

EMPLOYEE PROCESS

Employees will also need to create their own Marketplace username and password which should not be shared with anyone. This will create their "My Account." Employees have up to 90 days to complete their application once they start. The following information will be collected during the account creation and application process:

- Email (required)
- Username creation (required)
- Password (required)
- Answers to four security questions (required)
- First name
- Middle name
- Last name
- Suffix
- Physical address (required)
- Mailing address
- Social Security number (optional)
- Date of birth (required)
- Telephone number (required)
- Employer contact information (required)

Once finished the employee receives a system message asking them to complete the identity validation process by answering a series of real-time questions. Once this information is validated by the SHOP Marketplace the employee account will become active. Unlike the Individual Marketplace, the SHOP Marketplace does not access any external federal data to make eligibility determinations.

It's important for employees to know their enrollment isn't complete until their first monthly premium payment has been received by the health insurance company which provide their QHP. Employers will usually deduct this premium from their employees' paycheck and submit them to the QHP on behalf of the employees. It should also be stressed to employees that they need to submit their SHOP Marketplace applications during the enrollment window established by the employer. If they miss the enrollment window they may not be able to enroll until the next open enrollment period.

Appeals Process

Employees can be determined to be ineligible to participate. This may happen because the employee was not included on the employer's roster of employees which was submitted or the employer reported a change to the employee's full-time status. An employee has the right to appeal SHOP decisions in two cases:

- The employee received a notice which denies them SHOP eligibility.
- The SHOP Marketplace didn't make a SHOP eligibility determination in a timely manner.

The employee has 90 days from the date in the notice to request an appeal. The employee can file an appeal by completing and mailing an appeal request form or writing their own letter of appeal. This should include their name, address, telephone number where they can be reached and the reasons they believe the eligibility determination is wrong.

If a favorable ruling is made the appeal decision must be retroactive to the date the incorrect determination was made. The employee will be responsible for paying premiums back to the effective date. If eligibility is denied, the appeal decision is effective as of the date of the denial notice. Appeal decisions made by a state-based SHOP cannot be elevated to the federal SHOP Marketplace for reconsideration.

Special Enrollment Periods

Employees or if the employer offers dependent coverage, may enroll in or change QHPs outside of the annual enrollment period under certain circumstances. These Special Enrollment Periods (SEPs) are based on certain triggering events and apply to either a qualified individual or dependent.

- Marriage.
- Birth of a child.
- Adoption of a child.
- Loses minimum essential coverage under a group health plan.
- Loses coverage under Medicaid or CHIP.
- Makes a permanent move to an area where different QHPs are available.
- Other exceptional circumstances identified by the SHOP Marketplace.

The SHOP Marketplace would need to be notified within 30 days of a marriage for the qualified employee to enroll in the QHP or a spouse to be covered in the QHP. From the date of the marriage, if the SHOP is notified before the last day of the month, health insurance coverage will begin the 1st of the following month. If the SHOP is notified after the end of the month in which the marriage occurred, coverage will begin the 1st of the month following the notification.

In the case of a birth of a child or the adoption of a dependent, the effective date of coverage can be the date of birth or official date of adoption as long as the SHOP is notified within the 30 day period. Premiums will be pro-rated for the month based on when the child was added to the policy. In most cases, SEPs last for 30 days from the date of the triggering event.

One exception is if employees either become eligible for or lose eligibility for Medicaid or CHIP, then they have a 60 day SEP. If individuals do not take any action by the 30 day SEP deadline, they will have to wait until the next annual enrollment period to join a QHP.

After Initial Enrollment – Making Changes

What happens in the event an employee quits or moves and has a change of address or another employee is hired? The employer or employee would log into their My Account to make any changes. Employees who leave employment must be deleted from the employer's roster. Any newly-eligible or newly-hired full-time employees must be added to the roster through the employers My Account. These employees will then need to complete an employee application which is available on their My Account. The SHOP Marketplace or QHP issuer may request proof an employee is on payroll or that a dependent is eligible for coverage when they enroll.

Any changes going forward in the employee's status, such as address changes, addition of new dependent due to birth or adoption or plan changes during a Special Enrollment Period (SEP) due to triggering events such as marriage, loss of eligibility for public health insurance or loss of group coverage through another employer are made through the employee's My Account.

Annual Redetermination

Employers are notified, by SHOP, 90 days ahead of the annual renewal. Employers have 30 days to revisit health insurance coverage decisions from the previous year and to make any changes if desired. Before the plan renewal date each year, employees will have an open enrollment period (OEP) of at least 30 days as determined by the SHOP. Employees can change their enrollment selection or enroll an existing dependent, if applicable. The SHOP will notify each qualified employees about the annual open enrollment period before it begins. The employer must then submit the final renewal submission by the 15ᵗʰ of the month, prior to the end of the plan year. **Employees who do not confirm or switch health plans will be automatically re-enrolled in their existing plans.**

Annual redetermination may be based on whether the employer has agreed to continue to offer coverage to all full-time employees. Redetermination may be affected by an employer's work location.

COBRA Benefits in SHOP

The ACA does not change COBRA and related requirements for employers. FF-SHOPs will not notify employees about COBRA. It is the responsibility of the employer to notify employees terminated from coverage about their ability to extend health insurance coverage through COBRA. It is also the responsibility of the employer to collect COBRA premiums from terminated employees and submit these payments as part of their monthly QHP premium submission. If there is non-payment of COBRA premiums, the employer is responsible for terminating a COBRA enrollee. The employer is also responsible for terminating coverage when the former employee is no longer eligible to continue coverage.

An employee must enroll for COBRA benefits within 60 days of losing SHOP coverage if they so choose to extend health benefits. The effective date will be the day after SHOP coverage was terminated. COBRA enrollees need to continue their current SHOP plan but will be able to change plans during their previous employer's annual enrollment period if they are still on COBRA benefits. **It may be beneficial for COBRA enrollees and their dependents to seek lower-cost coverage through the Individual Marketplace.**

CHAPTER SEVEN

HEALTH CARE COVERAGE OPTIONS

According to the U.S. Census Bureau's website, the Census Bureau collects health insurance data using three national surveys: (1) the Current Population Survey's Annual Social and Economic Supplement (CPS ASEC), (2) the American Community Survey (ACS) and (3) the Survey of Income and Program Participation (SIPP). The CPS ASEC collects health insurance data on an annual basis at the national and state level geographies. The ACS collects data on an annual basis for all 50 states, the District of Columbia, Puerto Rico, every congressional district and all counties, places and metropolitan areas with populations of 65,000 or more. The SIPP collects longitudinal health insurance data at the national level of geography.

In an ACS brief released in 2011 titled, *Health Insurance Coverage of Workers Aged 18 to 64, by Work Experience: 2008 and 2010,* according to the Census Bureau 67.1% of all workers were covered by employer-based health insurance in 2010; down 2.1% from 2008. Another 13% were covered with non-employer health insurance; a marginal increase of 0.7% from 2008. In 2010, 19.8% of all workers were uninsured with no healthcare coverage at all; an increase of 1.4% from 2008.

COVERAGE OPTIONS

The enactment of the *Affordable Care Act* is changing the ways individuals obtain coverage and how small business owners offer coverage to their employees. Beginning in 2014, individuals must have health insurance as mandated by the ACA, unless they qualify for an exemption. If they do not obtain health insurance they will be required to pay a penalty when they file their federal tax return. When it comes to obtaining health care coverage for themself and their families, an individual usually has the following options depending upon their employment status.

- Large Employer-Sponsored Coverage
- Small Business Group Coverage (on exchange)
- Small Business Group Coverage (off exchange)
- Self-Employed & Individual Coverage (on exchange)
- Self-Employed & Individual Coverage (off exchange)

The previous two chapters dealt with a thorough discussion of the new Health Insurance Marketplaces for individuals and small business groups. This chapter covers the options an employee may see in their corporate benefits package.

LARGE EMPLOYER-SPONSORED BENEFITS

Large corporations have long offered health care benefit programs as an employee benefit. A large employer usually refers to companies which have greater than 200 employees. The most comprehensive health benefit packages are those offered by Fortune 500 type companies. The sheer number of employees allows them to negotiate the best rates for coverage for their employee group. The types of medical plans employees have access to have changed through the years. Health care inflation has outpaced the general CPI inflation rate for a number of years. Health care insurers have responded with more managed care alternatives. The employers that offer these health care benefits have embraced this managed care approach as a means to attempt to contain these rising costs.

Health Plan Enrollment and Coverage

Medical coverage is the benefit most employees want. Employer-sponsored health insurance plans offered to employees today include the following for medical coverage:

- Conventional Plan
- Health Maintenance Organization (HMO) Plan
- Preferred Provider Organization (PPO) Plan
- Point of Service (POS) Plan
- High Deductible Health Plan (HDHP)

The mix of these health insurance plans, which employees have enrolled in, has shifted over the past decade as both employers and employees have tried to contain their health insurance costs. In 1988, the majority of workers were enrolled in conventional plans. Since 2008, less than 1% of covered workers are now enrolled in this type of plan. As the costs associated with conventional plans escalated, both companies and employees began migrating to HMO and PPO plans to reduce their premium costs. Beginning in 2006, employers also began offering High Deductible Health Plans (HDHPs) as an option. From a 4% enrollment in 2006, HDHPs now account for 20% of enrollments as of 2013. Figure 7.1, on the next page, graphically displays the distribution of health plan enrollments for covered workers.

129

Figure 7.1 Distribution of Health Plan Enrollment for
Covered Workers, by Plan Type, 1988-2013

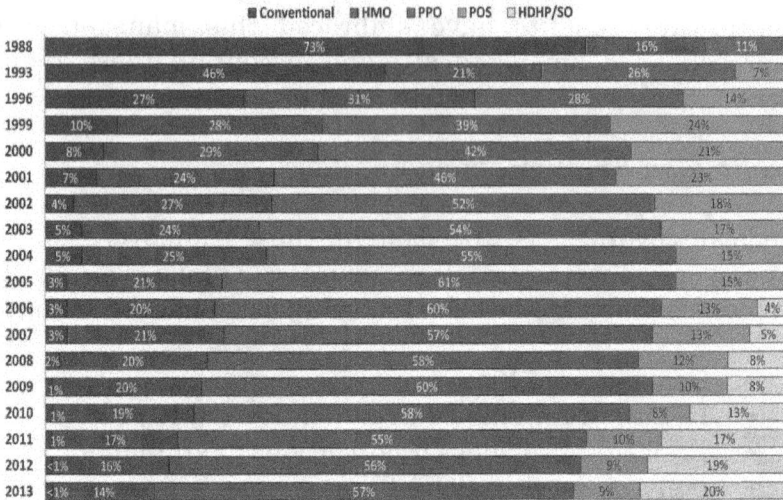

NOTE: Information was not obtained for POS plans in 1988. A portion of the change in plan type enrollment for 2005 is likely attributable to incorporating more recent Census Bureau estimates of the number of state and local government workers and removing federal workers from the weights. See the Survey Design and Methods section from the 2005 Kaiser/HRET Survey of Employer-Sponsored Health Benefits for additional information.

SOURCE: Kaiser/HRET Survey of Employer-Sponsored Health Benefits, 1999-2013; KPMG Survey of Employer-Sponsored Health Benefits, 1993, 1996; The Health Insurance Association of America (HIAA), 1988.

Courtesy: The Kaiser Foundation; 2013 Employer Health Benefit
Survey

As the costs to administer these programs, coupled with the rising cost of health care services in general, companies are now making the employees shoulder an ever increasing amount of those costs including reducing benefits. Figure 7.2, on the next page, graphs the average annual worker contribution paid by the employee for single coverage. From 1999 to 2011 premiums increased from $318 to $921, a 190% cumulative increase while family coverage rose from $1,543 to $4,129; nearly a 168% cumulative increase.

Figure 7.2 Average Annual Worker Premium
Contribution Paid by Covered Workers, 2013

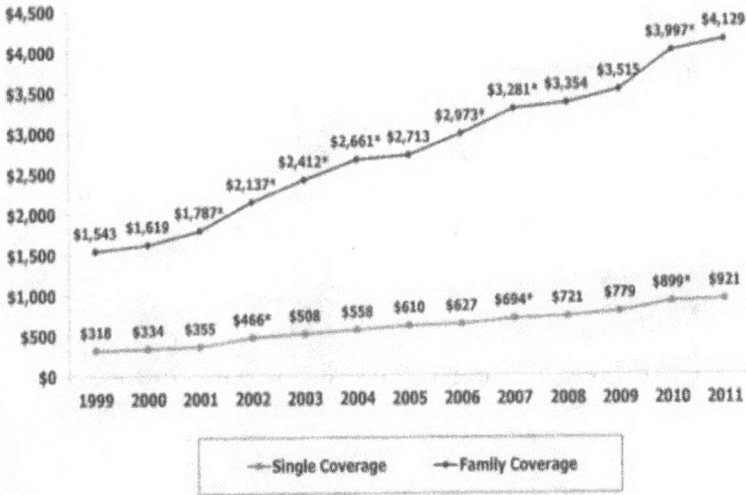

*Estimate is statistically different from estimate for the previous year shown (p<.05).

Source: Kaiser/HRET Survey of Employer-Sponsored Health Benefits, 1999-2011.

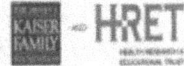

*Courtesy: The Kaiser Foundation; 2011 Employer Health Benefits
Survey*

Figure 7.3, on the next page, charts the average annual worker premium contributions and total premiums which are displayed by firm size for 2013. Small firms are those with between 3 and 199 workers while large firms are those with more than 200 workers. For 2013, worker contributions by small firms totaled $862 while those at large firms totaled $1,065 for single coverage. For family coverage, worker contributions totaled $5,284 at small firms and $4,226 at large firms.

Figure 7.3 Average Annual Worker Premium
Contributions and Total Premiums by
Firm Size, 2013

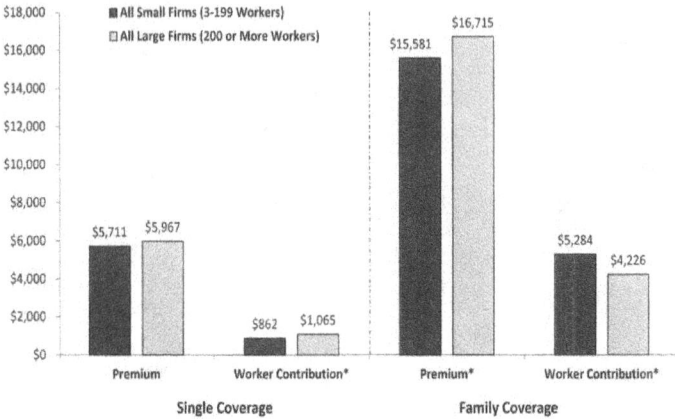

* Estimates are statistically different between All Small Firms and All Large Firms (p<.05).
SOURCE: Kaiser/HRET Survey of Employer-Sponsored Health Benefits, 2013.

*Courtesy: The Kaiser Foundation; 2013 Employer Health Benefit
Survey*

Very few companies today pay 100% of health care benefits. Most employees probably have no idea of the monetary value of this benefit. If you're fortunate enough to work for such a corporation, consider yourself in the elite minority when it comes to health care coverage. Many companies have reduced their contribution to as little as 25% of plan cost, leaving the employee to pay the remaining 75% of the cost of the group premium. There are many people out in the work force today who are working in jobs they don't necessarily want or enjoy but do so just to be able to get access to group health insurance. Why would someone do this? There were usually two reasons; either the cost to obtain coverage on their own is too expensive, or worst; some medical event has caused either them, their spouse or a child to most likely be uninsurable on their own and they can't obtain the needed coverage. The ACA changes this as pre-existing conditions will no longer preclude someone from getting health insurance.

COMPONENTS OF GROUP HEALTH CARE

A company's health benefits program may be assembled through the use of multiple health and life insurance carriers. Some carriers may specialize in a particular line of business. Having group health care coverage will typically be far less costly to you than if you have to buy individual coverage on your own. What you pay from one employer to another can vary significantly in terms its costs. If you work for an employer and you're covered by a very good health care program don't ever take it for granted. If you're going to change employers be sure you understand what the new employer's health benefits are. Otherwise you may end up paying far more for health care coverage than what you previously paid. If it's a promotion and/or salary increase it may be more than enough to offset any added benefit costs.

When you change firms, one of the first things you do, as part of the human resource process, is to select what options you want as part of their health insurance benefits package which is offered to you as a new employee. This assumes the employer offers such a package of benefits. In addition, anyone who has been employed with a medium or large sized company has probably gone through the annual process each year of either renewing or changing some of their health care benefits. Usually you have 4-6 weeks to make any changes, if you chose, to your benefits package for the upcoming plan year. This typically starts in mid-October and goes through the end of November each year.

Benefit Plan Eligibility

If you are a full-time employee you are eligible for whatever health benefits package is offered to the employee base. If you are a new employee to the company you could have a waiting period before benefits become effective. Under the ACA companies can have a waiting period no longer than 90 days. If you are a part-time employee, you may also be eligible for a benefits package depending on the number of hours you work. Some health benefits may only be available to full-time employees. The employee, their spouse or domestic partner and dependent children can be covered under the employee's plan. Eligible dependents include:

- Spouse or domestic partner.
- Dependent children up to their 26th birthday.
- Other minor children if you are the legal guardian
- In some cases older children with mental or physical impairments may be eligible.

Ineligible dependents include:

- Divorced spouses
- Parents
- Grandparents
- Siblings
- Aunts, uncles and cousins
- Spouses of dependent children

Many companies now allow employees to cover domestic partners for medical, dental, vision and life insurance. A domestic partner is an individual of the same or opposite gender as the employee with whom the employee shares their life. Typically to be eligible for domestic partner benefit coverage the employee and their domestic partner must:

- Be at least 18 years of age.
- Not be related by blood.
- Be each other's sole domestic partner and intend to remain so indefinitely.
- The same residence.

134

- Be financially independent.
- Not be legally married to anyone else.

Some companies may also allow the employee's domestic partner's biological or adopted children to be covered if:

- The employee covers their domestic partner.
- Children are under age 26.
- They live in the household of the employee and domestic partner.
- The employee provides more than 50% of the child's support.

Costs You Pay

Many programs are fully paid for by the employer while some program costs are shared with the employee. Other programs, like Dependent Life Insurance and Long-Term Care, are usually fully funded by the employee if they elect to participate in them.

Copays are a set dollar amount you pay for frequently used services such as physician office visits. Deductibles are amounts you must pay first before the health plan begins to cover their share of expenses. There is usually both an individual and family annual deductible. After the individual deductible is met you pay a coinsurance amount, which is a percentage amount for the covered care. Once combined eligible expenses for covered family members reach the family deductible, the plan pays benefits for all covered family members. You are protected from catastrophic medical expenses by your maximum out-of-pocket (MOOP) expenses. Should you incur a medical event where you reach your MOOP level, the health plan pays the full cost for any covered care you receive for the rest of the calendar year.

A trend in recent years, to help keep plan costs down, has been towards copays not counting towards the annual deductible and deductibles and coinsurance not counting toward reaching your annual MOOP expenses. These costs are eligible for reimbursement through a health care FSA if you participate in one.

The key benefit of group health care coverage was that you and your family qualified for health care coverage without having to go through a medical underwriting process. If you were not in the best of health or someone within your family unit wasn't, you were still able to get healthcare coverage by being an employee of the company. For individuals or immediate family members who fell into this category this was the best option they had to get affordable health care coverage. This changes as of January 1, 2014 with the ACA. As of that date you can no longer be denied health care coverage due to pre-existing health conditions. This does not apply to long-term disability, long-term care or life insurance where your current health and/or any pre-existing conditions could affect your ability to qualify for benefits and also affect the price you pay.

Covered Benefits

Corporate health benefit programs have changed through the years in terms of what they offer to employees. When one thinks of health insurance today, most individuals think about medical and prescription drug coverage since this is what is used the most by individuals. The benefit packages of today extend far beyond just medical and prescription drug coverage.

They can be grouped into two categories: (1) those that which are related to health care and includes medical coverage, dental coverage, vision coverage, dependent care flexible spending accounts, life insurance choices, dependent life insurance, accidental death and personal loss insurance, short and long-term disability coverage, long-term care coverage and (2) non-health related, which can include paid time-off, 401(k) choices, stock purchase plans (if the company's stock is publicly traded), educational assistance benefits, employee assistance programs and wellness programs. All these options may not be available in every corporate health benefits program you come across. The percentage of the costs you pay and the coverage you receive can vary significantly from one employer to another. The specifics of each option offered can also vary in terms of cost and coverage from one employer to the next.

Insuring against exposed risk is critical. It involves taking into account the family's ability to function without major interruption until planned retirement, no matter who you are working for. Each of the three risk scenarios: (1) loss of wages due to disability, (2) major costs due to long-term care of a loved one and (3) unexpected death are key issues you should think about when analyzing which benefits you should consider enrolling in.

Next we're going to take a comprehensive look at the various options you may have available to you in a group health care benefits package. We'll cover those options which are related to health care only. We'll also discuss what options you have if when you leave an employer or are between jobs.

Preventive Care – No Cost to You

Many company health benefit packages now include all preventive care which is covered at 100%, regardless of age or restrictions, based on American Medical Association (AMA) guidelines. This includes the cost of preventive care office visits and any related preventative care lab services. Examinations and procedures covered can include:

- Routine physicals.
- Routine PSA and DRE screenings.
- Well-child exams.
- Immunizations.
- Colonoscopies (may have a copay change for consultation with a specialist).
- Annual vision exams.

- Routine annual OB/GYN exams and Pap tests as well as mammograms.
- Routine hearing exams.
- Certain female contraception.
- Breast Feeding support.
- May cover aspirin, certain supplements and oral fluorides.

Your physician needs to code all eligible claims as preventative care in order to be eligible for the 100% cost coverage. This includes the five-digit Preventative Procedure Code that identifies the type of procedure and the three- to five-digit code which identifies the reason the service is being performed.

Types of Medical Coverage

Medical coverage will usually include four to five different plans. Some companies may simplify the terminology and call them a basic, enhanced, premium, out-of-network and high deductible. Below is a discussion of these plans.

Conventional Plan

These plans are also called indemnity plans or fee for service plan. Under this plan insured persons can contact any health care provider to address his medical or health problems. In most cases the provider will directly send circumstances you have to pay for service from your own pocket and submit claim with insurance company. Under this plan, the employee has to pay a regular fee called premium till he wants to remain covered. In addition to premium, deductibles are paid by the employee, before the insurance company commences payment under this plan. If deductibles are higher, the premium will be lower. After payment of deductibles, cost of medical and health services are shared proportionally between employee and insurance company. Mostly it is in the ratio of 30-70 but some companies and policies provide 20-80 ratio. This is the co-insurance. As before the higher the co-insurance, the lower will be the premium. Most policies under this plan have the clause life-time maximum, which is financial limit which company will pay for medical services, covered under specific policy, during entire life time of the employee. Few companies offer this today because of the significantly higher costs.

Health Maintenance Organization (HMO) Plan

An HMO is an organization that provides a broad range of health services to a group for a fixed periodic rate. The *Health Maintenance Organization Act of 1973* required employers with 25 or more employees to offer federally certified HMO options if the employer offers traditional healthcare options. Unlike traditional indemnity insurance, an HMO consists of comprehensive health care provided by contracted physicians and medical facilities for a pre-negotiated payment in accordance with the HMO's guidelines and restrictions in exchange for a steady stream of customers. HMOs cover emergency care regardless of the health care provider's contracted status.

Preferred Primary Organization (PPO) Plan

PPO is a managed care organization of medical doctors, hospitals, and other health care providers who have covenanted with an insurer or a third-party administrator to provide health care at reduced rates to the insurer's or administrator's clients. A PPO is similar to an HMO, except it allows the employee to receive care outside the network of PPO providers. Should the employee seek medical care outside of the PPO network, the insured will generally face higher deductibles and/or higher co-insurance rates for such care. PPO plans tend to have slightly higher premiums than HMOs and other more restrictive plans, but they offer the employee more flexibility overall in choosing their health care providers which they may place a high value on.

Point Of Service (POS) Plan

A POS plan is a type of managed care program. It combines the features of both a HMO and a PPO to create a hybrid plan. Those enrolled in a POS choose which option, HMO or PPO, they will use each time they seek health care services. They are required to choose a primary care physician (PCP) when they enroll. The PCP must be chosen from within the health care network. The PCP may then make referrals outside the network, but then only some compensation will be offered by the patient's health insurance company. For medical visits within the health care network, paperwork is completed for the patient. If the employee chooses to go outside the network, it is the employee's responsibility to fill out the forms, send bills in for payment, and keep an accurate account of health care receipts.

High Deductible Health Plan (HDHP)

An HDHP is a health insurance plan with lower premiums and higher deductibles than a traditional health plan. Since the deductibles can be quite high, these plans are more for catastrophic coverage. Some HDHP plans make available additional wellness benefits before the deductible is met.

For calendar year 2014, a HDHP is defined as a health plan with an annual deductible not less than $1,250 for self-only coverage or $2,500 for family coverage. The maximum amount out-of-pocket expenses (deductibles, copayments and other amounts but not including premiums) cannot exceed $6,350 for self-only coverage and $12,700 for family coverage. However, this limit does not apply to deductibles and expenses for out-of-network services if the plan uses a network of providers. These limits are modified each year by the IRS to reflect the change in the cost of living. If you are covered by an HDHP, you're eligible to have a tax-advantaged HSA to pay your medical care from. This type of account will be covered in more detail shortly.

Choosing Medical Coverage

Choosing your medical coverage can be the most confusing because of the number of choices you have. Each plan will have in-network costs and out-of-network costs. You can usually access the providers who are in-network to determine if the physicians you use are in-network providers. The key elements to focus on are the following:

- Calendar year deductibles – individual and family.
- Coinsurance out-of-pocket maximums.
- Procedures subject to deductible and coinsurance.

As you move up the plans which are offered in your health care benefit package the following is likely to occur:

- Monthly premiums will increase.
- Copays will decline.
- Your coinsurance portion, after the deductible is met, will decline.
- Size of the individual and family deductible will be smaller in dollar amount.
- Beginning in 2014, medical coverage will now have an unlimited maximum lifetime benefit across all plans.

Your best approach to medical needs planning is to understand the types of care you may need in the coming year, any specific medical procedures which might need to be done and what the frequency for the care will be. Then do the math to gauge a good understanding of which plan may be most cost effective for you and/or your family.

Prescription Drug Coverage

Prescription drug coverage is usually part of the medical coverage. Pharmacy coverage is usually the same across all medical plans. You do not have to enroll in it separately. The cost you pay will reflect the type of medication in your prescription. Prescription drug payments usually do not count toward the medical plan's annual deductible or the coinsurance out-of-pocket maximums. There are four levels of prescription drugs.

1. Tier 1 – Generic
2. Tier 1 – Formulary Brand
3. Tier 3 – Non-Formulary Brand
4. Specialty

Prescriptions in the first three tiers can usually be filled at any retail pharmacy which accepts your plan. If you are taking any Specialty medication they usually must be filled at a specific pharmacy denoted in the plan. If filled anywhere else the employee pays the full retail price of the medication. Generics generally cost between 20% and 70% less than their brand-name counterparts. Use the mail-order pharmacy for all maintenance prescriptions. Maintenance prescriptions are those you take to treat a chronic condition such as diabetes, high blood pressure, cholesterol levels, etc. You will spend much less than if you go to the retail pharmacy and get a 90-day supply.

Dental Coverage

For dental coverage, most companies will offer either a basic or enhanced plan. Both usually cover all preventative care at 100% while basic care is covered at between 70% and 80%. This includes the following procedures:

- Two Routine exams
- Two Cleanings

- X-rays
- Fillings
- Extractions
- Root canals
- Periodontal therapy
- Oral surgery

The difference in coverage comes into play with major dental work such as bridges, crowns, dentures and orthodontia work. A basic plan usually does not cover any of costs for this work, whereas an enhanced plan will cover between 50% and 60% of the costs.

Vision Coverage

If vision coverage is offered there is usually one plan offered. Shared costs will be determined by whether you use an in-network or out-of-network provider. In-network costs are usually covered at 100%, while some may require a copay or coinsurance. Out-of-network costs are covered by coinsurance where the employee pays a percentage of the covered costs. Items and procedures covered include:

- Eye exam every 12 months.
- One pair of frames every 12 or 24 months.
- Glasses.
- Anti-reflective coating (ARC).
- Plan contact lenses.
- Non-plan contact lenses.
- Medically-necessary lenses.

Flexible Spending Accounts

There are usually two flexible spending accounts (FSA) which are offered. One is a health care account while the other is for dependent care. A Health Care FSA allows employees to be reimbursed for qualified medical expenses not covered by their employer's main health plan. These medical expenses typically include deductibles, copays and coinsurance and various medical services and products from dental and vision care to eyeglasses and hearing aids. A Dependent Care FSA allows the employee to be reimbursed for their dependent care expenses. FSAs are usually funded through voluntary salary reduction agreements with the employer. The advantage of this account is its tax-advantage status. Money deducted from an employee's pay into an FSA is not subject to payroll taxes. This results in a payroll tax savings for the employee.

1. Health Care FSA

According to the human resources consulting firm Mercer, only 22% of eligible employee's at large companies contributed to an FSA in 2013. While this is down from 23% in 2012, it still leaves 78% of employees who are missing this tax savings benefit. For an individual in the 25% tax bracket, contributing the maximum $2,500 into the FSA could lower their income tax bill by $625. The average balance in 2013 was $1,349, down slightly from $1,484 in 2012. These accounts are offered by 85% of large companies with 500 or more employees. According to data from Alegeus Technologies, one in four FSA participants typically forfeits money at the end of the year. The average balance lost in just above $100. The analysis also found 38% of FSA dollars are spent on medical expenses, 28% at the pharmacy and 23% on dental expenses.

Since these elections need to be made during the open-enrollment period each year, one needs to plan ahead for what they think they will spend during the upcoming plan year. The big disadvantage to using an FSA has been that funds not used by the end of the year are lost to the employer. This is known as the "use it or lose it" rule. However, this is going to change.

In October 2013, the Treasury Department and the IRS issued a notice modifying the longstanding "use-or-lose" rule for health care FSAs. To make health FSAs more consumer-friendly and provide added flexibility, the updated guidance permits employers to allow plan participants to carry over up to $500 of their unused health FSA balances remaining at the end of a plan year. Some plan sponsors may be eligible to take advantage of the option to adopt a carryover provision as early as plan year 2013. In addition, the existing option for plan sponsors to allow employees a grace period after the end of the plan year remains in place. **However, a Health Care FSA cannot have both a carryover and a grace period: it can have one or the other or neither.** If an individual does carry over $500 into the next plan year they will still be able to contribute the maximum $2,500 in that plan year to have a pool of $3,000 to draw from for qualified medical expenses. They will need to use $2,500 before the year is up though. From a tax savings perspective, for that same individual in the 25% tax bracket, contributing $500 into the FSA could lower their income tax bill by $125.

Most plan participants access withdrawals through the use of an FSA debit card which simplified the substantiation requirement but did not eliminate it. Provisions of a medical FSA include:

- Pre-funded annual contributions for a medical FSA are available at the start of the plan year.
- If the employee experiences a qualifying event early in year, the entire amount of their annual contribution can be claimed against the FSA benefits.
- If the employee is terminated, quits or is unable to return to work, he or she does not have to repay the money to the employer.
- Expense must be incurred during the plan year.
- Most plans have a grace period allowing use of the funds for 2½ months after the end of the plan year.

- Over-the-counter (OTC) medical expenses qualify not distinguished as a drug or medicine with the exception of insulin.
- Contributions are made for the entire plan year or until employment terminates.
- Coverage period ceases upon termination of employment whether initiated by the employee or employer unless employee continues coverage with the company under COBRA.
- Contributions are federally capped, for 2014, at $2,500 per year. Employers are allowed to contribute an additional $1,000 to an employee's account.

2. Dependent Care FSA

A dependent care FSA covers qualified dependent care expenses incurred for care of one or more qualifying individuals.

- Before-school and after-school care
- Expenses for preschool/nursery school
- Extended day programs
- Au pair services (amounts paid for the actual care of the dependent)
- Baby sitter (in or out of the home)
- Nanny services (amounts paid for the actual care of the dependent)
- Summer day camp for your qualifying child under the age of 13
- Elder day care for a qualifying individual
- Most common expense is for child care for children under the age of 13.
- Used for children of any age who are physically or mentally incapable of self-care for themselves.
- Adult day-care for dependents that also live with the person, such as parents or grandparents.

- Person on whom funds are spent must be able to be claimed as a dependent on the employee's federal tax return.
- Contributions are federally capped, for 2014, at $5,000 per year and include both the employee and employer contributions. Married spouses can each elect an FSA but combined contributions cannot exceed $5,000 per year.
- Not pre-funded. Can only be reimbursed up to the amount already contributed so far into the plan year.

Ineligible expenses would include:

- Amounts paid to your spouse, your child under age 19, a parent of your child who is not your spouse or an individual for whom you or your spouse is entitled to a personal tax exemption as a dependent
- Expenses related to a disabled spouse or tax dependent living outside your household
- Educational expenses
- Tuition for kindergarten and above
- Food expenses (unless inseparable from care)
- Incidental expenses (such as extra charges for supplies, special events, or activities unless inseparable from care)
- Overnight camp

Expenses reimbursed under your dependent care FSA cannot be used to claim any federal income tax deduction or credit. **The new ruling from the Treasury Department regarding the $500 unused carryover does not apply to the dependent care FSA.**

Life Insurance

Life insurance options, in most corporate benefit packages, will include basic and supplemental term life insurance coverage. The basic coverage is one times (1x) pay and is usually provided automatically to the employee at no cost. Supplemental coverage can be purchased in increments from an additional 1x pay to as high as 6x pay, with a $1 million maximum coverage amount. Be sure to also clarify how the company defines "pay".

You may be required to go through medical underwriting for supplemental coverage or provide evidence of insurability (EOI). Many times, once an employee reaches certain ages past 65, the face value of the insurance coverage may be incrementally reduced. Milestones could be, for example, age 65, 70, 75, etc.

These policies are usually NOT portable so if you leave the company your life insurance coverage terminates. You can't take it with you. In addition, these policies are not usually convertible to permanent insurance. If you are contemplating the purchase of an individual policy, be sure to determine whether you can convert some or all of the coverage to a permanent solution, whether it seems necessary or not at the time of application.

Dependent Life Insurance

Some benefit packages offer the employee the ability to purchase term-insurance for their spouse, domestic partner or dependent children up to age 26. For the spouse or domestic partner the face amounts of the policies are usually $25,000 or $50,000 while those for children are usually in the amount of $10,000 for each dependent child. Any dependents in active, full-time military service are usually not eligible for dependent life coverage through the employer.

Your spouse or domestic partner may be required to go through medical underwriting for dependent coverage.

These policies are usually NOT portable so if you leave the company their life insurance coverage terminates. Coverage reduction can also apply to dependent coverage. Once the dependent reaches certain ages past 65, the face value of the insurance coverage is incrementally reduced.

Accidental Death and Personal Loss Insurance

Basic accidental death is usually provided in the amount of 1x pay at no cost to the employee. Some company benefit packages may also offer a supplemental plan which can be purchased by the employee with an additional 1x pay up to 5x pay. Coverage is for the loss of a hand, loss of a foot, loss of an eye or eyesight, loss of speech or hearing, loss of a thumb or index finger or multiple losses. Each loss has some percentage attached to it.

Disability Coverage

Disability insurance (DI) typically falls into two categories: (1) non-maternity related and (2) maternity related disabilities. Then there are two types of disability coverage: (1) short-term which covers a period of 6 months or less and (2) long-term which covers a period greater than 6 months. The benefit may also have a fixed number of days waiting period before you can begin receiving disability benefits. In most cases a short-term disability policy may be provided to the employee at no cost. It will replace a percentage of the employee's pay for up to 6 months if you are disabled. That percentage can vary from one company to the next.

Some benefit packages may also offer long-term coverage option. The percentage may begin, for example, with a 50% pay replacement, at no cost to the employee. Usually the percentage of pay replaced is a lower amount than with short-term disability coverage. In many instances, there will be an option to purchase additional supplemental long-term disability coverage to get the employee to a 70% pay replacement level.

Long-Term Care Coverage

The number of insurance companies which offer group long-term care (LTC) coverage has shrunk dramatically in the last few years. For those companies which stopped offering the option to new enrollees, these are now closed blocks of business which could be subject to multiple rate increases in the future. Some companies may still offer this option as part of their benefits package to the employee base.

Don't try to compare group coverage with that which you may see in individually owned policies. There can be significantly more limitations under most group LTC coverage policies. If you have had coverage under a group plan, as an employee for a significant period, now may be a good time to pull that policy out and review its details to see exactly what is covered. You want to know what type of care is covered, how much it pays for that care and what can trigger a claim for those benefits:

- Home health care
- Assisted living
- Nursing home
- Inflation coverage

LTC coverage helps to pay for care needed as a result of an illness, accident or advanced age. In addition to the employee, eligible family members can include spouse, parents, parents-in-law, grandparents and grandparents-in-law. Custodial care can be provided in the home, a nursing home or other facility. Assistance is received for activities of daily living (ADLs) which include bathing, eating, getting in or out of bed, dressing, toileting and continence.

The employee most likely will need to contact the insurance carrier directly who is offering the LTC benefit in the company's plan. Evidence of insurability is usually required for the employee and any family member who wants to enroll. If you are a new employee, depending upon the plan offered, you may be guaranteed coverage without evidence of insurability if you sign up within a certain time frame after beginning your employment with the company. If you are an employee and in your 50s or later, this is a benefit option you should definitely inquire about during the open enrollment period. See chapter 10 for a more thorough discussion on LTC coverage.

Health Savings Account

Health savings accounts (HSA) were established in 2003, as part of the *Medicare Prescription Drug, Improvement and Modernization Act,* to enable individuals who were covered by a high deductible health plan (HDHP) to receive tax-preferred treatment of money saved for medical expenses. **You must be covered under a HDHP and have no other health care coverage except permitted coverage.** If you are eligible for an HSA, anyone can contribute to it. You cannot be enrolled in Medicare or be claimed as a dependent on another person's tax return and be eligible for an HSA.

America's Health Insurance Plans (AHIP) is a national trade association representing the health insurance industry. According to a new census released by AHIP in June 2013, nearly 15.5 million Americans are now covered by HSA eligible health insurance plans. This is an increase of 15% from the previous year and 50% since the ACA was passed. Key findings from the census include:

- Enrollment has increased each year from 6.1 million in January 2008 to the 15.5 million in January 2013.
- Forty-nine percent of enrollees in the individual market (including dependents covered under family plans) were age 40 or over. The percentage under age 40 was 51%.
- Illinois has the most enrollees with 903,000, followed by Texas with 889,364, California with 808,019,

Ohio with 686,616 and Michigan with 577,208 enrollees.

- Preferred provider organizations (PPO) were the most popular HSA/HDHP product types representing more than 80% of plans.

The census also revealed the greatest enrollment increases were in the large group market, which represents nearly 70% of all enrollments in these HSA/HDHPs.

Devenir, which is based in Minneapolis, is a national leader in providing customized investment solutions to the HSA custodian marketplace. In their 6th semi-annual *Health Savings Accounts Survey*, conducted in July 2013 from data collected from approximately 50 providers in the HSA market, they estimated there is about $18.1 billion in combined assets from both deposit and investment accounts, representing over 9.1 million separate accounts residing in these HSAs. This is an increase of 29% from a year ago. Other findings from the survey include:

- Average account balance, halfway through 2013, grew to $1,981 from $1,879 from the same time last year. This is a 5% increase.
- Average account holder has a balance of $10,484.
- Total contributions to HSAs reached $16.7 billion, with account holders retaining approximately 23% of those contributions.
- Investment assets only reached an estimated $2 billion, up 14% from the end of 2012 and an increase of 26% from one year earlier.

The maximum amount that can be contributed to your HSA depends on the type of HDHP coverage you have. Effective for 2014, if you have self-only coverage, your maximum contribution is $3,300. If you have family coverage, your maximum contribution is $6,550. Additionally, there is a catch-up provision for those who are 55 and older, for either self-only or family, of $1,000. Withdrawals can be used to pay for qualified medical expenses, including prescription drugs, LTCI premiums and Medicare premiums but NOT supplement/Medigap premiums.

Deposits made into HSAs belong to the owner of the account and can be rolled each plan year if funds are left over. Funds in an HSA can be invested similar to investments in an IRA which gives the owner significant flexibility in investment choices. HSA's cannot be rolled into IRA's or 401(k)'s. Funds from these types of retirement investment accounts cannot be rolled into HSA's. However, the *Tax Relief and Health Care Act of 2006* added a provision allowing a one-time rollover of IRA assets to be used to fund up to one year's maximum HSA contribution.

In 2011 the IRS increased the penalty to 20% for nonmedical withdrawals and also included over-the-counter medications as ineligible medical expenses. If you or someone on your behalf made a contribution, you received HSA distributions, you failed to be eligible during testing period or you acquired an interest in an HSA as a result of the death of the owner you will have to file Form 8889 with your income tax return.

Qualified Medical Expenses

Generally, qualified medical expenses for HSA purposes are reimbursed medical expenses that could otherwise be deducted on Schedule A, Form 1040. Expenses incurred before you established your HSA are not qualified medical expenses. These would include expenses covered by the health plan but subject to cost sharing such as a deductibles, co-payments, co-insurance, dental, vision, and chiropractic care; durable medical equipment such as eyeglasses and hearing aids and transportation expenses related to medical care. Non-prescription medicines, other than insulin, purchased in tax years beginning after December 31, 2010, are not considered qualified medical expenses. You cannot treat insurance premiums as qualified medical expenses unless the premiums are for:

- Long-term care (LTC) insurance.
- Health care continuation coverage (coverage under COBRA)
- Health care coverage while receiving unemployment compensation under federal or state law.
- Medicare and other health care coverage if you were 65 or older. Premiums for a Medicare Supplemental/Medigap policy are not included.

Any part of a distribution not used to pay qualified medical expenses is includible in gross income and is subject to an additional tax of 20% unless an exception applies. This penalty is waived for persons who have reached the age of 65 or who have become disabled at the time of withdrawal. Then, only income tax is paid on the withdrawal which is included in gross income.

Owners of HSAs are required to retain documentation for their qualified medical expenses. Failure to do so could cause the IRS to rule the withdrawals were not for qualified medical expenses thus subjecting the taxpayer to additional penalties. When the owner of an HSA dies, the funds in the HSA are transferred to the beneficiary named for the account. If the beneficiary is a surviving spouse the transfer is tax free. State tax treatment of HSA's varies. As of January 25, 2011, only three states with income taxes do not conform to this Federal Tax treatment. Those are Alabama, California and New Jersey.

Before You Choose

Think carefully about the options you want from your health care benefit's package. Consider the following:

- Of your current paycheck, how much goes towards you and your family's day-to-day living expenses?
- Other coverage you may have through other individually owned policies or spouse's policies.

- How long could you pay household expenses from savings if you could not work?
- How many other individuals depend on you for financial support?

This is important to do because most benefit coverage is based on IRS rules. Once you make your decisions for the upcoming plan year, you generally CANNOT make any changes during that year. The exception is if you have a qualifying event in your family or employment status. These qualifying events include:

- Marriage or divorce.
- Death of a spouse or dependent.
- Gaining or losing a domestic partner.
- Birth or adoption of a child.
- Your spouse ending or starting employment when that affects coverage eligibility.
- The employee or spouse change from full-time to part-time employment status or vice versa and the change affects coverage eligibility.
- Change in health coverage or cost by the spouse's employer.
- Loss of eligibility for the employee's dependents because of exceeding the age eligibility requirements.
- Loss of eligibility (the employee or eligible dependents) for another group health plan or state/federal insurance program such as Medicaid or CHIP.

Be sure you're taking advantage of the 100% covered preventative services which are applicable to you.

Health Insurance Continuation - COBRA

There was a time when group health care coverage was only available to full-time employees and their families. If you lost your job, you had no health insurance coverage until you found another full-time job with an employer who offered group health care benefits. That changed with the passage of the *Consolidated Omnibus Budget Reconciliation Act of 1985 (COBRA),* a law passed by Congress on a reconciliation basis, and signed by former President Ronald Reagan. The statute became law on April 7, 1986. The law helps employees and their families keep their group health coverage during times of voluntary or involuntary job loss, reduction in the hours worked, transition between jobs and in certain other cases.

COBRA generally requires that group health plans sponsored by employers with 20 or more FTE employees in the prior year offer employees and their families the opportunity for a temporary extension of health coverage in certain instances where coverage under the plan would otherwise end. Part-time workers count as a 0.50 employee under the COBRA guidelines.

Qualified individuals may be required to pay 100% of the entire premium for group coverage. The employer may charge up to an additional 2% to cover administrative costs of the plan. Premiums may be higher for persons exercising the disability provisions of COBRA. Failure to make timely payments may result in loss of coverage. Premiums may be increased by the plan; however, premiums generally must be set in advance of each 12-month premium cycle. Individuals subject to COBRA coverage may be responsible for paying all costs related to deductibles, and may be subject to catastrophic and other benefit limits.

Several events can cause workers and their family members to lose group health coverage which may result in the right to COBRA coverage. These include:

- Voluntary or involuntary termination of the covered employee's employment for reasons other than gross misconduct.
- Reduced hours of work for the covered employee.
- Covered employee becoming entitled to Medicare.
- Divorce or legal separation of a covered employee.
- Death of a covered employee.
- Loss of status as a dependent child under plan rules.

However, COBRA also provides that your continuation coverage may be cut short in certain cases. Notification requirements include the following:

- An initial notice must be furnished to covered employees and spouses, at the time coverage under the plan commences, informing them of their rights under COBRA and describing provisions of the law. COBRA information also is required to be contained in the plan's summary plan description (SPD).
- When the plan administrator is notified that a qualifying event has happened, it must in turn notify each qualified beneficiary of the right to choose continuation coverage.
- COBRA allows at least 60 days from the date of the qualifying event to inform the plan administrator that the qualified beneficiary wants to elect continuation coverage. The individual then has 15 days to pay the premium for the period of coverage before the COBRA election was made.
- Under COBRA, the covered employee or a family member has the responsibility to inform the plan administrator of a divorce, legal separation, disability or a child losing dependent status under the plan.
- Employers have a responsibility to notify the plan administrator of the employee's death, termination

of employment or reduction in hours, or Medicare entitlement.

If covered individuals change their marital status, or their spouses have changed addresses, they should notify the plan administrator. The following table represents some basic information on periods of continuation coverage under the law.

Table 7.1 Continuation of Coverage Under COBRA

Qualified Beneficiary	Qualifying Event	Period of Coverage
Employee Spouse Dependent child	Termination Reduced hours	18 months (This 18-month period may be extended for all qualified beneficiaries if certain conditions are met in cases where a qualified beneficiary is determined to be disabled for purposes of COBRA.)
Spouse Dependent child	Entitled to Medicare Divorce or legal separation Death of covered employee	36 months
Dependent child	Loss of dependent child status	36 months

Source: U.S. Department of Labor

Health Insurance Portability and Accountability (HIPPA)

In 1996, Congress enacted the *Health Insurance Portability and Accountability Act* (HIPPA) which was signed by

President Bill Clinton in 1996. There were two parts to the law. Title I covered health care access, portability, and renewability. Title II covered preventing health care fraud and abuse, administrative simplification and medical liability reform.

Title I of the federal law protects health insurance coverage for workers and their families when they change or lose their jobs. HIPPA limits restrictions that a group health plan can place on benefits for pre-existing conditions. A pre-existing condition is defined as a medical condition for which medical advice, treatment or diagnosis was recommended or received within six months prior to the enrollment date in the new plan. HIPPA limits the pre-existing condition period to twelve months for most enrollees. This can be extended to eighteen months for late enrollment.

Individuals are able to reduce this exclusion period if they had group health plan coverage or health insurance prior to enrolling in the plan. HIPPA allows individuals to reduce the exclusion period by the amount of time that they had creditable coverage prior to enrolling in the plan and after any significant breaks in coverage. A significant break in coverage is if less than 63 days have elapsed since the employee lost coverage under a prior employer's plan or if COBRA continuation coverage expired. The employee's coverage under the former plan or COBRA can offset the preexisting condition exclusion period under the new plan.

An example will help clarify this. Michael had health coverage under a group plan with his employer where he has been employed for the last ten months. Michael quits his job and 55 days later begins working for a new employer who offers group health insurance. While he was between jobs, Michael had no health insurance coverage. Michael enrolls in his new employer's plan as soon as he is eligible. His new employer's plan imposes the maximum pre-existing conditions exclusion period allowed by HIPPA, which is twelve months. Since Michael's break in coverage was less than 63 days, his ten months of coverage at his

159

former job is credited toward the twelve month exclusion period. As a result, Michael is subject only to two months pre-existing conditions exclusion under his new employer's plan.

COVERAGE FOR INDIVIDUALS, FAMILIES AND THE SELF-EMPLOYED

The reality of why group healthcare works is because the healthy employees (those who use few medical and dental services) are subsidizing the welfare of the unhealthy ones (chronically ill who use lots of services) because both pay the same premiums for the same coverage.

There are significant changes occurring in the health insurance industry. Options for individuals and families not covered by an employer-based health plan and the self-employed will expand beginning in 2014. From analysis done so far, this may or may not be a good thing for some. You will be able to compare the cost of insurance for individual and family health care plans both off the exchange (the way shopping for health insurance was done before) and for health care plans on exchange, which are those available through the new Health Insurance Marketplace, covered in a previous chapter. It appears premiums for off exchange plans will be higher in 2014 than they were in 2013 for the most part.

Earlier in the chapter, basic plan design for medical insurance coverage was presented. Those basic concepts discussed there apply here also. This will be a general overview of plan coverage. Health care insurance providers may not offer plans in every state. Prices for coverage can vary widely from state to state. Health care plans offered in one state, by a carrier, may be different in another state. Also a carrier may not offer every plan available for a state, in every county within that state.

Another noticeable difference, compared to group coverage, is the number of plans available. Whereas we saw earlier, most group health care benefit programs will offer

4-5 different plan designs to the employee base. On the non-group side there may be more than 10 different health care plans available.

Coverage Prior to 2014

Generally plans available prior to 2014 fall into one of the categories below.

- PPO Open Access
- PPO Open Access – HDHP
- HMO Network
- HMO Network – HDHP
- HMO – Value
- HMO – Value – HDHP

Each plan offered may have a number next to it. This usually refers to the individual deductible of the plan. The PPO and HMO plans, which are not the high deductible health plans (HDHP), may have $1,500, $2,500 or $5,000 deductibles, for example. If the plan was for a family many health insurers just double the individual deductible. So in the example above, the family deductible would be $3,000, $5,000 and $10,000, respectively.

HDHPs usually begin at a higher deductible such as $3,500 deductible and include a $5,500 deductible plan for individuals. The family deductible would be $7,000 and $11,000, respectively. These plans would be compatible with a tax-advantage health savings account (HSA), which was discussed earlier in the chapter. With an HSA there are no income limits or phaseouts for tax deductions which make them especially attractive to high tax-bracket individuals. These deductions are above the line on the federal tax return, thus helping with loss of tax benefits which are tied to adjusted gross income or modified AGI. HSA deductions can also reduce exposure to the 3.8% surtax on net investment income. HSA's can be used to create a medical IRA which can be used to pay qualified medical expenses in later years. There is no use-it-loose-it timetable.

Lastly, there are the PPO and HMO Value plans which typically begin with an even higher deductible such as $5,000 and could include plans with deductibles of $7,500 and $10,000. The family deductible would therefore be $10,000, $15,000 and $20,000, respectively.

Because of the rising cost of health care premiums over the last few years many individual, especially the self-employed, opt for the high deductibles which result in the lowest premiums. Those individuals basically want health insurance that will insure them against a catastrophic medical event.

Coverage Beginning in 2014

If you read chapter 5, many plans you will see in 2014, off exchange will have a similar design to those plans which are available through the Health Insurance Marketplace. The "metallic color" of the plans described in chapter 6 are also used with many insurer for their plans off exchange. There will still be a variety of deductibles offered, though it appears that starting deductibles will be higher (in the $3,000s) than what existed in 2013. Health care plan design will include:

- Bronze
- Silver
- Gold
- Platinum

Bronze plans will have the lowest premiums but you will pay more for your deductible, copays and coinsurance. Platinum plan will have the highest monthly premiums but you will pay less for your deductible, copays and coinsurance. Not every health insurance carrier may offer every plan in every state.

CHAPTER EIGHT

UNDERWRITING AND THE MEDICAL INSURANCE BUREAU

With the implementation of various elements of the ACA; beginning January 1, 2014, medical underwriting for health insurance will essentially cease. Individuals can no longer be denied health insurance coverage due to either existing health or pre-existing conditions. For the most part the new health laws pertain to health insurance only, which in truth, really applies only to medical coverage and in some cases, dental coverage for children. It is those ten essential health benefits (EHBs) which must be covered and cannot be denied. Medical underwriting will still be used in qualifying an individual for the following:

- Disability Income Insurance
- Long-Term Care Insurance
- Life Insurance

Underwriting is the process which evaluates the risks and exposure of insuring a particular individual, assets or a business against some type of payout or loss. Underwriting involves measuring risk exposure and determining the appropriate premium which needs to be charged to insure that risk. The underwriter's role is to protect the insurance company's book of business from risks they feel will make a loss and issue insurance policies, at premiums, which are commensurate with the exposure presented by those risks.

Underwriting Process

Every insurance company has its own set of underwriting guidelines to help the underwriter determine whether or not the company should accept the risk and if so what premium they should charge. Underwriters use a variety of information to set premium prices for insurance policies. For life, health or disability insurance this could include actuarial data, health status, tobacco usage, weight, age and occupation, to name a few, which help to determine the likelihood and magnitude of a payout over the life of the policy.

Once you have completed an application and submitted it to the insurance company that application will then go through their underwriting process. After the underwriter reviews your application, the insurance company will respond in one of four ways:

1. Approved as submitted.
2. Approved with uprating.
3. Approved with exclusion(s).
4. Rejected.

Approved as submitted is just that. How ever you have filled out the application, the insurance issuer is accepting that application. *Approved with uprating* indicates the insurance issuer is accepting your application but they are charging you a higher premium for the policy. This can typically be 15% to 30% higher than a standard rating. If you don't want to accept the terms, always find out the specific reason for the uprating. *Approved with an exclusionary rider* indicates that your application has been approved. However, the insurance issuer is going to exclude coverage for a specific illness or disease. This could be for a specific period of time or for the life of the policy. Lastly, if your application was *rejected* you definitely want to understand why. The reason for this is just about every insurance application you fill out and submit will ask the question - have you been previously rejected, uprated or had an exclusion placed on an offer for a policy?

Ratings Class

Insurance companies generally assign one of the following rating classes to new policies.

- Preferred Plus (also known as Preferred Best, Super Preferred, Premier & Elite)
- Preferred
- Standard Plus (also known as Select)
- Standard
- Sub-Standard (also known as Tables A-H)

Many people think a Preferred Plus rating class is considered to be the normal rating class, and then feel somewhat offended if this is not the rating class they are assigned. In reality, the Standard rating class is given to people who have an average mortality risk. As you might expect, the price of your term insurance policy will go up as your mortality risk goes up. A Preferred Plus rating will be the least expensive while a Sub-Standard class rating will be the most expensive. If a ratings class cannot be approved, based on your mortality risk, the insurance company is likely to decline to issue the policy.

In many cases, ads you see for insurance may seem to be a very cheap price. Unless you read the fine print that quote is usually for a Preferred Plus rating class. If you are rated less than Preferred Plus the premium you are quoted most likely will be higher.

Insurance underwriters have several tools available to them to confirm information by prospective applicants. One of those is the Medical Information Bureau (MIB). No, this is not the Men in Black secret organization. MIB maintains a record on almost everyone who has applied for an *individually* underwritten life, health, critical illness, disability or long-term care insurance policy within the last seven years. So if you've done this the MIB probably has a file on you.

Medical Information Bureau

The MIB Group, Inc. is a member-owned corporation that has operated on a not-for-profit basis in the United States and Canada since 1902. The Medical Information Bureau's (MIB) Underwriting Services are used exclusively by MIB's member life and health insurance companies to assess an individual's risk and eligibility during the underwriting of life, health, disability income, critical illness, and long-term care insurance policies. These services alert underwriters to errors, omissions or misrepresentations made on insurance applications. By mitigating the risk of applicant errors, omissions and misrepresentations, MIB may help lower the cost of life and health insurance for consumers. Insurance companies cannot rely solely on a report from the MIB to make a coverage decision.

The MIB does not collect, maintain or store any medical records such as examination reports, attending physician statements, x-rays and results from laboratory tests, underwriting files or reasons for denial of insurance. Instead, MIB's members agree to share information of underwriting significance in the form of brief medical and avocation "codes," which are a simple form of encryption. These codes do not indicate what action a member company took with respect to an application for insurance (i.e., approval, denial, approved with a substandard rating, etc.).

The MIB also does not maintain prescription drug history or credit information on individuals.

MIB's business model is sometimes described as an "information exchange" because its members contribute underwriting information to the MIB database that may be useful to other members who later search the database with the authorization of the insurance applicant. The information in MIB's database is maintained and safeguarded in a coded format that is accessible only to authorized personnel of the member company to which an individual has applied for insurance and has authorized the use of MIB as an information source. In addition to MIB's use of highly confidential and proprietary codes to protect the privacy of individuals, MIB also implements and enforces robust security standards and policies that are designed to protect the security and confidentiality of any individually identifiable information in MIB's database.

MIB only shares an individual's file with its member life and health insurance companies (with the individual's authorization) or with the individual directly, unless otherwise required or allowed by law. Employers, vendors, physicians and non-members do not have access to MIB files and MIB does not sell any personally identifiable information (PII) to any non-member third parties. Further, the federal *Fair Credit Reporting Act* and the Privacy Rule under the *Health Insurance Portability and Accountability Act (HIPAA)* severely restrict the use and dissemination of individually identifiable information, and MIB complies with both the letter and spirit of these laws.

MIB has long provided consumers with the right to obtain their MIB Consumer File (if one exists) in order to ensure its accuracy and completeness. **Individuals who have not applied for individually underwritten life or health insurance in the last seven years will NOT have an MIB Consumer File.** As a practical matter, individuals who are in good health, approved for a policy as a standard or preferred risk, typically will not have any information reported to MIB.

Since its establishment, MIB has been committed to maintaining the confidentiality and security of the information entrusted to it and to protecting the privacy of the individuals to whom it pertains. This commitment is as important to us today as it was when the organization was founded. Consumer privacy is a priority to MIB, and they go to great lengths to protect it by acting in accordance MIB's Consumer Privacy Policy.

There is no charge to request a copy of your MIB Consumer File (if one exists) once per year directly from MIB. In addition, in the event that you have received an adverse underwriting decision letter from an insurer indicating that an MIB record influenced the underwriting process which resulted in your application being rated or declined, then MIB will provide you with a free copy of your MIB Consumer File in addition to your free annual copy.

You can request a copy of your MIB Consumer File at http://www.mib.com/request_your_record.html. This can be done either online or by telephone, using their toll free line, 800-692-6901. If you call be prepared to give the following information:

- Social Security number.
- First, middle and last names, as well as any other surnames.
- Date of birth.
- Place of birth.
- Occupation.
- Recent addresses.
- Telephone number.

Upon verification of your identity, MIB will process your request in a timely fashion and send you your MIB Consumer File. If you do not have an MIB Consumer File, MIB will provide a "no record" letter explaining that a record does not exist. An MIB Consumer File includes:

- The nature and substance of information, if any, that MIB may have in its database pertaining to you.
- The name(s) of the MIB member companies, if any, which reported information to the MIB.
- The name(s) of the MIB member companies, if any, that received a copy of your MIB Consumer File during the three (3) year period preceding your request for disclosure.
- The name(s) of the MIB member companies, if any, which made an inquiry to the MIB about you within the past two (2) years.

The MIB and its member companies are fully committed to ensuring that only accurate, timely, verified and complete information is reported to MIB. According to the MIB, out of all the free disclosures that are provide to consumers, they find that only 1-2% of these Consumer Files have to be amended due to inaccurate or incomplete information. Based on the very low incidence of corrections that are made to MIB Consumer Files, the MIB is confident that their files are highly accurate and reflect the uncompromising efforts of MIB and its member companies to report information that is accurate, timely, verified and complete, as required by MIB's General Rules, Internal Procedural Rules and federal regulations (the Fair Credit Reporting Act).

The mission of the MIB is to prevent fraud and misrepresentation. The reports can tip-off an insurance company as to whether an applicant may be lying. For example, if an individual was denied by Insurance Company A for life insurance because they had congestive heart failure, then went to Insurance Company B to apply for life insurance and "failed" to disclose the medical diagnosis on the application, that individuals MIB repo would probably expose the fraud to the other insurer.

"Good health is not something we can buy. However, it can be an extremely valuable savings account."

Anne Wilson Schaef
Author with Ph.D. in Clinical Psychology

CHAPTER NINE

DISABILITY INCOME INSURANCE

Disability income (DI) insurance is another specific category of insurance coverage like property and casualty, life, health or long-term care. Should you lose your income due to accident or illness and suddenly there is no incoming cashflow to fund your monthly expenses; your continued health care coverage could be at risk. Disability income insurance is designed to protect your most important asset – you and your ability to earn an income. DI replaces lost income when an individual becomes disabled. I know what your first thought is; what, me disabled? It happens more frequently than most individuals think. A few statistics will bear this out.

According to a February 7, 2013 Fact Sheet, from the Social Security Administration, just over 1 in 4 of today's 20 year-olds will become disabled before they retire. From the U.S. Census Bureaus' American Community Survey, 2011, over 37 million Americans are classified as disabled; about 12% of the total population. More than 50% of those disabled Americans are in their working years, ages 18-64.

From the Social Security Administrations' Disabled Worker Beneficiary Data, December 2012, 8.8 million disabled wage earners, over 5% of U.S. workers, were receiving Social Security Disability (SSDI) benefits at the end of 2012. Also from that same report, in December 2012, there were over 2.5 million disabled workers in their 20s, 30s and 40s receiving SSDI benefits.

An example will help to illustrate what can possibly happen. John is a small business owner who has built a very successful business over the years. His income from that business has allowed him and his family to maintain a very comfortable lifestyle. The downside has been that John has worked long hours, reinvested significant amounts of cashflow back into the business to grow it, not maintained good eating habits, doesn't exercise and over the years has gained more weight than he would have liked and stress has been a constant issue. His kids are now in college; they don't have a lot of investments except the value of the business and they have a high level of monthly expenditures. John is now in his mid-40s, living the high-life and the unthinkable occurs. John has a severe stroke though he is still alive. His wife calls their insurance agent. She knows that John has several insurance policies and wants to know which will take care of his family's need for income while he is incapacitated and going through several months physical therapy. Her shock as she gets the call from the insurance agent. None of them will. Three life insurance policies with a total death benefit of $975,000. But John isn't dead. He has several business insurance policies, group hospitalization and others which cover the home, cars and personal possessions. John has no disability income coverage. With no business partner and the absence of Johns' leadership and management skills the business quickly suffers as does its' value. The family is forced to sell the business at a loss to make up for the extended loss of income. John was very diligent about protecting everything except his most important asset. That was himself and his ability to earn an income. In this case, John's family would have been better off financially had he died from the stroke.

According to the Council for Disability Awareness (CDA), illnesses like cancer, heart attack or diabetes cause the majority of long-term disabilities. Back pain, injuries and arthritis are also significant causes. Most are not work related and are not covered by workers' compensation. According to their 2013 Long-Term Disability Claims Review, the following were the leading causes of new disability claims in 2012:

- Musculoskeletal/connective tissue disorders (28.5%)
- Cancer (14.6%)
- Injuries and poisoning (10.6%)
- Mental disorders (8.9%)
- Cardiovascular/circulatory disorders (8.2%)

The most common causes of existing disability claims in 2012 were:

- Musculoskeletal/connective tissue disorders (30.7%)
- Disorders of the nervous system and sense organs (14.2%)
- Cardiovascular/circulatory disorders (12.1%)
- Cancer (9.0%)
- Mental disorders (7.7%)

Approximately 90% of disabilities are caused by illnesses rather than accidents.

Most individuals are destined to become millionaires. That is, over our lifetime up to age 65, our ability to earn an income will generate more than $1,000,000 of earnings over that period. Table 9.1, on the next page, illustrates the potential earnings of someone to age 65 at various monthly income levels.

Table 9.1 Potential Earnings to Age 65, Total Dollars
Based on Monthly Income

Age	$2,000	$4,000	$6,000	$8,000
25	960,000	1,920,000	2,880,000	3,840,000
30	840,000	1,680,000	2,520,000	3,360,000
35	720,000	1,440,000	2,160,000	2,880,000
40	600,00	1,200,000	1,800,000	2,400,000
45	480,000	960,000	1,440,000	1,920,000
50	360,000	720,000	1,080,000	1,440,000

Source: Florida School of Insurance

The financial impact from total disability may be greater than the financial impact of death. You may live many years totally disabled with no ability to generate an income to pay for the higher medical costs and ongoing living expenses caused by the disability. When disability occurs, life insurance usually isn't of much help. Other than the cash value, which the policy may have built up, the insurance benefits aren't available. Pension benefits, if any, usually aren't available. Even if you qualify for Social Security disability benefits, actual receipt of the money may be at least a year away. However, if the disability arises from a work-related accident or illness, benefits to the injured employee are generally paid by workers' compensation.

Your ability to earn an income is a much greater asset than any other material possessions or assets you have. The risk of losing this ability is substantial during your lifetime. When one looks are probabilities, the probability of a disability occurring is many times greater than the probability of having a pre-mature death over the same period of time. Table 9.2, on the next page, illustrates the probability of disability compared to death at specific ages.

Table 9.2 Probability of Disability Compared to
Death at Specific Ages

Age	# per 1,000 Disabled	# per 1,000 Deaths	Ratio
32	6.87	1.74	4 to 1
37	7.75	2.27	3.5 to 1
42	9.46	3.39	2.8 to 1
47	12.00	5.00	2.4 to 1
52	15.78	7.36	2 to 1

Source: Commissioners Individual Disability Table
Commissioners Standard Ordinary Mortality Table

The risk of a disability occurring to someone during their working years is much greater than the risk of pre-mature death. The impact of a disability can result in an enormous financial burden for that family.

If you don't have any DI and you become disabled the question you need to ask is; how will I replace my lost income? Sources of funds could include:

- Cash savings
- Investments
- Business assets
- Government and state programs
- Borrowings

How long will my savings last? How liquid are my investments or business assets? Will I qualify for any government or state sponsored programs? These are all questions you need to have answers to.

BENEFITS UNDER SOCIAL SECURITY

To be eligible to receive disability benefits under Social Security, you must be both fully insured and disability insured. Fully insured status means you have paid Social Security taxes for 40 calendar quarters or for 10 years. Disability insured requires you have paid Social Security taxes in at least 20 out of 40 calendar quarters (5 out of 10 years) prior to filing a claim. In addition, you must be under the age of 65 and the disability must be expected to last at least 12 months or end in death.

The disability must satisfy the definition of total disability in accordance with Social Security law. Total disability is the inability to engage in any substantial gainful activity by reason of a medically determined physician or mental disability relative to an individual's education and prior work experience. What this means is you must unable to perform your previous job or any other substantial work which exists in the national economy relative to your age, education and prior work experience.

There is a 5-month waiting period before any benefits can be paid. Due to this waiting period plus the time it takes to process the initial claim, the first Social Security disability check which an individual receives may not be until near the end of the first year of disability.

BENEFITS UNDER WORKERS' COMPENSATION

Workers' comp provides another source of disability income. The intent of the workers comp system is to make the employer liable for occupational disabilities without fault having to be proved by the injured worker. Workers comp offers benefits to workers who have job-related disabilities due to an accident or illness received while on the job. Worker comp laws and the benefits provided can vary from state to state. The basic requirement to be eligible for these benefits is that the disability has to be work related.

BENEFITS UNDER DISABILITY INSURANCE

The primary purpose of disability income coverage is to replace personal income due to a disability. A DI policy can be purchased through either a group plan, such as an employer-sponsored, labor union or association plan or as an individual plan. Coverage under a group plan is sometimes broader than that under an individual plan. In addition, most group coverage is less expensive than individual coverage. Benefits paid are in accordance with the policy's provisions and to a degree your loss of income.

According to the *Journal of the American Society of Certified Life Underwriters*, estimating the duration of a disability, which lasts for more than 90-days at its onset, the age and average duration of the disability could be:

- Age 30 – 4.7 years
- Age 35 – 5.1 years
- Age 40 – 5.5 years
- Age 45 – 5.8 years
- Age 50 – 6.2 years
- Age 55 – 6.6 years

Disability Income Needs

The process of determining your disability needs is similar to identifying what your life insurance or health insurance needs might be. A key difference is disability insurance considers your annual income as part of the equation. Assessing the affordability of the premium requires you to have a good understanding of your circumstances from both a financial and personal perspective. You need to be concerned with what you make and what you have to protect. What you make is typically your salary and other earned income you expect to have during a specific period of time. You'll need to also consider any non-earned income such as interest income, dividends, rental income, deferred compensation, residual commissions, royalties and any other miscellaneous income.

The insurance company should ask for some kind of proof of income like an IRS W-2 form or other tax document. If a company doesn't do some type of income due-diligence, make sure you read the fine print of the contract very closely or you may never collect on a legitimate disability claim you file with the insurance company.

Need for Protection

The factors which will most directly impact your disability needs are your fixed or essential expenses. These are expenses which must be paid each month. These would include the mortgage or rent payment, car payments, utilities, food, any installment purchases such as credit cards, insurance premiums, transportation expenses, tuition or educational expenses, etc.

Another factor would be variable expenses which are unexpected, non-fixed expenses. These could include car repairs, medical and dental expenses, home repairs, prescription drugs and those nasty miscellaneous expenses which seem to be a fixed expense each month.

In addition, there might be added expenses resulting from the disability itself. This may include additional prescriptions, the need for specialists, the need for prosthetic devices such as braces, rental of a wheelchair or hospital bed and possible hospital expenses which are not fully covered by your hospitalization insurance.

Partnerships and Small Business Owner Considerations

For a partnership or small business dealing with the death of a partner or principal is usually relatively straightforward. While not to minimize the seriousness of the situation or the emotional toll incurred by the family, most partnerships or small business ownerships usually have life insurance policies in place to deal with these situations. Dealing with a partner or small business owner who becomes disabled can be a much more difficult issue. That is because many partnership/small business agreements will cover what happens in the event of death, but fail to address the possibility of a partner or principal becoming disabled. Yet as we saw earlier, a disability event has a higher statistical probability of occurring than death.

Another aspect to consider is the tax consequences involved in how the policy is paid for. Many partnerships and small businesses will pay for LT disability coverage then write it off as a business expense. While this may amount to a small benefit for the company it could become a huge disadvantage for the business owner should they become disabled and need to claim benefits.

Many of these LT disability policies typically provide 60% of the disabled person's salary as the benefit amount. If the firm pays for the policy, the beneficiary will end up having to pay federal and state income taxes on the benefit amount received. Thus, on an after tax basis the 60% policy becomes even less. Will this after-tax benefit amount cover your required expenses? If the partner or principal pay the premium themselves they will not have to pay the taxes and this could result in a higher net amount being received by the beneficiary. The math needs to be done to determine which may be the better situation for you.

Analyzing Coverage

Once you have completed your needs analysis, your focus now turns to comparing different disability income policies. The cost of DI varies depending on a variety of factors including:

- Occupational classification.
- Age.
- Sex of insured.
- Length of the waiting or elimination period (EP).
- Length of the benefit period (BP).
- Monthly benefit amount.
- Any optional benefits such as inflation protection, options to increase the amount of the benefit over time, cost of living rider, lifetime accident and

sickness benefit, Social Security rider and hospital confinement or non-disabling injury.

The most important differentiator in comparing and analyzing policies is how the policy defines "disability" in the first place. This is critical and why it is important to read the contract carefully.

Elimination Period

The EP is the waiting period between when you make a disability income insurance claim and when the coverage begins. A plan with a 30-day EP will have a considerably higher premium than a plan with a 90 or 120-day EP. The longer you can wait without collecting benefits the smaller the premium will be. This is why you want to complete a thorough income and expense needs analysis. Even though a longer EP will result in premium savings, it may not be in your best interest. Most disability policies can have EPs as short as 30-days to as long as two years. The other thing to remember is how the initial benefit is paid by the insurance company. For example, if you choose a 90-day EP, you will not begin to accrue an income benefit until the 91st day of a disability. Most insurance companies don't issue their benefit checks until the end of the month. Thus, you could wait up to 120 days, from the onset of your disability, before you receive your initial income benefit check. The question you need to ask yourself is; how long can I go without income from my disability income plan?

Benefit Period

Like the elimination period, the benefit period (BP) is a reflection of the premium which you'll pay. The longer the BP the higher the premiums will be. The potential loss of income due to a permanent and total disability could be millions of dollars. For example, a 40-year old individual earning $50,000 per year who becomes totally disabled stands to lose more than $1.2 million before age 65 if the disability becomes permanent.

Disability insurance also makes a distinction between short-term (S-T) and long-term (L-T) disability coverage. Short-term disability can provide coverage up to two years; however most policies only cover a few weeks. Long-term disability coverage can provide benefits for either a maximum number of years or until the insured reaches a certain age. An individual who has DI coverage may have both policies which cover both term periods of coverage. Or they might have just one type of coverage, either a short-term or long-term policy.

Benefit Amount and Participation Limits

The insurance company's issue and participation limits, as well as any applicable state laws, will determine the maximum amount of monthly benefits which may be issued. When applying for disability income insurance the insurance company will want to know how much earned income you make each year. Another factor which is considered by the insurance company is the existence of any other disability income policies currently in force. Any other coverage will cause the amount requested to be limited to the insurer's underwriting limits.

If this seems confusing an example should help to clarify this information. Robert, a lawyer with earned income of $5,000 per month has a disability policy with Company A, his employer which will pay $1,500 per month. In addition, Robert purchases another policy with Company B which will pay a benefit of 70% of his grossed earned income or $3,500 per month. It will participate with other insurers' coverage up to this 70% maximum. He discloses on the application his other policy he has through his company. Robert files a claim due to a disability. Since 70% of his earned income is $3,500, Robert will receive $1,500 from Company A. The maximum benefit Company B will pay Robert is $2,000 per month. Both these amounts total the $3,500.

Tax Considerations

Premiums paid for an individually owned disability income policy are not tax-deductible. Since the benefits received are from a personally paid policy the benefits are not taxable income and thus are tax-free. This would also apply to a sole-proprietorship since it is a non-incorporated business entity owned by one individual.

If benefits received from an employer-provided policy and the employer paid all the disability premiums, all income replacement benefits received are included as taxable income in lieu of wages. If the policy is partially paid for by the employer and employee, benefits will be taxable up to the extent of the employer pro-rata share of the premiums.

Contestable Period

An insurance company cannot contest or challenge any statement on the application or deny a claim after the policy has been in force for two years from the effective date of coverage. After this two year period the policy becomes incontestable. Some states may elect a time limit which is more favorable to the issuer such as three or four years.

There are two exceptions to this. The first is a misstatement of age or sex. This can be corrected at any time in which it is discovered. The second is in the case of fraud. Fraud can void an insurance policy whenever it can be proven by the insurance company.

Pricing Disability Coverage

Underwriting is the process of selection, classification and rating of risks. An underwriter's source of information includes:

- The agent, also known as a field underwriter.
- The application, including the agent's statement.
- Inspection reports.
- Medical information and attending physician's reports.
- Other information including occupational or avocational questionnaires.

The application is the main tool used by the underwriter. It contains the important information about risk including:

- Age, sex and occupation of the applicant.
- Past medical history and current physical condition.
- Moral habits.
- Information regarding other insurance owned.
- Family history.
- Unusual hobbies or avocations.

Most insurance companies group jobs according to the degree of injury risk they pose. These groups are usually identified as classes 1, 2, 3 or 4. Class 1 occupations are the least hazardous while Class 4 occupations are the most hazardous. As an underwriting factor, occupation is more heavily weighted in terms of disability income insurance coverage than it would be in life insurance underwriting. We'll take a look at a few occupations by class.

- *Class 1:* Physicians, dentists, lawyers, accountants, school teachers, actuaries, insurance sales representatives, corporate officers, most engineers.
- *Class 2:* General clerical employees, bank tellers, inside salespersons, outside salespersons with limited travel, most building contractors, electricians, registered nurses, practical nurses.
- *Class 3:* Bartenders, waiters and waitresses, cooks, salespersons with extensive travel, plumbers, mechanic and most factory workers.

- *Class 4:* Bridge workers, construction workers, truck drivers, sanitation workers, firefighters, police personnel, mine workers.

The occupations listed above are not all-inclusive. Some insurance companies may classify the same occupation differently. Pricing models for disability income insurance are not standard among different insurance companies.

Insurance underwriters will try to determine whether an applicant presents a moral hazard or a morale hazard. *Moral hazard* relates to how an individual behaves and does it suggest claims problems or invites disability risk. Evidence of a moral hazard could include the loss of a driver's license, a history of substance abuse or a record of criminal activity. A *morale hazard* is an indifferent attitude displayed by an individual that increases the risk of loss. For example, an individual regularly receives speeding tickets or has had a couple of DUI's may be demonstrating an indifferent attitude toward the risk of injury due to high speeds or drinking and driving. If the insurance company concludes that an individual poses any of these additional risks it may add a surcharge to the disability premium or even just reject the application.

Hazardous hobbies are a pricing factor related to occupational risk. Hobbies such as skin diving, scuba diving, sky diving, flying or auto racing are inherently more dangerous than golf or tennis. The insurance company will ask you to list any such high-risk hobbies when considering your application for disability income insurance. In addition, the insurance company may have you fill out an avocation questionnaire which provides more specific information concerning the hobby. Most disability insurers will offer coverage equal to 60% to 70% of earned income.

Risk Classification

Once the insurance company reviews all the underwriting information, it will make a decision about the acceptance of

184

the risk. For DI policies most applicants are classified as a standard risk. This means they fit the profile of an average policyholder. If approved, the policy will be issued as applied for by the applicant.

In some cases, the applicant may be classified as a substandard risk. This could result from any of the factors we discussed earlier such as past or current medical history or evidence of a moral hazard. If you are classified as a substandard disability risk, many insurance companies have alternatives available for issuing a policy including:

- Charging an extra premium to compensate for the higher risk involved.
- Attaching a rider to modify the coverage of the policy. For example, a full back exclusion for chronic back disorders or full injury exclusions related to any sky diving incident.
- A qualified condition exclusion to exclude coverage for a specific medical problem for a specific period of time.
- Changing the Elimination Period or Benefit Period related to a specific medical condition. The EP could be increased and/or the BP could be shortened to compensate for the medical disorder.

The final alternative is to simply reject the application.

The underwriting factors which impact DI insurance are different from the factor which might influence life insurance or other types of insurance coverage. For example, if an individual suffers from chronic back problems they may have no problems getting life insurance but a lot of trouble getting DI policy.

Summary

Pricing models for disability insurance coverage are not standard, but there are provisions that are common to both group and individual policies. Some of these include:

- Definition of disability. These definitions can be own occupation (most expensive), any occupation, Social Security or some form of hybrid definition.
- The elimination period. This usually is 30, 60, 90, 180 or 365-days.
- The benefit amount or percentage. S-T policies usually are limited to 60% of wages while L-T policies can provide up to 75-80% of monthly gross wages.
- The benefit period (BP).
- The coverage or perils insured against.
- Some L-T policies reduce benefits, dollar for dollar, if receiving disability from Social Security.

The following are factors to consider in evaluating the appropriateness of long-term disability coverage:

- It is income replacement therefore, the amount of the benefit must be appropriate.
- The term of the benefit should match the term of work-life expectancy.
- The policy should cover both sickness and accidents.
- The definition of disability should be appropriate to the insured.
- The policy should be non-cancelable or guaranteed renewable.
- Consider the elimination period. Do you have sufficient emergency funds to cover this period plus 30 days; as benefits most likely will be paid in arrears?
- Does the policy have a Social Security disability benefit offset? Is that an important consideration?

If you have applied for disability income insurance and received a quote which seems too high or too restrictive, ask the company's agent or customer service to explain the reasons for the quote. While you can't change your age, sex, occupation and health, there are factors you can change which could reduce the premium you're charged including:

- Increase the Elimination Period.
- Reduce the Benefit Period.
- Reduce the benefit amount.
- Eliminate optional benefits, if any.

GROUP UNDERWRITING

Many individuals have at least a small amount of disability income insurance with the benefits offered by their employer. Group policies are typically underwritten on very liberal terms. Group underwriting is usually accomplished without any reference to an individual's medical information. Many insurance companies require a minimum number of employees participate in the group plan for it to be issued without evidence of insurability. Most group disability coverage will be limited to not more than 70% of earned income and usually subject to a low maximum benefit amount such as $1,000 or $2,000 per month for up to a year. Another type of group coverage is association coverage. This form of coverage is for individual policies which are administered as group insurance. If the association is to offer a guaranteed-issue plan, then there is no medical underwriting. If some medical underwriting is required it is referred to as simplified or progressive underwriting. Premiums for association types of coverage are normally banded by ages and amounts. For example, individuals between ages 25 to 31 would pay the same premium for a 30-day EP with a monthly benefit amount of $1,000 payable to age 65. Individuals between the ages 31 to 35 would have a different band of premiums applied.

"If we don't make great breakthroughs on Alzheimer's, we are going to be sunk in 30 years; the costs to our society are going to be immeasurable."

Tom Harkin
Democratic U.S. Senator - Iowa
Chairman - Senate Health Education Labor and
Pensions Committee
Speech - Co-sponsored by TIAA-CREF Institute and the Alfred Sloan Foundation

CHAPTER TEN

CHOICES FOR LONG-TERM CARE

If you don't meet all the requirements for Medicaid, what is your plan for long-term care should the need arise? **Medicare is not going to cover what you're going to need, if you need it.** Many individuals may not need long-term care (LTC) until they reach their 70s, 80s or 90s. However, if you wait that long until you actually need it, the costs involved in obtaining the needed coverage may be cost prohibitive or you may not even be able to qualify for LTC coverage. This doesn't even consider the possibility of a sudden event occurring much earlier in life requiring LTC. LTC is a health issue that should be planned for in advance because of the escalating costs involved as you get older and potentially less healthy.

Like the Medicare health plans, LTC insurance can vary from state to state; in what is sold, the coverage and benefits the policy provides and the premiums you pay. We're going to cover LTC in general, solutions for getting LTC other than with insurance and LTC insurance. We'll conclude with a look at the issues facing LTC insurance right now in wake of the Great Financial Crisis and a

Federal Reserve that has now implemented a zero-rate monetary policy going on nearly 5 years. This has severely impacted the yields insurance companies, who provide LTC insurance, can obtain on their fixed income portfolios which account for up to 60% of their revenues to pay benefits. The last five years have brought seismic changes to this industry.

LONG TERM CARE SURVEYS

Let's take a look at a few surveys which were done within the past two years on attitudes, beliefs and behavior regarding long-term care and the need for it. Surveys have a value in accessing perception, at a specific point in time, even though they may present conflicting conclusions depending on who conducted them.

In the fall of 2012, John Hancock released its *Study of Consumer Behavior*, prepared by The Forbes Consulting Group, which was an online survey of 305 individuals aged 45-65 who had household incomes greater than $70,000 and investable assets of over $100,000. Of those who indicated they would NOT consider purchasing a LTC policy, 74% cited cost of the policy as the primary reason. Major reasons for considering purchasing an LTC policy pertained to the need for planning and to protect one's family. LTC insurance as an important part of financial planning for retirement was identified by 77% of respondent versus only 23% who would consider purchasing because of a personal experience. Those who indicated their primary goal in considering purchase was to avoid becoming a burden to their family was identified by 62% of respondents. Only 38% would buy to retain control over their care. Those who said their primary goal for purchasing was to protect their family was 54% while only 46% indicated their goal was to protect their assets. An insurance carrier's reputation and financial strength was also found to be a critical factor in purchasing LTC insurance.

In November 2012, a study from Northwestern Mutual, *The Long-Term Care Awareness Study*, was conducted by Harris Interactive and surveyed 2,516 adults. The study found that a third haven't factored their LTC needs into their retirement planning. Nearly a quarter aren't sure how they'll address LTC needs and 8% say they're not going to address them at all. This is despite the fact that 55% of respondents think they will need LTC at some point in their lives. The study also found less than half of the respondents felt financially prepared to live beyond age 75 and only 38% say they are prepared to live beyond 85.

In February 2013, Nationwide Financial released a survey regarding perceptions of long-term care among baby boomers. Their survey included 813 respondents, 50 years of age and older and who have at least $150,000 in annual income or in investible assets. Most respondents think of long-term care as nursing home care or assisted living. The fact: nearly half of LTC is done in the home by a home health-care worker or is adult day care. When asked to estimate how much nursing home care will cost a year in 2030, respondents estimated an average of $111,507. This is less than half the actual estimated costs, which are projected to be $265,000 a year. In 2013 it is currently about $67,000 a year. According to John Carter, president and chief operating officer of retirement plans for Nationwide Financial, nursing home costs have increased more than 4% annually since 1974. Other findings include those aged 50 or older who have not retired believe they will live an average of only 20.7 years in retirement, while those already in retirement believe they will live 27.1 years in retirement. Most respondents indicated they have a plan for their finances in retirement but 57% admitted they had not taken long-term care costs into consideration.

U.S. Trust, a unit of Bank of America, surveyed 711 high-net worth individuals with over $3 million in investable assets. LTC costs were unseen risks which were not well reflected in the financial planning process. Even though 47% of the respondents had created a financial plan

191

to address LTC needs they and their spouse/partner might need; only 18% had a financial plan that accounts for their parents' LTC costs. Of these respondents, 46% indicated they have provided substantial financial support to adult family members with 69% indicating they do not have a financial plan which accounts for the financial needs of any of these other adult family members.

NO PRIOR EXPERIENCE

The real perception for most individuals in their 40s, 50s and even into their 60s is, *"nothing is going to happen to me so why would I want to pay for a product I'll never need."* Most individuals feel this way because they have no prior experience. By no prior experience I mean they have never been **directly** involved as the **primary caregiver**, NOT to be confused with the primary earner. Knowing someone who has acted in this capacity or even another individual within your extended family does not count. Once you have gained prior experience you now understand the emotional, physical and financial consequences the event poses to the family. You have experienced the fear. Those you love have no choice but to set aside their lives to provide assistance and/or supervision on a 24 hour basis.

Extended care usually results from two impairments. One is physical; where a chronic medical condition compromises the individual's ability to get through most of their activities of daily living. The other is cognitive; where there is a measurable decline in intellect. Of claims which are filed, 80-85% of the LTC claims are from the neck up.

How individuals response to the possibility of an unexpected death or disability is based on their role in the family. Whether this is the other spouse or an adult child, some individuals are more emotionally mature than others within the family. **Unlike primary earners' who view the risk of an unexpected death or disability as negligible; primary caregivers view them as events with serious consequences to their ability to**

continue providing for the day to day needs of the family. Providing care to those who are chronically ill often makes a healthy caregiver chronically ill. These situations can tear them apart both physically and emotionally.

In October 2013, Genworth Financial released a report, *Beyond Dollars: A Way Forward*, which surveyed more than 1,200 caregivers and recipients receiving LTC. Those who identified themselves as caregivers; more than 50% said they had lost income because of those responsibilities. Thirty-eight percent of caregivers indicated they could have avoided a lot of stress if they had started planning for care earlier while 35% of recipients agreed. Many of those who participated said they made a mistake by not purchasing LTC insurance. Almost 60% of respondents, who didn't have a LTC policy, wished they had purchased one. Of those, nearly 60% felt it would have been easier on their finances and would have put less strain on their family. According to the report, Genworth believes families could save almost $11,000 per year on out-of-pocket expenses for LTC if they started planning earlier.

The need for LTC is a very real potential risk. In many ways LTC insurance is no different than life insurance, homeowners insurance or car insurance. Pay the premiums now and transfer the risk to an insurance company, which covers you and pays you benefits should you need them. Or you don't pay the premiums and pray you never need the coverage. If you do you're probably screwed if you don't have the cash reserves available. Your retirement plan then implodes and you're suddenly faced with a radically different lifestyle ahead of you than what you had expected for your later years. Not an enjoyable scenario.

LTC OVERVIEW

Despite medical improvements and advances in pharmacology, health conditions for a majority of the U.S. population are getting worse. As the population ages and life expectancies increase, there is an increased risk for the need for long-term care. According to the CMS, almost 70% of individuals aged 65 can expect to eventually require some level of services and support to meet personal care needs over an extended period of time. Those who reach 65 will likely have a 40% chance of entering a nursing home. About 10% of the individuals who enter a nursing home will stay there five years or more.

According to the American Association for Long-Term Care Insurance (AALTCI), in 2013, LTC insurers paid $7.5 billion in long-term care insurance benefits to approximately 273,000 individuals, an increase of 13%. Claimants rose 3% as well over 2012. Insurers paid $6.6 billion to some 264,000 policyholders in 2012. **The most common reasons for claims were Alzheimer's disease, stroke, arthritis and cancer.** In-home care accounted for about half of all new LTC insurance claims and two-thirds of benefit recipients were women. In a separate report released by the AALTCI, in August 2013, it was estimated insurers will pay $15 billion by 2023 and $34 billion by 2033 in LTC benefits when today's 60 year olds, in 2014, reach their 80s.

In their 2012 annual report, the Life Insurance and Market Research Association reported that about seven million individuals, including about 12% of Americans over age 65, have long-term care coverage.

In an interview with AARP, Susan Collins, a Republican senator from Maine who is on the Senate Aging Committee noted, there are over 5 million Americans who have Alzheimer's disease. There is $200 billion being spent each year caring for these individuals. Medicare and Medicaid account for $142 billion of that being spent and yet only $500 million is invested into researching Alzheimer's.

COST CONCERNS FOR LTC

The costs associated with LTC are quite high. LTC costs generally range from $30,000 - $100,000 per year, depending on the region where you live and the level of care provided. According to the Department of Health and Human Service (HHS), for 2010, the average costs for long-term care in the United States were:

- $205 per day or $6,235 per month for a semi-private room in a nursing home,
- $229 per day or $6,965 per month for a private room in a nursing home,
- $3,293 per month for care in an assisted living facility (for a one-bedroom unit),
- $21 per hour for a home health aide,
- $19 per hour for homemaker services and
- $67 per day for services in an adult day health care center

For comparison since 2010, each year insurance carrier Genworth Financial releases its *Cost of Care Survey*, which looks at home care providers, adult day health care facilities, assisted living facilities and nursing homes. The 2013 survey conducted by CareScout included nearly 15,000 LTC providers from all 50 states and Washington, D.C., divided into 437 regions across the country. The study, in its 10th year, included the following findings in the report:

- Licensed Homemaker Services: National median hourly rate is $18, a 1.39% increase over 2012, with a 5-year annual growth rate of 0.84%.
- Licensed Home Health Aid Services: National median hourly rate is $19, a 2.32% increase over 2012, with a 5-year annual growth rate of 1.0%.
- Adult Day Health Care: National median hourly rate is $65, a 6.56% increase over 2012, with a 5-year annual growth rate of 1.61%.
- Assisted Living Facility (One Bedroom – Single Occupancy): National median monthly rate is $3,450, a 4.55% increase over 2012, with a 5-year annual growth rate of 4.26%. Annual cost: $41,400.

- Nursing Home (Semi-Private Room): National median daily rate is $207, a 3.30% increase over 2012, with a 5-year annual growth rate of 4.22%. Annual cost: $75,555.
- Nursing Home (Private Room): National median daily rate is $230, a 3.60% increase over 2012, with a 5-year annual growth rate of 4.45%. Annual cost: $83,950.

The five year percentage increases listed above represent the compound annual growth rate for surveys conducted from 2008 to 2013. The room you might have had in 2008, at a cost of $67,525 for the year will now cost you $83,950 for the year in 2013; an additional $16,425 per year. The average yearly cost of assisted living is $39,600 for a single room with a single occupant.

According to the Genworth report, the cost of care for Alzheimer's disease, which affects 5.1 million Americans, is projected to rise to $1.2 trillion annually by 2050. This only includes the cost for paid health care, LTC and hospice. The unpaid caregiver's contribution was some 17.5 billion hours of care, valued at more than $216.5 billion for just 2012 alone. Which states had the least expensive (average annual) costs for LTC in 2013?

1. Missouri - $35,645
2. Louisiana - $35,749
3. Alabama - $35,963
4. Oklahoma - $36,936
5. Arkansas - $37,535
6. Texas - $37,751
7. Georgia - $38,713
8. South Carolina - $40,315
9. Iowa - $40,536
10. Kansas - $40,686

States most expensive (average annual) for costs in 2013?

1. Alaska - $103,336
2. Connecticut - $68,983
3. Hawaii - $66,910
4. Massachusetts - $65,212
5. New Jersey - $65,203
6. New York - $59,598
7. Delaware - $59,003
8. Vermont - $58,581
9. New Hampshire - $57,689
10. Maine - $57,628

According to Genworth, though women own about 58% of in-force LTCI policies, they account for nearly 67% of all claims and 71% of all claim dollars paid.

The National Clearinghouse for Long Term Care has a website which gives you a representation of the costs for LTC in various states. Clicking on the link, http://www.longtermcare.gov/LTC/Main_Site/Tools/State_C osts.aspx, takes you to the website which allows you to interact and click on the state where you live to quickly see the costs for long-term care there. Here you can track and project average nationwide costs for home care, adult day care, assisted living facilities and nursing homes. Based on their predicted long-term care needs and lifespans, individuals can estimate inflation-adjusted costs for up to 30 years.

These costs can vary significantly from state to state. For example, the cost of private care in Missouri is about $56,000 a year. In North Carolina it is about $75,000 a year and in New York as much as $120,000 each year. The biggest mistake individuals make in planning for LTC is underestimating these costs.

LTC can be provided at home, in the community, in assisted living or in a nursing home. In 2012, it's estimated about nine million men and women over the age of 65 will need LTC. By 2020, an estimated 12,000,000 individuals may need LTC. Most will be cared for at home. Family and friends are the sole caregivers for 70% of the elderly.

TRIGGERING AN LTC EVENT

LTC constitutes a variety of services which includes medical and non-medical care to individuals who have a chronic illness or disability. Many individuals who require LTC are generally not sick in the traditional sense. Instead they are old and frail and unable to perform some of the basic activities of daily living (ADLs). The six ADLs include:

1. Dressing
2. Bathing
3. Eating
4. Toileting
5. Continence
6. Transferring (getting in and out of a bed or chair)

If you have LTC insurance, you usually become eligible to receive benefits when either of the following events occur and are certified by a Licensed Health Care Practitioner.

- When an illness or accident prevents an individual from performing at least **two activities of daily living** for at least 90 days. Events triggering an LTC event could include heart attack, cancer and other chronic health conditions.
- Substantial supervision to protect yourself from threats and safety due to severe cognitive impairment such as Alzheimer's disease, brain injury, stroke or dementia.

LONG-TERM CARE CHOICES

If you find yourself having to deal with a LTC situation, it helps to have a number of care options available so you can decide which arrangements will work best for you and your family members. Figure 10.1, on the following page, provides a summary view of the comparative levels of assistance.

Figure 10.1 Comparison of LTC Types and Assistance

	Help with activities of daily living	Help with additional services	Help with care needs	Range of Costs
Community Based Services	Yes	Yes	No	Low to Medium
Home Health Care	Yes	Yes	Yes	Low to High
In-Law Apartments	Yes	Yes	No	Low to High
Housing for Aging and Disabled Individuals	Yes	Yes	No	Low to High
Board and Care Homes	Yes	Yes	Yes	Low to High
Assisted Living	Yes	Yes	Yes	Medium to High
Continuing Care Retirement Communities	Yes	Yes	Yes	High
Nursing Homes	Yes	Yes	Yes	High

Courtesy: Medicare; Long Term Care

Each of these options will be discussed in more detail below and we'll provide some insight into how you can get assistance with your long-term care needs.

Community-Based Services

- Adult day care
- Senior centers
- Transportation
- Meals On Wheels
- Telephone reassurance
- Case management

Adult day health care provides social and other related support services in a community-based, protective setting during any part of the day, but is less than 24 hour care.

Home Health Care

- Homemaker services
- Home health aids
- Personal care aide services
- Skilled nursing care
- Respite care
- Medical equipment
- Home repair and modification
- Hospice

Licensed homemaker services provide hands-off care such as helping with cooking and running errands. They are also referred to as personal care assistance or personal care companion. Licensed home health aide services provide hands-on personal care but not medical care in the home. This assistance includes help with daily activities of living such as bathing, dressing, etc.

In-Law Apartments

An in-law apartment is a separate housing arrangement within a single family home or on your lot. It is a complete living space which includes a private bath and kitchen. They are sometimes referred to as a second unit, accessory apartment or accessory dwelling. An in-law apartment may provide a living space for a caretaker or may be rented to provide additional income to you.

Housing for Aging and Disabled Individuals

The Federal government and most states have certain programs which help pay for housing for older people with low or moderate incomes, usually less than $46,000 if single or $53,000 if married. An application must be filled out and many of these programs have a waiting list. Many times these programs also offer assistance with meals and other activities such as housekeeping, shopping and laundry.

Board and Care Homes

This is a group living arrangement which provides help with activities of daily living such as eating, bathing and using the bathroom. These are individuals who typically can't live on their own but do not need nursing home services. This type of care is sometimes called a "group home". In some cases, private long-term care insurance and other types of assistance programs may help pay for this type of living arrangement. Since many of these homes do not receive payments from either Medicare or Medicaid they are not strictly monitored. The monthly charge for this type of arrangement is usually a percentage of your income.

Assisted Living

This group living arrangement provides help with activities of daily living such as eating, bathing, and using the bathroom, taking medicine, and getting to appointments as needed. Residents often live in their own room or apartment within a building or group of buildings and have some or all of their meals together. Social and recreational activities are usually provided. Some assisted living facilities have health services on site. Costs for assisted living facilities can vary widely depending on the size of the living areas, services provided, type of help needed, and where the building is located. Residents usually pay a monthly rent and then pay additional fees for the services that they get. In 2001, the typical cost of living in an assisted living facility ranged from $900 to $3,000 per month. They have increased significantly since then. Costs can be higher in urban areas or in upscale facilities.

Continuing Care Retirement Communities (CCRC)

CCRCs are housing communities which have different levels of care based on your needs. Within the same community, there may be individual homes or apartments for residents who still live on their own, an assisted living facility for people who need some help with daily care, and a nursing home for those who require higher levels of care. Residents are able to move from one level of care to another based on their needs but still stay in the same CCRC.

If you are considering a CCRC, be sure to check the record of its nursing home. Your CCRC contract usually requires you to use the CCRC nursing home if you need this level of care. CCRCs generally charge a large payment before you move in (called an entry fee) and then charge monthly fees. In 2004, entrance fees range from $38,000 to $400,000. Monthly payments can then range from $650 to $3,500 per month.

Nursing Homes

These facilities provide care to those individuals who can't be cared for at either home or in the community 24 hours a day. Nursing homes provide a wide range of personal care and health services. This care generally is to assist people with activities of daily living such as dressing, bathing, and using the bathroom and for individuals who can't take care of themselves due to physical, emotional, or mental problems. **Medicare doesn't pay for this type of care and doesn't pay for most nursing home care.** Some nursing homes may provide skilled care after an injury or hospital stay. Medicare will pay for skilled nursing facility care for a limited period of time if you meet certain conditions.

Generally, Medicare doesn't pay for LTC. Medicare pays only for a medically-necessary skilled nursing facility or home health care. You must meet certain conditions for Medicare to pay for these types of care. Most LTC is custodial care which assists individuals with support services such as dressing, bathing and using the bathroom. **Medicare doesn't pay for custodial care.**

SOLUTIONS OTHER THAN LTC INSURANCE

When planning for the possibility of a potential LTC event occurring you need to ask the following three questions:

1. Who is going to take care of me when I can't do it myself any longer?
2. Where will I be taken care of?
3. How will I pay for this care?

The questions sound very simple but the answers and solutions can be extremely complex and filled with significant emotion. These conversations need to take place between spouses and for many baby-boomers with their aging parents. The cost of long-term care can vary considerably depending on what kind of care you need, where you get care and where you live. To put it simplistically, there are only 4 ways to pay for care if or when you need it.

1. Through family and their financial support.
2. Government programs may be a possibility. Medicaid does if you are in poverty or an indigent.
3. Self-insure – pay for care by depleting your existing financial resources.
4. LTC insurance.

Before we look at LTC insurance itself, let's first explore what options are available other than obtaining the insurance for LTC needs.

Family

Traditionally, families usually bore the cost of taking care of older family members when they could no longer maintain their independence. In the early stages for the need of LTC, family assistance may be the only viable option in that it requires the family to minimally assist the older individual. This might include helping with activities such as shopping, home cleaning and cooking. In some cases the family may opt to have the older individual move into the home of younger family members to provide more assistance.

Personal Assets

Many times older individuals don't feel comfortable relying on their children or other family members for support and decide to use their own assets to pay for LTC. One problem that can arise is the assets may not be sufficiently liquid (readily converted to cash without loss) to provide the resources for immediate or long-term needs. They may also significantly deplete their assets, leaving very little left as a legacy to their children or grandchildren.

Medicare

Can provide some benefits for LTC but its restrictive and limited in its scope of care. **It covers nursing home and home health care but is limited to skilled nursing care that is rehabilitative. The individual may not be sufficiently ill enough to require skilling nursing care.** Medicare will not cover aid associated with ADLs. A physician is required to certify the need for skilled nursing care and any nursing home must be certified by Medicare. Medicare only covers a maximum of 100 days of skilled nursing care and only the first 20 days are covered at 100%.

LTC INSURANCE

Age is not a determining factor in needing long-term care. Being older though definitely increases your risk that you may need it because of a LTC event. According to the U.S. Department of Health and Human Services, in their *Medicare & You, National Medicare Handbook, Centers for Medicare and Medicaid Services, Revised November 2012*, about 70 percent of individuals over age 65 will require at least some type of long-term care services during their lifetime. About 40% of those receiving long-term care today are between 18 and 64. Once a change of health occurs as a result of an LTC event obtaining long-term care insurance (LTCI) may no longer be an available option because of the now pre-existing health condition.

LTCI policies are not standardized. LTCI rates are determined by seven main factors:

1. The person's age.
2. The daily (or monthly) amount of benefit. Benefit can vary depending on whether it is for nursing home care, assisted living or home care, for example.
3. Duration of how long the benefits are paid. These usually start at 12 months and can last as long as the individual lives. The average is about 5 years. The longer the duration the more costly the premiums.
4. The elimination or waiting period. This is the period of time before benefits are paid. Common periods are 30, 60, 90 and 180-days.
5. Maximum policy benefits once an individual begins receiving benefits.
6. Any inflation protection.
7. Health rating (preferred, standard, sub-standard).

Coverage and caregiver options are most critical when you are evaluating policies. You want as much flexibility as possible. The policy should cover all types of situations whether it is to stay at home or go into a facility. Does the caregiver have to be a licensed caregiver or can it be someone in the family.

Most LTCI companies will offer couples and multi-life discounts on individual policies. Some will define "couples" as not only spouses but also as two people who meet criteria for living together in a committed relationship and sharing basic living expenses. Individuals who probably shouldn't consider purchasing any LTCI are those individuals:

- Who may soon begin receiving Medicaid benefits.
- Having limited assets and not being able to afford the premiums over the lifetime of the policy.
- Your only source of income is a social security benefit or supplemental security income.

Insurance companies and the *National Association of Insurance Commissioners* say you should not spend more than 7% of your income on long-term care insurance.

The average age of purchasers has dropped from 68 years in 1990 to 61 years in 2005, and the number of purchasers who are under age 65 has increased significantly. The qualifying process to get a LTC insurance policy is somewhat similar to qualifying for a large life insurance policy. That means you'll most likely have to go through the insurance company's underwriting process. There will be a fairly lengthy application to flush out your current health status. You might also be required to have lab work done to assess your blood chemistry panels. Individuals who have certain health conditions may not qualify for LTCI. Common reasons could include:

- Currently using LTC services.
- Already need help with certain ADLs.
- Have AIDS or AIDS Related Complex (ARC).
- Have Alzheimer's disease or any form of dementia or cognitive dysfunction; a stroke within the past year to two years or a history of strokes.

206

- Have metastatic cancer.

Once an individual purchases a LTC policy, the language cannot be changed by the insurance company. The policy is usually guaranteed renewable for life and it can never be canceled by the insurance company for health reasons. **The only reason it can be canceled is for non-payment of premiums.**

Payout Options for Long Term Care Policies

The payout options for LTCI policies include:

- **Indemnity Policy:** The indemnity policy is used by chronic illness riders. An indemnity or per diem policy pays up to a fixed amount irrespective of what you spend. Benefits are paid in a lump sum. Once received these funds can be used for any purpose.
- **Reimbursement or Expense Incurred Policy:** With a reimbursement policy you choose the benefit amount when you apply for the policy and you are reimbursed for actual expenses for services rendered up to the monthly maximum, which is a fixed dollar amount per day, week or month. Payments are made as expenses are incurred. Any portion of the monthly maximum amount not used is typically available for future benefits.
- **Integrated Policy:** An integrated policy has pooled benefits. This type of policy provides a total dollar amount which may be used for different types of LTC services. There is usually a daily, weekly or monthly dollar limit for your covered LTC expenses.

If you have legally given control of your finances to a care-giver, who is going to be responsible for the payment of your LTC expenses, be sure it is an individual you can trust unequivocally and who will look out for your best interests. There can be a dark side, especially for indemnity policies.

Don't make any assumptions just because it may be a family member that you are entrusting. I am aware of situations where caregivers, who were family members, suddenly having a new car appear in their driveway or are taking expensive vacations, which would normally appear out of the realm of their own financial situation.

Benefits and Eligibility

Many LTCI policies have limits on how long or how much the policy will pay. Most policies will pay the costs of your LTC for two to five years. There are some insurance companies which offer policies that will pay your LTC costs for as long as you live, no matter how much it costs, though there are very few companies today that offer such unlimited or lifetime policies. Some insurance companies have a high coverage option, which offer a $1 million lifetime limit.

Most LTCI policies sold today are comprehensive policies. That is the policies generally cover all types of LTC we discussed earlier such as home care, assisted living, adult daycare, respite care, hospice care, nursing home and Alzheimer's facilities. If home care coverage is purchased, LTCI can pay for home care, often from the first day it is needed. It will cover the cost for a visiting or live-in caregiver, companion, housekeeper, therapist or private duty nurse up to seven days a week, 24 hours a day (up to the policy benefit maximum). Other benefits of long-term care insurance include:

- Many individuals may feel uncomfortable relying on their children or family members for support. LTCI can help cover out-of-pocket expenses. Without this type of coverage, the cost of providing these services may quickly deplete the savings of the individual and/or their family.
- Premiums paid on a LTCI product may be eligible for an income tax deduction. The amount of the

deduction depends on the age of the covered person. Benefits paid from a LTCI policy are generally excluded from income.

- Business deductions of premiums are determined by the type of business. For corporations paying premiums for an employee, they are generally 100% deductible if not included in employee's taxable income.

You qualify for covered benefits with most LTCI plans when you need help with two or more of six activities of daily living (ALDs) or when you have a cognitive impairment.

Most policies have an elimination period or waiting period. This is the period of time that you pay for care before your benefits are paid. The elimination period for most LTCI policies can be from 20 to 120 days. Longer elimination periods can result in lower premiums. Some policies can require intended claimants to provide proof of 20 to 120 service days of paid care before any benefits will be paid. In some cases, the option may be available to select zero elimination days, when covered services are provided in the home in accordance with a physician's Plan of Care.

Medicaid provides some benefits for LTCI. As a welfare program, Medicaid provides medically necessary services for people with limited resources who need nursing home care but can stay at home with special community care services. However, Medicaid generally does not cover LTC provided in a home setting or for assisted living.

Tax Advantages

There can be tax advantages associated with purchasing LTCI. As LTCI relates to personal income taxes there are two types of LTC policies which are offered.

- Tax Qualified (TQ): These policies are the most common policies offered. A TQ policy requires that a person meet either of two conditions. (1) they be expected to require care for at least 90 days and be **unable to perform 2 or more ADLs** such as eating, dressing, bathing, transferring, toileting, continence without substantial assistance (hands on or standby) or (2) for at least 90 days they need substantial assistance due to a severe cognitive impairment. In either case a physician must provide a Plan of Care. Benefits from a TQ policy are non-taxable.

- Non-tax Qualified (NTQ): These policies were formerly called traditional long term care insurance. The policy includes a trigger called a medical necessity trigger. What this means is the patient's own physician, or a physician in conjunction with someone from the insurance company can state that the patient needs care for any medical reason and the policy will pay. NTQ policies include walking as an activity of daily living and usually only require the **inability to perform 1 or more ADLs**. The Treasury Department has not clarified the status of benefits received under a non-qualified LTCI plan. Therefore, the taxability of these benefits is open to further interpretation. This means that it is possible that individuals who receive benefits under a NTQ long-term care insurance policy risk facing a large tax bill for these benefits.

If your LTCI premiums are paid by yourself and are not part of a business expenses, there is a partial inclusion you can receive on your federal tax return if you itemize your deductions on Schedule A - Form 1040. You can include your premium payments, per limits below, as medical expenses on Schedule A. One of the IRS tax changes beginning in 2013 affects those under the age of 65. With your 2013 federal tax return you'll be able to deduct on Schedule A only the amount of your medical and dental expenses that is more than 10% of your adjusted gross income (AGI) from Form 1040, line 38. This increases from the 7.5% in previous years.

However, there is a temporary exemption from January 1, 2013 to December 31, 2016 for individuals age 65 and older and their spouses. If you or your spouse is 65 years or older or turned 65 during the tax year you are allowed to deduct unreimbursed medical care expenses that exceed 7.5% of your adjusted gross income. The threshold remains at 7.5% of AGI for those taxpayers until December 31, 2016.

If you elected to pay your LTCI premiums with tax-free distributions from a retirement plan made directly to the insurance provider and these distributions would otherwise have been included in income, these premiums cannot be included as a medical expense on Schedule A.

A qualified long-term care insurance contract provides only coverage of qualified long-term care services. The contract must:

- Be guaranteed renewable,
- Not provide for a cash surrender value or other money that can be paid, assigned, pledged, or borrowed,
- Provide that refunds, other than refunds on the death of the insured or complete surrender or cancellation of the contract, and dividends under the contract must be used only to reduce future premiums or increase future benefits and
- Generally not pay or reimburse expenses incurred for services or items that would be reimbursed under Medicare, except where Medicare is a secondary payer or the contract makes per diem or other periodic payments without regard to expenses.

The amount of qualified long-term care premiums you can include on Schedule A is limited by IRS guidelines. For the tax year 2014, the following amounts can be included.

1. Qualified long-term care premiums up to the amounts shown below for attained age before the close of the taxable year:

   - Age 40 or under – $370
   - Age 41 to 50 – $700
   - Age 51 to 60 – $1,400
   - Age 61 to 70 – $3,720
   - Age 71 or over – $4,660

2. Unreimbursed expenses for qualified long-term care services.

The limit on premiums is for each person. For example, both the husband and spouse have qualified LTCI policies and are both aged 65. His annual premium is $5,000/year while that of his wife's policy is $4,000/year. Though their combined premiums are $9,000/year, the maximum they could include on Schedule A, for medical and dental expenses, for 2014, would be $7,440 ($3,720 x 2). For more information on medical, health care and LTC expense deductibility you can refer to the IRS Publication 502, *Medical and Dental Expenses (including the Health Coverage Tax Credit)*.

LTCI State's Partnership Program

The federal *Deficit Reduction Act of 2005* authorized states to establish a Long-Term Care Insurance Partnership Program. A Partnership Program brings together a state government, private insurance companies that sell long-term care insurance, and residents who want to buy long-term care partnership policies. The purpose for creating this program is intended to alleviate the financial burden on states' Medicaid programs by encouraging individuals to purchase private LTCI. Four states; California, Connecticut, Indiana, and New York established partnership programs as part of a pilot project that began in 1987. However, the passage of the *Omnibus Budget Reconciliation Act (OBRA) of 1993* prohibited the program's expansion into other states. Today, all but 10 states have a Partnership LTCI Program. Except for California, these plans are also reciprocal among participating states. States must certify that partnership policies meet the specific requirements for their partnership program, including those who sell partnership policies are trained and understand how these policies relate to public and private coverage options.

A Partnership-qualified policy allows you to apply for Medicaid under modified eligibility rules that include a special feature called an asset disregard. These programs provide lifetime asset protection from the Medicaid spend-down requirement. What this means is that in return for purchasing partnership policies, a portion of the policyholders' assets will be disregarded when determining their eligibility for Medicaid LTC services, if and when they apply for such services. When applying for Medicaid LTC benefits, the partnership program allows individuals who purchase qualifying insurance policies to retain one dollar in assets for each dollar of long-term care insurance benefits paid by the policy. For example, the typical asset limit for an individual applying for Medicaid nursing home services is $2,000. If an applicant received $100,000 in benefits through a partnership program insurance policy, they may retain up to $102,000 of their assets when applying for Medicaid.

Qualifying LTCI policies must meet certain minimum requirements. Policies must be federally tax-qualified, provide inflation protection for policyholders of certain ages and only provide coverage to residents of the state where the policy coverage was offered. Often the only difference between a partnership-qualified policy and other long-term care insurance policies is the amount and type of inflation protection that the state requires.

LIFE INSURANCE AND LTC

If you don't have a LTCI policy there might be alternatives for paying the costs for LTC. Many life insurance products can pay a benefit through a policy rider to help cover LTC expenses. This living benefit enhances the value of life insurance to those seeking more than just a death benefit. Others allow you to sell your policy under certain circumstances. You'll need to review the language of your specific life insurance contract or call the insurance company who you have the policy with. You may be able to use your life insurance policy to help pay for long-term care services through the following options:

- Accelerated Death Benefits (ADB)
- Chronic Illness Rider
- Long-Term Care Rider
- Life settlements
- Viatical settlements

The first three bullet points cover these policy riders while the last two present situations allowing you to sell your life insurance policy to raise cash for LTC expenses. Some policy riders cover chronic illness situations, though some have broader coverage for long-term care services and can be marketed as long-term care insurance under many state regulations. Each rider opens accelerated access to a policy's death benefit while the insured is living. The qualification requirements for underwriting as well as for use and the benefits offered can differ significantly.

Accelerated Death Benefit

An accelerated death benefit (ADB) is a feature included in some life insurance policies that allows you to receive a tax-free advance on your life insurance death benefit while you are still alive. Sometimes the insurance company includes it in the policy for little or no cost. Other times the insurance

214

company may require you to pay an extra premium to add this feature to your life insurance contract. There are different types of ADBs, each of which serves a different purpose. Depending on the type of policy you have, you may be able to receive a cash advance on your life insurance policy's death benefit if:

- You are terminally ill.
- You have a life-threatening diagnosis, such as AIDS.
- You need long-term care services for an extended amount of time.
- You are permanently confined to a nursing home and incapable of performing activities of daily living, such as bathing or dressing.

The amount of money you receive from these types of insurance policies varies, but typically the ADB payment amount is capped at 50 percent of the death benefit. The payments received from an ADB policy, while you are alive, are subtracted from the amount that will be paid to your beneficiaries when you die. However, there may be some policies out there which allow you to use the full amount of the death benefit.

For ADB policies that cover LTC services, the monthly benefit you can use for nursing home care is typically equal to two percent of the life insurance policy's face value. The amount available for home care (if it is included in the policy) is typically half that amount. For example, if your life insurance policy's face value is $200,000, then the monthly payout available to you for care in a nursing home would be $4,000, but only $2,000 for home care. Some policies may pay the same monthly amount for care regardless of where you receive the care.

Life Insurance with Chronic Illness Rider

An insurance rider, which is attached in a life insurance contract, refers to extra coverage or protection offered by the insurance contract aside from the primary coverage indicated in the policy. Since the rider is not originally covered in the policy, the insured might have to provide an additional payment for such rider. Some insurance policies may include this at no initial cost. However, administrative fees and expenses are usually triggered if the rider is activated by a chronic illness diagnosis. The cost may not be known until coverage is activated. This type of rider cannot be marketed as long-term care insurance and is usually an indemnity policy. The IRS enforces limits on the amount on income tax-free benefits that can be paid under the indemnity model. Any payments above this indemnity limit may be taxable to the insured. Currently, amounts paid over $320 per day or $116,800 per year may be taxable income unless receipts can be provided. If you have this rider, consult your tax specialist. The benefit is usually paid as a monthly, semi-annual or annual lump sum.

With a Chronic Illness Rider, a chronic illness is defined as a one-time permanent situation. It must be certified by a physician and the chronically ill individual must have a severe cognitive impairment or require substantial assistance with at least two activities of daily living **for the rest of their lifetime**. The benefit is usually available once in a lifetime. The Elimination Period may be 90 days or higher. Any remaining death benefit not accelerated through the rider will be paid as a death benefit.

Life Insurance with LTC Rider

The Long-Term Care Rider is usually a lower-cost method of providing some LTC insurance due to the fact that the insurer is simply paying out the life policy's proceeds before death, versus actually increasing the specified cash value amount of the policy. The rider could provide accelerated access up to 100% of the life insurance policy's specified amount if the insured suffers a qualified LTC event. With this rider there is usually an additional cost of insurance charge and expenses are based on the insured's age and

216

their underwriting class. Costs are known at the time the policy is issued. Benefits under the LTC rider are income tax-free long term care payments under IRS code. Unlike the Chronic Illness Rider, **benefits for one or more LTC events are available throughout the insured's lifetime under the same LTC rider.**

Coverage becomes available when an insured is diagnosed with an illness or suffers an accident that requires substantial assistance with at least two ADLs for at least 90-days. The Elimination Period can depend on where LTC is received. Some policies may have 0 days for home care and 90 days for facility care. When looking at these LTC riders, as an alternative to "stand-alone" LTCI, make sure you completely review the features, benefits and premiums which are offered. This includes whether the rider pays in a reimbursement or first dollar basis, whether it pays the insured directly, as most do, or actually pays only to the facility providing care. A LTC rider normally allows the policyholder to utilize some or all of the policy's specified amount, or death benefit, for long term care costs, either for a period of time or until the available coverage amount has been exhausted, under stated terms; usually 2% or 3% of the specified amount per month. Make sure you are clear on how much the rider will pay and how, to whom and when. Premiums are often not the critical issue.

It's essential to make certain you understand that any pay-outs made for LTC under the LTC rider are deducted from the specified amount (and sometimes the cash-value amount as well) of the life insurance policy. At death the amount paid to your beneficiaries will be reduced, typically dollar for dollar, by the amount of LTC disbursements.

Life Settlement

Many individuals in their 60s, 70s and 80s were whipsawed by the Great Financial Recession of 2008-2009. More than one out of eight Americans, aged 40-60, is both raising children and caring for a parent. A life settlement may be a creative income generating option for some individuals. The Life Insurance Settlement Association, the national trade association, lists common reasons seniors sell their life insurance policies:

- A change in estate planning needs.
- The life insurance policy is no longer needed or wanted.
- Premium payments have become unaffordable.
- Changes in financial and life circumstances such as divorce, financial hardship or death of a beneficiary.
- The policy is about to lapse or surrender.

Life settlements allow you to sell your life insurance policy an agreed upon value to raise cash for any reason. There are no restrictions on how you chose to use the money. You may choose to use the proceeds to pay down loans or other outstanding debts, pay for essential expenses during your retirement or pay for long-term care services. A life settlement is usually only available to women age 74 and older and to men age 70 and older. The process can be very time consuming. There are items you should think about before you go this route. If you sell your life insurance policy, there may be little or no death benefit left for your heirs when you die. This could eliminate any legacy plans which you might have.

The Conning Research & Consulting 2011 study on life settlements found the average life settlement is 20% of the policy face value. Settlement offers can vary substantially depending on a policyholder's life expectancy and the premium costs. A shorter life expectancy means the provider pays the policy seller's premiums during a shorter period of time. The fewer costs associated with holding an active policy by the life settlement provider, the more cash a provider can return to the policyholder. The Conning 2011 study also found the average cash surrender value is only 10% of a policy's face value. In another study conducted in 2010, by the U.S. Government and Accountability Office, revealed consumers who sold their policies in a life settlement received an average of 700% more than if that same consumer had sold the policy back to the insurer for the policy's cash surrender value.

Once you find a life settlement provider you'll need to complete an application. The timeframe this entire process can take could be between 10-15 weeks, so this is NOT a quick way to receive cash proceeds. During this process the provider will collect medical information and obtain a copy of the life insurance policy. Once all the necessary documents are received, the provider will determine a settlement value and make an offer to the policyholder. If the policyholder accepts the offer, documents are prepared to transfer ownership of the policy. Once document are signed, the funding organization will submits these and requests a change of policy ownership. In the final step the ownership and beneficiary changes are verified and recorded and settlement funds are wire transferred into the account designated by the policyholder.

There may be tax consequences as proceeds may be taxed. The IRS can consider some or all funds from a life settlement as taxable. The amount recouped up to the cumulative premiums, which have been paid by the policyholder, are usually tax-free. Additional monies received up to the cash surrender value can be treated as ordinary income. Any excess cash above the cash surrender value could be considered a capital gain. Considering all the taxes which could be paid on a life settlement, the costs could outweigh the benefit. If you're considering a life settlement you should definitely consult with a tax expert.

Life settlements are labor-intensive during which the policyholder must be evaluated and submit medical records. Even after the transaction is complete, the policy seller must provide regular health updates. How does the life settlement provider get paid? After the policyholder receives his life settlement, the provider finances the premium payments until the policy seller dies, then redeems the insurance contract for its full face value.

Many individuals will eventually need to rely upon Medicaid coverage for their long-term care services in a nursing home. In a twist in Medicaid planning, several states, including Florida, Kentucky and Texas have proposed legislation which would allow the consumer to use a life settlement to help fund long-term care. These assets would not count in determining Medicaid eligibility whereas in their life insurance form they would. The proceeds from the life settlement would be held in an irrevocable state or federally insured account with a schedule of payments to provide for LTC. All of these proposals include a provision that any amounts remaining in the individual's account with the state be refunded as a death benefit if they are not needed to cover LTC costs. This would be an alternative to surrender the life insurance policy which could provide the policyholder with a greater cash benefit. For now, Florida's proposal *HB 535-Medicaid Eligibility* died in the Health Innovation Subcommittee on Friday, May 03, 2013.

Viatical Settlement

A viatical settlement allows you to sell your life insurance policy to a third party and use the money you receive to pay for care. Most viatical settlement companies pay a lump sum typically up to 75% of the face value of your policy, depending on your life expectancy and the expected policy premiums for the remainder of the life of the insured.

The viatical settlement industry got started in the 1990's. In the early days you could have gotten a higher percentage in your settlement. However, as of 2010, several factors have changed the rules of the game. Adjustments to Life Expectancy Tables, medical advances, and industry trends have all resulted in a lowering of the payoff values for policies. The benefit you receive is based on your life expectancy as illustrated in Figure 10.2 on the next page.

Somewhat like ADBs, a viatical settlement is only possible if you are terminally ill. Viatical settlements can be done by someone of any age who has been diagnosed with a life-threatening illness and is expected to die within twenty-four months. Since one of the key variables in pricing the deal is estimating how long you've got left, do **not** rely on life expectancy estimates provided by viatical medical underwriting companies without first speaking with your own physician. If you accept the terms of the offer, the viatical company becomes the owner of your policy and is its beneficiary. The viatical company also takes over payment of premiums on the policy. As a result, you get money to pay for LTC costs and the viatical company receives the full death benefit after you die.

The National Association of Insurance Commissioners (NAIC) provides guidelines as to how that percent should vary based on your remaining life expectancy.

Figure 10.2 Viatical Benefits Received Based on Life Expectancy

Life Expectancy	Benefit (%)
1 – 6 months	80
6 – 12 months	70
12 – 18 months	65
18 – 24 months	60
Over 24 months	50

Courtesy: National Clearinghouse for Long Term Care Information

Don't accept partial payment or installment payments from a viatical provider, and insist that all the money be placed in an escrow account until the transaction is completed. Your heirs will not receive a death benefit if you use the viatical settlement option.

The proceeds received from a properly executed viatical settlement is tax-free, if you have a life expectancy of two years or less or are chronically ill, and the viatical company is licensed in the state in which it does business. You should know that viatical companies approve less than 50% of applicants. Viatical settlements are complicated contracts with both legal and financial elements.

Take Advantage of Age and Health

For the most part the old saying is probably true. You're never going to be in better shape, then the shape you're in right now! You're also never going to be any younger than you are right now. Many experts believe that between 45 and 55 is the idea age to begin the planning process. Figure 10.3 below illustrates an example of the premiums for a LTCI policy for a couple based on various ages.

Figure 10.3 Premium Based on Age for 2 Policies

Age of Couple (same age)	Combined Monthly Premium for Couple
40 years old	$83
45 years old	$94
50 years old	$110
55 years old	$123
60 Years old	$162
65 years old	$225

Source: Kiplinger and American Association for Long-Term Care Insurance (AALTCI)

The calculations above are based on preferred rates, $150 daily benefit, 3-year benefit period, 90-day elimination period, $164,250 total pool of money and a future benefit growth option. Figures are based on leading insurers in a September 2012 survey.

According to the American Association for Long-Term Care Insurance (AALTCI) the older you are, the greater the likelihood is your application for coverage could be denied.

Figure 10.4 below illustrate the percentage of those individuals who receive good health discounts and those whose applications were denied because of health reasons.

Figure 10.4 Good Health vs. Bad Health

Age When Applying	% Receiving Good Health Discount5	% Denied Coverage for Health Reasons
40 – 49	42%	11%
50 – 59	32%	16%
60 – 69	21%	24%

Source: AALTCI 2012 Long-Term Care Insurance Sourcebook

In the long run, retirees of all income levels will need to better plan for their futures. Even seemingly secure families can lose a great deal of their savings through unexpected LTC expenses. While retirements are typically funded by long-term investments and Social Security, the sudden and unexpected need for assistive services can quickly drain savings and place seniors into the low-income brackets necessary to qualify for Medicaid.

Final Thoughts Concerning LTCI

The final decision whether or not to buy LTCI comes down to 2 main issues. The first is your mental disposition. The first wave of the Baby Boom generation turned 65 in 2011. There will be 78,000,000 turning 65 over the next 17 years. I am in this generation, though later in time. This was a generation who once believed; never trust anyone over 30. A generation who loved its music and never thought they would get old. That was then and this is now. Like other risks you need to decide if you have the ability to "self-insure" if the time comes. Sudden, unexpected events can have a long lasting impact. Where will the financial assistance come from to pay for this ongoing care?

The second decision is based on income levels and cash flow needs. If you have the financial assets and resources, you should at least consider insuring some of the LTC risk. The three most important reasons why not to wait are:

1. The longer you wait, the greater the chance you have of becoming uninsurable due to a medical event or chronic illness. Your eligibility is based on your current physical health and mental acuity at the time of your application submission.
2. Your LTCI premiums are based on your age at the time you submit your application. The longer you wait the more it will cost when you apply.
3. Once you're approved, your premium rate does not increase as you age or if your health deteriorates. The insurance company can increase premiums on an entire class basis but not on just your policy.

2013 – THE CURRENT ENVIRONMENT

Over the last ten years the number of carriers who provide LTCI has dropped from over a hundred companies to about two dozen key players. In 2009, Allianz Life Insurance Company of North America got out. In 2010, MetLife exited the business. In 2011, Guardian Life Insurance Company of America stopped offering the policies. In 2012, Unum Group dropped out of the group LTC business and Prudential Financial Inc. stopped offering individual LTC insurance but continued to provide coverage for employer-based groups. According to Moody's Investor Service, in 2012 Genworth and John Hancock (a subsidiary of Manulife Financial Corporation) represented 23% and 16% of the LTCI market share, respectively. Aegon NV's Transamerica unit, Bankers Life and Casualty, Northwestern Mutual Life Insurance Company and Mutual of Omaha Insurance Company are the other major players in the market today.

What's causing this seismic shift in the business? Three major forces are currently squeezing the LTC business.

- Increases in life expectancies of the individuals buying the coverage.
- Underpricing of premiums on in-force policies.
- Low returns on the fixed-income portfolios that pay claims.

Many insurance companies made miscalculations or used overly optimistic assumptions about these issues and offered policies at lower prices, expecting to make money by paying fewer claims and getting higher returns on their investment portfolios. In addition, the lapse rate on issued policies has been falling. The lapse rate is, the number of policyholders, who stop paying their premiums and let their policies expire. Underwriters anticipated 5% to 6% of policyholder's would let their plans lapse. Actually experience has been closer to 1% to 2%, according to insurance commissioner for the state of Nevada. Together these factors are creating a block of business which is building sizable liabilities for the LTCI insurers.

The Federal Reserve has pumped trillions of reserves into the banking system to keep short-term interest rates low to support the fledgling economy and repair the banking system. Low inflation, a desire for safety plus massive bond purchases by the Fed have resulted in long-term interest rates falling also. The current interest rate environment is creating havoc within the insurance industry. According to the *American Association for Long-Term Care Insurance (AALTCI)* 40%-60% of the money insurers accumulate to cover future claims comes from the investment returns of their portfolios. Insurance portfolio managers are now seeking higher returns by increasing their credit risk exposure and/or lengthening the duration of their holdings by assuming increased interest rate risk.

With LTC increasing at an average of 4.7% to 6.6% a year, LTC insurance providers have now begun changing their assumptions. According to the AALTCI this is leading to higher costs for new LTC policies. New policies are 17% higher in price that they were one year ago. Besides premium increases, another major change that's already occurring is gender-distinct pricing. Genworth was the first to introduce this in April 2013, followed later by Transamerica, John Hancock and Mutual of Omaha. Studies show women are two to three times more likely than men to require LTC and, on average, require that care for a longer period. Women accounted for 66% of the $6.6 billion in LTCI claim benefits paid out in 2012. Unisex pricing is still available in 25 states, including California, Florida and New York though it's just a matter of time before more states adopt this trend. According to the AALTCI, earlier this year these insurers introduced new policies which charged single women an average of 40% and 60% more than a comparably aged single man.

In its January 2014 release of its *2014 National Long-Term Care Insurance Price Index*, the AALTCI indicated that a 55-year old, single male purchasing new LTCI protection can expect to pay $925 per year for $164,000 of benefits. He'll pay $1,765 for coverage which increases the benefit pool to $365,000 at age 85, a 14.5% decline from the previous year's average. A 55-year old, single female, would pay an average of $1,225 per year for the same level of $164,000 in benefits. The typical woman will pay an average of 12% more than in 2013. For a couple where both spouses are age 60, purchasing $164,000 of immediate coverage will cost about $2,000 per year. For the same age couple purchasing $164,000 of immediate coverage which grows to a combined benefit pool of $730,000 ($365,000 each) at age 85 is about $3,840 in premium costs per year. The range of coverage cost was as wide as $2,700 to $5,400 per year. According to the National Association of Insurance Commissioners (NAIC), a 50-year old buying a new policy will pay an average of $888 a year; a 65-year old average of $1,850 and a 75-year old, $5,880. The NAIC also recommends that consumers should typically spend no more than 7% of their income on long-term care insurance.

Many companies are becoming less willing to insure individuals with health issues. Some of the most popular policy features such as lifetime benefit period and limited pay are no longer available in some policies. In addition, carriers are re-evaluating the inflation protection feature of these policies. It was very common in older policies to have a 5% compounded inflation rider. How can the insurance company increase your benefit at 5% when long-term U.S. Government bond yield about 3.5%. This is what has been responsible for much of the premium increases. Look at a simple inflation rate as opposed to a compound rate. Consumers need to be creative when look for LTC coverage.

The real problem is the business which has been written over the course of the last two decades. To raise premiums on existing policies the LTCI providers must file requests with state insurance regulators. Many LTCI providers are now raising prices on existing in-force business. The rate hikes in LTC premiums over the past few years have been staggering. Earlier in 2013, Genworth indicated it had requested premium increases of up to 95% on some of its individual LTC products. John Hancock recently indicated they would file requests with state insurance regulators to raise premiums on 50% of its in-force business by an average of 25%. This comes three years after the insurer asked state regulators for rate hikes averaging 40%. Genworth Financial started filing for rate increases of 6% to 13% on its in-force business which was purchased between 2003 and 2012.

Before the last 3-5 years, LTC insurance had been priced much like life insurance policies, where premiums remained the same over time. With the massive rate increases which have been see in premiums and those requested by LTCI carriers over the last 3-5 years, we may begin to see premiums stabilize in a sense. LTCI may begin to be priced more like traditional health insurance going forward where periodic rate increases of 2% to 4% may be seen. If premiums rise by too much it could cause healthy policyholders to drop their coverage due to cost, thus creating a larger pool of policyholders who most likely will need LTC.

Will you really need LTC? No one knows for certain but specific factors may increase your odds of some medical event occurring. The older you get the more likely you'll need some sort of assistance. If you live alone, you're more likely to need paid care as opposed to if you're married. Women are more likely to need LTC, simply because women tend to live longer than men. A chronically poor diet along with bad exercise habits will increase your chances. Your family medical history may give clues as to past conditions among family members or relatives. The industry is totally different than it was twenty years ago and LTC facilities are different also.

FINAL THOUGHT

Let's look at the following situation. Your father passed away a number of years ago. Your mother's health subsequently deteriorated and she's now been in a nursing home for a few years. Her cost of care has been rising steadily over the years and she has limited financial resources. You realize her expenses are now exceeding her ability to pay and begin to look into Medicaid as an alternative. Can you, as the adult child, be held fiscally responsible for your mother's nursing bills?

Believe it or not the answer is yes! Even if you have other siblings, you _could_ be singled out and held fiscally responsible for your parent's nursing home and other LTC expenses. There is a law which is on the books' in about 30 states and can vary somewhat from state to state. These laws are known as *filial support laws*. The law generally provides that a spouse, child and/or parent have the responsibility to maintain or financially assist an indigent person. These are two exceptions in the law. The first is if an individual doesn't have sufficient financial ability to support the indigent person. The second would be the case where a child would not be liable for the support of a parent who abandoned the child when he or she was a minor for a specific period of time. While these laws have been on states' books for decades, they were rarely enforced until recently. The *Deficit Reduction Act of 2005*, signed by President Bush, made it more difficult for individuals to transfer assets before qualifying for Medicaid coverage of nursing home costs. Filial laws are being enforced more frequently to make children of LTC recipients responsible for their parents' LTC costs.

This was recently highlighted in a 2012 Pennsylvania case, *Health Care & Retirement Corporation of America v. Pittas*, which received national attention. The case went to an appeals court where it ruled that John Pittas, 47, was liable for his mother's $93,000 nursing home bill under Pennsylvania's filial laws. This was despite the fact that the mother had applied to Medicaid to cover her cost of care, the son had done nothing wrong and there were three other potentially responsible individuals; the mother's husband and two other adult children. The law does not make all family members responsible, let alone equally.

This case highlights the fact that many companies in the nursing home care business, when given a choice, might prefer private pay over Medicaid reimbursed expenses. The nursing home company can pick and choose who they sue without regard for family discord which will likely ensue. With chronic federal government deficits and a Medicaid program whose costs are going to explode in some states due to the implementation of the ACA, a rise in filial law cases may be just on the horizon.

If you are reasonable well off financially, you need to check your state laws and if you have aged parents, include them in your own planning process for LTC. If you're going to purchase a LTCI product, take the time to read the fine print. You may be purchasing the policy but somewhere down the road it may be your adult-child filing the claim. If you don't include them in your planning process they may not be familiar with the intent of your original plan.

"I will never turn Medicare into a voucher. No American should ever have to spend their golden years at the mercy of insurance companies. They should retire with the care and dignity they have earned."

Barack Obama
44th President of the United States of America
Democratic U.S. Senator – Illinois
Illinois State Senator
13th State District

CHAPTER ELEVEN

ORIGINAL MEDICARE

According to the *2013 Annual Report of the Boards of Trustees of the Federal Hospital Insurance and Federal Supplemental Medical Insurance Trust Funds*, in 2012, Medicare covered 50.7 million people: 42.1 million aged 65 and older, and 8.5 million who were disabled. About 27 % of these beneficiaries have chosen to enroll in Medicare Part C private health plans that contract with Medicare to provide Part A and Part B health services. Total expenditures in 2012 were $574.2 billion. Total income was $536.9 billion, which consisted of $523.5 billion in non-interest income and $13.4 billion in interest earnings. Assets held in special issue U.S. Treasury securities decreased by $37.3 billion to $287.6 billion.

THE AFFORDABLE CARE ACT

There is much confusion among many individuals who are on Medicare as to whether the Health Insurance Marketplace is something they either need to worry about or enroll in. The answer is very simple – **No and No**. If you are enrolled in original Medicare, have a Medicare Advantage plan, have a Medicare Supplement plan or enrolled an employer-sponsored retiree health plan you do have to be concerned with the Health Insurance Marketplace.

OVERVIEW

This chapter presents a general overview of the original Medicare program. If you are enrolled in Medicare or approaching the age you can qualify for Medicare and want a more in-depth discussion, I have written a companion book titled, "*Navigating the Maze of Medicare*", which goes into significantly more detail than what will be presented here and is updated annually. The book is available on Amazon.com as well as in digital format on Kindle, Apple and Nook platforms.

Many believe that Medicare is completely free and covers everything. Wrong! Original Medicare is composed of two programs: Part A and Part B. What they cover is very specific. There are few restrictions on where you get care and coverage is flexible. This is why it is sometimes known as a fee-for-service program. The downside to original Medicare is that it can leave significant out-of-pocket costs you are responsible for if you have a major medical event.

Individuals, who are eligible for Medicare coverage, have their Medicare Part A premiums entirely waived if the following circumstances apply:

- Are 65 years or older and U.S. citizens or have been permanent legal residents for 5 continuous years, and they or their spouse has paid Medicare taxes for at least 10 years (40 quarters).
- Are under 65, disabled, and have been receiving either Social Security Disability Insurance (SSDI) benefits or Railroad Retirement Board disability benefits; they must receive one of these benefits for at least **24 months** from date of entitlement (first

disability payment) before becoming eligible to enroll in Medicare.

- Are receiving continuing dialysis for End Stage Renal Disease (ENRD) or need a kidney transplant.
- Are eligible for SSDI and have amyotrophic lateral sclerosis (ALS, or Lou Gehrig's disease).

Those who do not meet these criteria and are 65 and older must pay a monthly premium to remain enrolled in Medicare Part A, if they or their spouse have not paid Medicare taxes over the course of 10 years while working. According to the Centers for Medicare and Medicaid Services (CMS), 99% of Medicare beneficiaries do not pay premiums for Part A.

MEDICARE ENROLLMENT

Enrollment for Part A and/or Part B can occur in one of four ways:

1. Under 65 and already enrolled in Social Security or the Railroad Retirement Board.
2. Turning Age 65 - Initial Enrollment Period (IEP).
3. General Enrollment Period (GEP).
4. Special Enrollment Period (SEP).

You can sign up for Medicare when you first become eligible during what is called the Initial Enrollment Period (IEP). This is a 7- month period that begins 3-months before the month you turn 65, the month you turn 65 and 3-months after the month you turn 65. If you do not enroll in Medicare during your IEP you may have to pay a penalty unless you're eligible for an SEP. This penalty may apply to both Part A and Part B of Medicare.

MEDICARE PART A: HOSPITALIZATION INSURANCE

Medicare Part A covers five areas of health care.

- Inpatient Care in Hospitals
- Inpatient Care in a Skilled Nursing Facility
- Home Health Care Services
- Hospice Care Services
- Inpatient Care in a Religious Nonmedical Health Care Institution

Medicare Part A provides coverage for hospital care. This includes:

- Inpatient hospital care
- Skilled nursing facility care
- Long-term care hospitals

Inpatient Care in Hospitals

Hospitalization covers inpatient care in hospitals such as critical access hospitals and inpatient rehabilitation facilities. These costs include:

- Semi-private room
- Meals
- General nursing
- Medications as part of your inpatient treatment
- Hospital services and supplies
- All but the first three pints of blood. However, if the hospital gets blood from a blood bank at no charge, you shouldn't have to pay for it or replace it.

Medicare does not cover and **excludes:**

- Private duty nursing.

234

- Private room unless medically necessary.
- Television and telephone in your room (if there's a separate charge for these items.
- Personal care items, such as slippers or razors.
- First three pints of blood if needed.

Inpatient mental health care coverage is limited 190 days per lifetime.

There are deductibles and coinsurance amounts you're responsible for. For each benefit period, Medicare pays all covered costs except the Medicare Part A deductible, which for 2014 is $1,216, during the first 60 days and coinsurance amounts for hospital stays that last beyond 60 days and no more than 150 days. For each benefit period you pay:

- A total of $1,216 for a hospital stay lasting from 1-60 days.
- $304 per day for days 61-90 of a hospital stay.
- $608 per day for days 91-150 of a hospital stay (Lifetime Reserve Days).
- All costs for each day beyond 150 days.

Lifetime reserve days are additional days Medicare will pay for when you're in the hospital for more than 90 days. You have a total of 60 reserve days which can be used during your lifetime. For each lifetime reserve Medicare pays all covered costs except for a daily coinsurance.

Skilled Nursing Care

For qualified skilled nursing care it must be a Medicare-certified facility. There needs to be a 3-day prior hospitalization. Transfer within 30 days from hospital discharge to Medicare-certified facility. The services in nursing home must be for a condition that was treated during hospitalization (conditions test apply). Medicare coverage will pay in full the first 20 days. For 2014, the skilled nursing facility coinsurance is $152.00 per day for days 21 through 100 for each benefit period. There is no coverage after 100 days. **The deductible for Part A is not an annual deductible but per episode of care deductible.** Part A doesn't cover copays, long-term care or custodial care such as a nursing facility.

Home Health Care

To qualify for home health care the beneficiaries' physician must have determined medical care is needed in the home and the physician has prepared a written plan of care. Needed care must include intermittent (not full time) skilled nursing care or physical and/or speech therapy. The beneficiary must be home-bound. Absences from home must be infrequent and of short duration to receive medical care. If a Home Health Care Agency is used it must be Medicare approved. Homemaker services such as cooking, cleaning or shopping **are not covered**.

Medicare Part A will cover 100% of **medically necessary**, Medicare approved home health care visits. Any Durable Medical Equipment (DME), such as wheelchairs, hospital beds, oxygen and walkers, Medicare will pay 80% of approved charges, leaving you responsible to pay the remaining 20%. Medicare does not cover or pay for:

- 24 hour-a-day care at home.
- Meals delivered to your home.
- Homemaker services such as cooking, cleaning or shopping.
- Personal care.

Hospice Care

If you qualify for hospice care, you'll have a specially trained team and support staff to help you and your family cope with your illness. The beneficiary must have their physician certify that they're terminally ill and have 6 months or less to live. If you're already getting hospice care, a hospice physician or nurse practitioner will need to see you about 6 months after you entered hospice to recertify that you're still terminally ill. Hospice care is usually provided for in your home and includes the following services when your physician includes them in the plan of care for palliative care for your terminal illness. You pay nothing for hospice care but there is a copayment for drugs and a coinsurance charge for inpatient respite care. Coverage includes:

- Physician services.
- Nursing care.
- Medical equipment.
- Medical supplies.
- Medications for symptom control of pain.
- Hospice aid and homemaker services.
- Physical and occupational therapy.
- Speech language pathology services.
- Social work services.
- Dietary counseling.
- Grief and loss counseling for you and your family.
- Short-term inpatient care.
- Short-term respite care.
- Any other Medicare covered services needed to manage your pain and other symptoms related to your terminal illness, as recommended by your hospice team.

Hospice care doesn't pay for your stay in a facility (room and board) unless the hospice medical team determines that you need short-term inpatient stays for pain and symptom management that can't be addressed at home. Drugs for symptom control and pain relief are subject to a copay of up to $5.00 per prescription.

Medicare also covers inpatient respite care which is care you get in a Medicare-approved facility so that your usual caregiver can rest. You can stay up to 5 days each time you get respite care. Inpatient respite care is subject to 5% coinsurance payment. You can continue to get hospice care as long as the hospice medical director or hospice physician recertifies that you're terminally ill.

When you make the decision to choose hospice care, you have decided that you no longer want care to cure your illness and/or your physician has determined that efforts to cure your illness are not working. Medicare will not cover any of these once you choose hospice care:

- Treatments intended to cure your illness.
- Prescription drugs to cure your illness.
- Care from any hospice provider that was not set up by the hospice medical team.
- Room and board.
- Care in an emergency room, inpatient facility care or ambulance transportation unless it's either arranged by you hospice team or is unrelated to your terminal illness.

Some additional resources which may help include:

- National Hospice and Palliative Care Organization (NHPCO)
- Hospice Association of America (HAA)
- Hospice Foundation of America (HFA)

Religious Nonmedical Health Care Institution

The only coverage Medicare provides for non-medical, non-religious health care items and services, such as room and board, in this type of facility is if you qualify for hospital or skilled nursing facility care, but your medical care isn't in agreement with your religious beliefs. Medicare doesn't cover the religious portion of care.

PREMIUM COSTS IF YOU PAY FOR PART A COVERAGE

If you aren't eligible for premium-free Part A, you may be able to buy Part A if you meet one of the following conditions:

- You're 65 or older, and you have (or are enrolling in) Part B and meet the citizenship and residency requirements.
- You're under 65, disabled and your premium-free Part A coverage ended because you returned to work. If you're under 65 and disabled, you can continue to get premium-free Part A for up to 8 1/2 years after you return to work.

The monthly premium for 2014 is $234.00 for individuals having 30-39 quarters of Medicare-covered employment or a monthly premium of $426 for those who are not otherwise eligible for premium-free hospital insurance and have less than 30 quarters of Medicare-covered employment.

MEDICARE PART B: MEDICAL INSURANCE

Original Medicare Part B is a voluntary program which covers the medical services component of your health care. Everyone pays the Part B monthly premium. Part B helps cover medically-necessary services like physician's services, outpatient care, durable medical equipment, home health services, and other medical services. Part B also covers some preventive services. Part B covers two types of services:

- Medically-necessary services: services or supplies that are needed to diagnose or treat your medical condition and that meet accepted standards of medical practice.

- Preventive services: health care to prevent illness (like the flu) or detect it at an early stage, when treatment is most likely to work best.

If you obtain these preventive services from a health care provider who accepts assignment you usually pay nothing.

Medicare may cover some services and tests more often than the timeframes listed if needed to diagnose a condition. Part B premiums increased in 2012 for the first time since 2009. Such increases used to be routine before that. There is a law that prevents premiums from rising if Social Security's cost-of-living adjustment isn't enough to cover the increase. During the low inflation environment which prevailed following the Great Financial Crisis there were no increases because there were no increases in Social Security payments.

PREMIUM COSTS

The standard Part B premium for 2014 is $104.90. The last five years have been among the slowest periods of average Part B premium growth in the programs' history. According to Jonathan Blum, CMS principal deputy administrator, he noted that for the third year in a row Medicare premium costs are meeting or beating expectations. Medicare premiums for 2014 are lower than the $109.10 they were projected to be in 2014.

If you are considered a high earner you will pay the standard premium plus a fixed dollar amount based on your modified adjusted gross income (MAGI), as reported, **on your federal tax return from 2 years ago**. It is a two year period because that is the most recent tax return information provided to Social Security by the IRS. MAGI is the total of your adjusted gross income (gross income minus adjustments to income) plus tax-exempt interest income. For 2014, your premium would be based on your 2012 federal tax return, which was filed in 2013, to determine if you are considered a high earner.

High income beneficiaries are defined as singles earning more than $85,000 and couples exceeding $170,000. Currently only 4% of beneficiaries make that much. If you're a high income beneficiary and you are single and filed an individual tax return, or married and filed a joint tax return, the following premiums will apply for 2012:

- Individuals with a MAGI above $85,000 up to $107,000 and married couples with a MAGI above $170,000 up to $214,000. Standard premium + $42.00. **Total monthly premium $146.90**.
- Individuals with a MAGI above $107,000 up to $160,000 and married couples with a MAGI above $214,000 up to $320,000. Standard premium + $104.90. **Total monthly premium $209.80**.
- Individuals with a MAGI above $160,000 up to $214,000 and married couples with a MAGI above $320,000 up to $428,000. Standard premium + $167.80. **Total monthly premium $272.70**.
- Individuals with a MAGI above $214,000 and married couples with a MAGI above $428,000. Standard premium + $230.80. **Total monthly premium $335.70**.

If you are married and lived with your spouse at some time during the taxable year, but filed a separate tax return, the following premiums will apply:

- Individuals with a MAGI of $85,000 or less. **Standard monthly premium $104.90**.
- Individuals with a MAGI above $85,000 up to $129,000. Standard premium + $167.80. **Total monthly premium $272.70**.

- Individuals with a MAGI above $129,000. Standard premium + $230.80. **Total monthly premium $335.70**.

States have programs that pay some or all of beneficiaries' premiums and coinsurance for certain individuals who have Medicare and a limited income. Information is available at 1-800-MEDICARE (1-800-633-4227). For individuals who have hearing difficulties and/or are speech impaired, information is available at TTY/TDD 1-877-486-2048.

If you're receiving Social Security, RRB or Civil Service benefits your Part B premium will be deducted from your benefit payment. If you don't get these benefit payments and choose to sign up for Part B you will receive a bill. If you choose to buy Part A because you don't qualify for premium-free Part A you will always receive a bill for your premium.

MEDICAL SERVICES

One of the things you will learn as a Medicare recipient is whether or not your health care providers accept assignment. Assignment is an agreement by your physician, other health care provider or supplier who will be paid directly by Medicare, to accept the payment amount Medicare approves for the service, and not to bill you for any more than the Medicare deductible and/or co-insurance. You most likely will pay more for physicians or providers who don't accept assignment.

If the Part B deductible applies you must pay all costs until you meet the yearly Part B deductible before Medicare begins to pay its share. The deductible for Part B is $147.00 for 2014. Then, after your deductible is met, you typically pay 20% of the Medicare-approved amount of the service, if the physician or other health care provider accepts assignment. **There is no yearly limit or cap for what you can pay out-of-pocket for health care expenses.**

COVERED SERVICES

Medicare may cover some services and tests more often than the timeframes listed if needed to diagnose a condition. You pay nothing for most preventive services if you get the services from a physician or other health care provider who accepts assignment. However, for some preventive services, you may have to pay a deductible, co-insurance, or both. Listed below are some of the medical services which Medicare covers.

- Abdominal Aortic Aneurysm Screening
- Alcohol Misuse Counseling
- Ambulance Services
- Ambulatory Surgical Centers
- Blood
- Bone Mass Measurement (Bone Density)
- Breast Cancer Screening (Mammograms)
- Cardiac Rehabilitation
- Cardiovascular Screenings
- Cervical and Vaginal Cancer Screening
- Chemotherapy
- Chiropractic Services (limited)
- Clinical Research Studies
- Colorectal Cancer Screenings
- Defibrillator (Implantable Automatic)
- Depression Screening
- Diabetes Screenings
- Diabetes Self-Management Training
- Diabetes Supplies
- Durable Medical Equipment (like walkers)
- EKG (Electrocardiogram) Screening
- Emergency Department Services
- Eyeglasses (limited)
- Flu Shots
- Foot Exams and Treatment
- Glaucoma Tests

- Hearing and Balance Exams
- Hepatitis B Shots
- HIV Screening
- Home Health Services
- Kidney Dialysis Services and Supplies
- Kidney Disease Education Services
- Laboratory Services
- Medical Nutrition Therapy Services
- Mental Health Care (outpatient)
- Obesity Screening and Counseling
- Occupational Therapy
- Outpatient Hospital Services
- Outpatient Medical and Surgical Services and Supplies
- Physical Therapy
- Pneumococcal Shot
- Prescription Drugs (limited)
- Prostate Cancer Screenings
- Prosthetic/Orthotic Items
- Pulmonary Rehabilitation
- Rural Health Clinic Services
- Second Surgical Opinions
- Speech-Language Pathology Services
- Surgical Dressing Services
- Tobacco Use Cessation Counseling
- Tests (other than lab tests)
- Transplants and Immunosuppressive Drugs
- Urgently-Needed Care
- "Welcome to Medicare" Preventive Visit Yearly "Wellness" Visit

NON-COVERED SERVICES

Medicare does not cover the following items or services.
- Most prescriptions
- Long-term care
- Custodial care

- Routine dental or eye care
- Cosmetic surgery
- Acupuncture
- Hearing aids
- Exams for hearing aids
- Routine foot care
- Custodial care is non-skilled personal care. It is designed to help individuals with six activities of daily living like bathing, dressing, eating, toileting, continence and transferring (getting in and out of bed or a chair).

PRESCRIPTION DRUG COVERAGE

For the most part, Medicare doesn't cover most prescription drugs. If you're currently not taking many prescription drugs this may not be an issue at the moment. However, if you are taking an extensive list of prescription drugs as you turn 65 you may want to consider alternative health care coverage. Most Medicare Advantage Part C plans will include prescription drug coverage. Your other choice will be a standalone Medicare Prescription Drug Part D plan to work in conjunction with original Medicare.

MEDICARE SAVINGS PROGRAMS

The federal government offers Medicare Savings Programs for low-income individuals which the states' administer through Medicaid that pay some or all of beneficiaries' premiums and coinsurance. The programs are called Qualified Medicare Beneficiary (QMB), Specified Low-income Medicare Beneficiary (SLMB), Qualifying Individual (QI) and Qualified Disabled Working Individuals (QDWI). If an individual can answer yes to the following 3 questions, call your State Medicaid Program to see if you qualify for a Medicare Savings Program in your state:

1. Do you have or are you eligible for Medicare Part A?

2. Is your income for 2013 at or below the income limits below?
3. Do you have limited resources below the limits listed?

Resource limits for the QMB, SLMB, and QI Medicare Savings Programs are $7,080 for one person and $10,620 for a married couple. Resource limits for the QDWI program are $4,000 for one person and $6,000 for a married couple. These values listed below are for the 48 contiguous states and the District of Columbia. Alaska and Hawaii (not shown) have their own values.

- QMB: $11,736 ($978 monthly) for a single individual and $15,756 ($1,313 monthly) for a married couple. Program helps pay Part A and Part B premiums plus deductibles, copays and coinsurance is guaranteed if you meet the qualifications.
- SLMB: $14,028 ($1,169 monthly) for a single individual and $18,852 ($1,571 monthly) for a married couple. Program helps pay Part B premium and has no fixed budget. Everyone who qualifies gets the benefit.
- QI: $15,756 ($1,313 monthly) for a single individual and $21,180 ($1,765 monthly) for a married couple. Program helps pay Part B premium but program has a fixed budget. When the money is exhausted no one else can qualify that year.
- QDWI: $46,980 ($3,915 monthly) for a single individual and $63,060 ($5,255 monthly) for a married couple. Program helps pay for Part A premiums only.

Information is available at 1-800-MEDICARE (1-800-633-4227), Social Security at 1-800-772-1213. For individuals who have hearing difficulties and/or are speech impaired, information is available at TTY/TDD 1-877-486-2048. Ask for information about Medicare Savings Programs.

FURTHER QUESTIONS

If you have further questions about Medicare, Social Security, Railroad Retirement, Medicaid or the Veterans Affairs, the following resources may be helpful.

1. Visit www.medicare.gov:

- For Medigap policies in your area, visit www.medicare.gov/medigap.
- For updated phone numbers, visit www.medicare.gov/contacts.

2. Call 1-800-MEDICARE (1-800-633-4227):

- For general or claims-specific information, customer service representatives are available 24 hours a day, 7 days a week. TTY users should call 1-877-486-2048. You can get information 24 hours a day, including weekends. If you need help in a language other than English or Spanish, let the customer service representative know the language.

3. Social Security (1-800-772-1213)

- Get a replacement Medicare card.
- Change your name or address.
- Eligibility, entitlement and enrollment information for Part A and/or Part B.
- Apply for Extra Help with prescription costs.
- TTY users should call 1-800-325-0778.
- Visit www.socialsecurity.gov.

4. Coordination of Benefits Contractor

- Find out if Medicare or your other insurance pays first and to report changes in your insurance information.
- Call 1-800-999-1118.
- TTY users should call 1-800-318-8782.

5. Department of Defense

- Information about the TRICARE for Life (TFL) and the TRICARE Pharmacy program.
- TFL call 1-866-773-0404.
- TTY users should call 1-866-773-0405.
- Pharmacy, call 1-877-363-1303.
- TTY users should call 1-877-540-6261.
- Visit www.tricare.mil/mybenefit.

6. Department of Health and Human Services – Office for Civil Rights

- Think you were discriminated against or if your health information privacy rights were violated.
- Call 1-800-368-1019.
- TTY users should call 1-800-537-7697.
- Visit www.hhs.gov/ocr.

7. Department of Veterans Affairs

- You're a veteran or have served in the U.S. military.
- Call 1-800-829-4833.
- TTY users should call 1-800-829-4833.
- Visit www.va.gov.

8. Railroad Retirement Board (RRB)

- Receiving benefits from the RRB.

- Call 1-877-772-5772.
- Visit www.rrb.gov.

9. Below are some additional telephone numbers that may be useful.

- Senior Medicare Patrol: 877-808-2468; to find out location of nearest office.
- Medicare Fraud Hotline: 800-447-8477; if you suspect fraud.
- Do Not Call Registry: 888-382-1222.

"It is time that we provide clarity for our seniors, informing them of the services available that will lower the costs of their prescription drugs and strengthen the overall integrity of the Medicare entitlement."

Olympia Snowe
Republican U.S. Senator from Maine
Chairman of the Senate Committee on Small
Business and Entrepreneurship
First Lady of Maine
U.S. House of Representatives – Maine's 2nd District

CHAPTER TWELVE

MEDICARE ADVANTAGE, SUPPLEMENT/MEDIGAP AND PRESCRIPTION DRUG PLANS

This chapter will again present a general overview of Medicare Advantage Part C, Supplement/Medigap and Prescription Drug Part D plans. There is simply too much information to present in one chapter. If you are enrolled in Medicare or approaching the age you can qualify for Medicare and want a more in-depth discussion, I have written a companion book titled, "*Navigating the Maze of Medicare*", which goes into significantly more detail than what will be presented here and is updated annually. The book is available on Amazon.com as well as in digital format on Kindle, Apple and Nook platforms.

MEDICARE PART C: MEDICARE ADVANTAGE (MA)

Medicare Advantage plans are offered by private insurance companies approved by and contracted with Medicare you can choose from. You will also hear them referred to as Part

C or MA plans. Medicare Advantage combines both Part A hospital and Part B medical services into one package for individuals. The plans must provide coverage at least equally to what coverage is provided by Part A and Part B of Medicare. The individual does not lose Medicare Part A and Part B coverage and continues to pay their Part B premium. With Medicare Advantage the insurance company now pays all claims instead of Medicare. Medicare pays a monthly fee to the insurance company for each enrollee. These insurance companies must follow rules set by Medicare and plans are filed on an annual basis with Medicare. According to a report from the Kaiser Family Foundation 28% of the Medicare population, over 14 million beneficiaries are now enrolled in a Medicare Advantage plan. Since 2010, total enrollment has grown by 30% or 3.3 million individuals.

Not all Medicare Advantage plans work the same way so before you join discuss the plan's rules, what the costs will be and whether the plan will meet your health care needs. These plans can and do change each year. Each MA plan can charge different out-of-pocket costs and have different rules for how you get services (like whether you need a referral to see a specialist or if you have to go to only doctors, facilities, or suppliers that belong to the plan for non-emergency or non-urgent care). Future cuts in subsidies to the health insurance providers are scheduled so this may affect the level of benefits offered in the future.

Types of Medicare Advantage Plans

There are different types of MA plans which are offered by private health insurance companies. These plans may vary in terms of costs and benefits offered from one health insurance provider to another. Not all Medicare Advantage plans work the same way so before you join take the time to find and compare Medicare health plans in your area. Not all plans may be available in your area.

Health Maintenance Organization (HMO, HMO-POS)

An HMO plan must cover all Medicare Part A and Part B health care services. Some HMOs also cover additional benefits, like additional days in the hospital. In most HMOs, you can only go to physicians, specialists, or hospitals on the plan's list of contracted network providers. The one exception is in the case of emergency care. The member must choose a primary care physician (PCP) and referrals may be required for specialist visits. Some services may require pre-authorization.

In the case of a HMO Point-of-Service (POS) plan, the member may obtain certain services out-of-network at a higher cost. Your initial costs may be lower than in the original Medicare program. These plans may or may not include Part D prescription drug coverage.

Preferred Provider Organization (PPO)

With this type of plan, you use physicians, hospitals, and providers that belong to your designated PPO contracted network for the lowest out-of-pocket expenses. Usually these networks are geographically regional or local for the health care providers who are included. You don't have to have a PCP designated and there is no requirement for referrals. You may use physicians, hospitals, and providers outside of the network, but there will be an additional cost. This plan may or may not include Part D prescription drug coverage.

Special Needs Plan (SNP)

These plans generally limit membership to people with specific diseases or conditions. They tailor their benefits, choose their providers, and create their list of covered drugs to best meet the specific needs of the groups they serve. Since they offer all health care services through a single plan, Medicare SNPs can help you manage your different services and health care providers. This is usually a network based plan with a required PCP to be designated. Three types of special needs plans exist.

- Chronic Condition (C-SNP): You have one or more of the following severe or disabling chronic conditions such as chronic alcohol and other drug dependence, autoimmune disorders, cancer, cardiovascular disorders, chronic heart failure, dementia, diabetes, end-stage liver disease, end-stage renal disease, severe hematologic disorders, HIV/AIDS, chronic lung disorders, chronic and disabling mental health conditions, neurological disorders and stroke.
- Institutional (I-SNP): You live in a nursing home or you require nursing care at home where a long-term care setting is required.
- Dual-Eligible (D-SNP): You have both Medicare and Medicaid which coordinate costs and services.

Each Medicare SNP limits its membership to individuals in one these above groups. All Medicare SNPs include Medicare prescription drug coverage.

Private Fee-for-Service (PFFS)

In this type of plan, you can go to any Medicare-approved physician or hospital that accepts the plan's terms and conditions of payment. The insurance plan, rather than the Medicare program, decides how much it will pay and what you pay for the services. You may pay more or less for Medicare-covered benefits. You may also have more benefits than original Medicare Part A and Part B.

Medicare Medical Savings Account (MSA)

A MSA plan combines a high deductible health plan with a bank account. Medicare gives the plan an amount each year for the member's care, and the Plan deposits a portion of this money into the bank account. You can use the money to pay for your health care services during the year. For more information about MSAs, visit http://go.usa.gov/irD, to view the booklet, *Your Guide to Medicare Medical Savings Account Plans*.

Covered Benefits

Medicare Advantage plans must cover all of the services that original Medicare covers in Part A and Part B, except hospice care. Original Medicare covers hospice care even if you're in a Medicare Advantage plan. In addition most plans include prescription drug coverage. Some plans also provide additional benefits such as vision, hearing and dental.

Enrollment Periods

Individuals may generally join a Medicare Advantage plan if they meet the following conditions. These conditions are:

- You must be entitled to and enrolled in Medicare Part A **and** Part B.
- The beneficiary of the plan must permanently reside in the MA plan's service area, which is usually county-based. Also the beneficiary must be able to make an informed decision.
- In most cases if you have End-Stage Renal Disease (ESRD) you can't join a Medicare Advantage Plan.

As with Medicare Part A and Part B, there are specific times you can enroll for a MA plan or make changes to the coverage you already have. These periods include:

1. Initial Enrollment Period (IEP)
2. General Enrollment Period
3. Annual Enrollment Period (AEP). Also called Open Enrollment Period (OEP)

4. Special Enrollment Period (SEP)

Each year members have two separate enrollment periods to make changes to their Medicare Advantage coverage for the coming plan year.

1. October 15 – December 7

Changes made during this period will take effect on January 1st. During this period you can do the following:

- Change from original Medicare to a Medicare Advantage plan.
- Change from a Medicare Advantage plan back to original Medicare.
- Switch from one Medicare Advantage plan to another Medicare Advantage plan.
- Switch from a Medicare Advantage plan that doesn't offer drug coverage to a Medicare Advantage plan that offers drug coverage.
- Switch from a Medicare Advantage plan that offers drug coverage to a Medicare Advantage plan that doesn't offer drug coverage.

2. January 1 – February 14

This is a 45 day period when a member can disenroll from their current MA plan. During this period you can do the following:

- If you're in a Medicare Advantage plan, you can leave your plan and switch to original Medicare. Your original Medicare coverage will begin the first day of the following month.
- If you switch to original Medicare during this period, you have until February 14 to also join a Medicare Prescription Drug plan to add drug coverage. Your

prescription drug coverage will begin the first day of the month after the plan gets your enrollment form.

During this period, you **can't** do the following:

- Switch from original Medicare to a Medicare Advantage plan.
- Switch from one Medicare Advantage plan to another.

MEDICARE SUPPLEMENT/MEDIGAP PLANS

Original Medicare pays for many but not all health care services and supplies. What if you want additional coverage for those benefits and services that original Medicare might not cover? There are supplement policies, also sold by private health insurance companies, which can help pay for some or all of the health care costs gaps that original Medicare doesn't cover. Medicare Supplement/Medigap plans provide this additional coverage. They pay the costs; some or all copays, coinsurance and deductibles not covered by original Medicare Part A and Part B. Medicare doesn't pay any of the costs for you to get a Medigap policy. Therefore, **you will also pay a monthly premium for your Medicare Supplement/Medigap policy in addition to your monthly Part B premium.** These policies usually don't cover long-term care, vision or dental care, hearing aids, eyeglasses or private-duty nursing. The terms Medicare Supplement, Med Supp and Medigap are all used interchangeably and mean the same.

Med Supp policies sold after January 1, 2006 are not allowed to include prescription drug coverage. If you want a drug coverage plan you can join a Medicare Prescription Drug Part D plan to be discussed later. You can't have prescription drug coverage in both your Med Supp policy and a Medicare prescription drug plan.

A Med Supp policy only covers one person. Spouses must buy separate policies. If you're under 65 and have Medicare because of a disability or ESRD, you might not be able to buy a Medigap policy until you turn 65. Federal law doesn't require insurance companies to sell Med Supp policies to individuals under 65, however, some states may require the insurance company to offers plans to those who are under 65 and disabled. It's important to compare Med Supp policies since the costs can vary and may go up as you get older. Some states limit Med Supp costs.

Enrollment Period

You must be enrolled in original Medicare Part A **and** Part B in order to purchase a Med Supp plan. The initial Open Enrollment Period (OEP) is one-time only. By federal law, this 6-month period gives you guaranteed acceptance, regardless of your health status, to buy any Med Supp policy that is sold in your state. The period begins with the first day of the month in which you are both age 65 or older and enrolled in Medicare Part B. There is no medical underwriting. Some plans may have a waiting period for pre-existing conditions.

If you apply for coverage after your Med Supp OEP ends there is no guarantee that an insurance company will sell you a policy if you don't meet the medical underwriting requirements for eligibility. There are limited situations where an insurance company can't refuse to sell you a Med Supp policy.

Premium Costs

At age 65, costs for these programs can range from $65-$275/month, depending on the plan type chosen. If you are a tobacco user, premiums will be significantly higher. You'll also want to know if premiums can increase with your age. A high-end Med Supp plan will protect you more than a Medicare Advantage plan but it will also cost you more.

Premiums can vary by insurance provider. Benefits are standardized and coded by a letter so you can compare one provider's C plan, for example, with that of another provider's C plan. If you buy a Med Supp plan within the first six months of going on original Medicare Part B; the Med Supp Open Enrollment Period, you can't be turned down or charged more because of your health. If you wait until after your open enrollment period, the insurance company will use medical underwriting requirements and there is no guarantee the insurance company will sell you a Med Supp policy if you don't meet the necessary medical requirements.

How do insurance companies set premiums for their Med Supp policies? These policies can be priced in three ways to determine premiums:

- *Community-no age Rated:* Generally the same monthly premium is charged to everyone who has the Med Supp policy regardless of age. Your premium isn't based on your age but may go up because of inflation and other factors but not because off your age.
- *Issue-age Rated:* Your premium is based on the age you are when you purchase the policy. Premiums are thus lower for individuals who buy at a younger age and won't change as you get older. As with community rated, premiums can go up because of factors other than your age.
- *Attained-age Rated:* Your premium is based on your current or attained age and will go up as you get older. Premiums are low for younger buyers but premiums go up as you get older. This rating process may be the least expensive in the beginning but could end up being the most expensive based on how old you get and other factors such as inflation.

This is important to understand since the way they set premiums determines how much you pay now and in the future. This is critical in incorporating your future premiums into your financial plan. Other factors such as geographical rating, medical underwriting, discounts and future inflation can affect the amount of your premiums.

Medicare Supplement/Medigap Plan Types

Every Med Supp policy must follow Federal and state laws designed to protect you and it must be clearly identified as Medicare Supplement Insurance. Health insurance companies can sell you only a "standardized" policy identified in most states by letters A–N. Any standardized Med Supp policy is guaranteed renewable even if you have health problems. In other words, the insurance company can't cancel your policy as long as you pay the premiums.

Health insurance companies selling Med Supp policies are required to make Plan A available to consumers. If they offer any other Med Supp plan, they must also offer either Plan C or Plan F. Plans D and G, effective on or after June 1, 2010, have different benefits than D or G Plans bought before June 1, 2010. Plans E, H, I, and J are no longer available to buy but if you already have one of those policies you can keep it. All policies offer the same basic benefits but some offer additional benefits so you can choose which one meets your needs.

In some states, you may be able to buy another type of Med Supp policy called Medicare SELECT. It is a policy that requires you to use specific hospitals and, in some cases, specific doctors or other health care providers to get full coverage, except in the case of an emergency. These policies, if available to you, generally cost less than other Medicare policies. However, if you don't use the Medicare SELECT health care providers you will have to pay some or all of what Medicare doesn't cover. If you buy a Medicare SELECT policy, you have the right to change your mind within 12 months and switch to a standard Med Supp policy.

Figure 12.1 below displays the basic information about the different benefits that the various Med Supp policies cover. If a check mark appears, the plan covers the described benefit 100%. If a percentage appears, the plan covers that percentage of the benefit.

Figure 12.1 Medicare Supplement/Medigap Plan Comparisons

Medigap Benefits	Medigap Plans									
	A	B	C	D	F	G	K	L	M	N
Medicare Part A Coinsurance and hospital costs up to an additional 365 days after Medicare benefits are used up	✓	✓	✓	✓	✓	✓	✓	✓	✓	✓
Medicare Part B Coinsurance or Copayment	✓	✓	✓	✓	✓	✓	50%	75%	✓	✓***
Blood (First 3 Pints)	✓	✓	✓	✓	✓	✓	50%	75%	✓	✓
Part A Hospice Care Coinsurance or Copayment	✓	✓	✓	✓	✓	✓	50%	75%	✓	✓
Skilled Nursing Facility Care Coinsurance			✓	✓	✓	✓	50%	75%	✓	✓
Medicare Part A Deductible		✓	✓	✓	✓	✓	50%	75%	50%	✓
Medicare Part B Deductible			✓		✓					
Medicare Part B Excess Charges					✓	✓				
Foreign Travel Emergency (Up to Plan Limits)			✓	✓	✓	✓			✓	✓
							Out-of-Pocket Limit**			
							$4,660	$2,330		

*Plan F also offers a high-deductible plan. If you choose this option, this means you must pay for Medicare-covered costs up to the deductible amount of $2,070 in 2012 before your Medigap plan pays anything.

**After you meet your out-of-pocket yearly limit and your yearly Part B deductible ($140 in 2012), the Medigap plan pays 100% of covered services for the rest of the calendar year.

***Plan N pays 100% of the Part B coinsurance, except for a copayment of up to $20 for some office visits and up to a $50 copayment for emergency room visits that don't result in an inpatient admission.

Courtesy: Centers for Medicare & Medicaid Services; 2013 Choosing a Medigap Policy

Med Supp plans which are available in Massachusetts, Minnesota and Wisconsin are standardized in a different way. There are 2 plans in Massachusetts; Minnesota has 2

Medicare Advantage, Supplement/Medigap & Prescription Drugs

plans with mandatory riders while Wisconsin has 1 plan with optional riders.

MEDICARE PART D: MEDICARE PRESCRIPTION DRUG PLANS (PDP)

According to the Centers for Disease Control and Prevention (CDC), 2.6 billion prescriptions were ordered or provided in the U.S. in 2010. Those orders were placed from a list of 35,574 human prescription drugs which are available according to the National Drug Code Directory. Medicare offers voluntary prescription drug coverage to everyone with Medicare. To obtain the prescription drug coverage you must join a plan administered by either a health insurance company or other private company approved by and contracted with Medicare. Each plan can vary in cost and specific drugs covered. If you are enrolled in a Medicare Advantage plan, which includes prescription drug coverage, and you join a Medicare PDP, you'll be dis-enrolled from your Medicare Advantage Plan and returned to original Medicare.

Even if you don't take a lot of prescriptions now, it's important for you to consider joining a Medicare drug plan if you do not have other creditable drug coverage. If you decide **not to join** a Medicare drug plan when you're first eligible, and you don't have other creditable prescription drug coverage you will likely pay a late enrollment penalty.

There are two ways to get Medicare prescription drug coverage:

1. Medicare Advantage Plans (MA-PD)

These plans add drug coverage to the Medicare Advantage plans. To join an MA-PD, individuals must have both Medicare Part A **and** Part B. In both instances the individual must also live in the service area of the Medicare Advantage plan they wish to enroll in. There's no additional

262

cost for drug coverage other than copays and each type of Medicare Advantage plan will have its own specific formulary.

2. *Medicare Prescription Drug Plan (PDP)*

These plans add drug coverage to original Medicare, some Medicare Cost Plans and Medicare Private Fee-for-Service Plans (PFFS). In addition you must be entitled to Medicare Part A and/or enrolled in Medicare B. Having a Medicare Supplement plan provides no prescription drug coverage.

Enrollment Periods

For the most part, the enrollment period for PDPs is the same as they are Medicare Advantage plans. These periods include:

- Initial Enrollment Period (IEP)
- General Enrollment Period
- Annual Enrollment Period (AEP). Also called Open Enrollment Period (OEP)
- Special Enrollment Period (SEP)

For individuals navigating the enrollment process for the first time, many find the prescription drug program to be the most confusing. **You need to pay attention to the details in what each drug plan offers, which drugs are covered, what tiers those drugs are in and where you can buy your prescription drugs.** Anyone who is entitled to Medicare Part A and/or is enrolled in Medicare Part B is eligible. Like Medicare Advantage plans, PDPs can change their plans every year, with new plans coming out. You also need to permanently reside in the service area of the plan you choose.

Premium Costs

Most prescription drug plans (PDPs) charge a monthly premium that varies by plan. You pay this premium in addition to the Medicare Part B premium. The Part D base beneficiary premium in 2014 is $32.42. This is a 4% increase from the $31.17 premium in 2013. Individuals have four options on how to pay for their Part D plan:

- Auto deduction from Social Security. This is usually the most preferred method.
- Auto pay from their bank.
- Auto deduction from a credit card.
- Direct monthly billing.

Contact the drug plan provider you chose if you want your premium deducted from your monthly Social Security payment. Don't call Social Security. Your first deduction will usually take three months to start and three months of premiums will likely be deducted at once. After that, only one premium will be deducted each month. You may also see a delay in premiums being withheld if you switch plans. If you want to stop premium deductions and get billed directly, contact your drug plan.

Like Medicare Part B, there are also five household income levels for Medicare Part D. The average premium for a drug plan is $32/month. As with Medicare Part B, beginning January 2014, an individual's Part D monthly premium could be higher based on their income. High income earners can expect to pay just over $12 to slightly more than $69 each month based on their income. Figure 12.2, on the next page, illustrates the additional premium high earners will need to pay based on their income levels for the federal tax year 2012.

Figure 12.2 Additional Premiums for High Income
Earners

	If your yearly income in 2012 was		
File individual tax return	File married & separate tax returns	File married joint tax returns	You pay in 2014
$85,000 or less	$85,000 or less	$170,000 or less	Your plan premium
Above $85,000 up to $107,000	Not applicable	Above $170,000 up to $214,00	$12.10 + your plan premium
Above $107,000 up to $160,000	Not applicable	Above $214,000 up to $320,000	$31.10 + your plan premium
Above $ 160,000 up to $214,000	Above $85,000 up to $129,000	Above $320,000 up to $$428,000	$50.20 + your plan premium
Above $214,000	Above $129,000	Above $428,000	$69.30 + your plan premium

*Courtesy: Centers for Medicare and Medicaid Services; Guide to
Medicare Prescription Drug Coverage*

Standard Benefits

Eligible Medicare Part D prescription drug plans can have an annual deductible, a copayment/coinsurance up to an initial coverage limit, a coverage gap and catastrophic coverage for the rest of the year after an individual incurs out-of-pocket expenses above the annual out-of-pocket threshold. Standard benefit levels are adjusted annually, including all the expenses just previously mentioned.

The yearly deductible is the amount you must pay before your drug plan begins to pay its share of your covered drugs. For 2014 this deductible is $310, down from $325 in 2013. Some PDPs don't have a deductible, though these PDPs will typically have higher monthly premiums. The copayments and coinsurance are amounts you pay for your covered prescriptions after the deductible has been met. These are amounts you pay for your share and your drug plan pays its share for covered drugs. Your actual drug plan costs will vary depending on:

- The drugs you use.
- The plan you choose.
- Whether you go to a pharmacy in your plan's network.
- Whether your drugs are on your plan's formulary.
- Whether you get "extra help" paying your Part D costs.

Is your local pharmacy is on the preferred list? Is there a limit to the number of prescription you can get? Do you have to try less expensive alternatives before paying for your current prescription? These are questions you should inquire about.

Formularies and Tiers

A formulary is a list of medications covered within the benefit plan. This often represents the level of cost-sharing associated with different groupings of medications. There are five pharmacy tiers in most prescription drug plans. There are also copays and coinsurance expenses, depending on the tier in question. These tiers are:

- Tier 1: Preferred Generic; lowest copayment.
- Tier 2: Non-Preferred Generic; low copayment.
- Tier 3: Preferred Brand; medium copayment.
- Tier 4: Non-Preferred Brand; higher copayment.
- Tier 5: Specialty; coinsurance.

TrOOP

True out-of-pocket (TrOOP) expenses are costs used to move the individual through the coverage gap phase and into the catastrophic phase. These costs can be incurred by the individual or another person on behalf of the individual. TrOOP expenses include:

- Deductible.
- Copayments paid up to the coverage gap.
- While in coverage gap, individuals pay 72% of generic drugs and 47.5% of brand name drugs

While in the catastrophic phase an individual pays 5% coinsurance or a fixed dollar amount, whichever amount is greater.

The Donut Hole

Medicare prescription drug plans have a coverage gap. This gap is also known as the "donut hole". While in this donut hole there is a temporary limit on what the drug plan will cover for drug costs. The coverage gap begins after you and your drug plan have spent a certain amount for covered prescription medications. For 2014, you're responsible for the first $310 of prescriptions you pay for before coverage begins and your plan starts to pay some of the costs.

During the initial coverage phase, you'll pay a copay which is a flat dollar fee or coinsurance which is a percentage of the drug's total cost for each prescription medication you fill, depending on the plan. The PDP pays the rest until your total drug costs (paid by you and the plan) reach $2,850. Then you hit the donut hole or coverage gap. Once you enter the coverage gap, you pay 47.5% of the total cost for brand name drugs and 72% of the total cost for generic drugs in 2014. Figure 12.3, on the next page, illustrates a standard Medicare Part D plan and what you'll pay in 2014, depending on the amount of money you end up spending for prescription drugs.

Figure 12.3 Donut Hole Dilemma

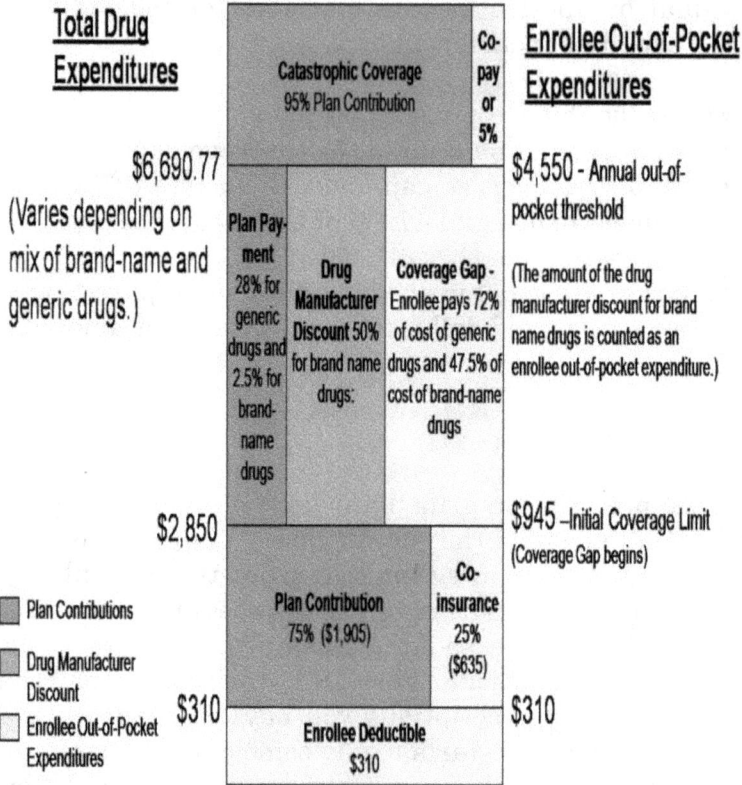

Total Drug Expenditures

$6,690.77
(Varies depending on mix of brand-name and generic drugs.)

$2,850

☐ Plan Contributions
☐ Drug Manufacturer Discount
☐ Enrollee Out-of-Pocket Expenditures

$310

Catastrophic Coverage
95% Plan Contribution

Co-pay or 5%

Plan Payment 28% for generic drugs and 2.5% for brand-name drugs

Drug Manufacturer Discount 50% for brand name drugs:

Coverage Gap - Enrollee pays 72% of cost of generic drugs and 47.5% of cost of brand-name drugs

Co-insurance 25% ($635)

Plan Contribution 75% ($1,905)

Enrollee Deductible $310

Enrollee Out-of-Pocket Expenditures

$4,550 - Annual out-of-pocket threshold

(The amount of the drug manufacturer discount for brand name drugs is counted as an enrollee out-of-pocket expenditure.)

$945 – Initial Coverage Limit
(Coverage Gap begins)

$310

Courtesy: AHIP 2013

Not everyone will enter the coverage gap. The following items all count toward you getting out of the coverage gap; your yearly deductible, coinsurance, copayments, the discount you get on brand-name drugs in the coverage gap and what you pay in the coverage gap. The drug plan premium and what you pay for drugs that aren't covered don't count toward getting you out of the coverage gap.

If your out-of-pocket drug costs should reach $4,550 in 2014, you exit the coverage gap and move into catastrophic coverage. In this phase you either pay a copay of $2.25 for generic drugs or $6.35 for brand name drugs or a 5% coinsurance amount to fill prescriptions, whichever is greater. The PDP or MA-PD pays the rest of your drug costs until the end of the calendar year.

Drug Coverage Rules

Medicare Part D drug plans may have the following rules regarding drug coverage:

- Prior authorization: You and/or your prescriber must contact the drug plan before you can fill certain prescriptions. Your prescriber may need to show that the drug is medically necessary for the plan to cover it.
- Quantity limits: Limits on how much medication you can get at a time. These are set by private insurance companies and/or regulations set by the government. These limits may be in place to ensure safe and efficient use of the medication.
- Step therapy: There are effective, clinically proven, lower-cost alternatives to some medications that treat the same health condition. You must try one or more similar, lower cost drugs before the plan will cover the prescribed drug. If the individual has already tried other medications or a provider thinks other drugs are not right for the situation, the individual or his/her physician can ask the plan to cover these medications.

If you or your prescriber believe that one of these coverage rules should be waived, you can ask for an exception. Except for vaccines covered under Medicare Part B, Medicare drug plans must cover all commercially-available vaccines, such as the shingles vaccine, when medically necessary to prevent illness.

A recent study from the University of Pittsburgh found that 95% of Medicare beneficiaries do not choose the most cost-effective plan. In another analysis by the Kaiser Family Foundation, of the vast majority of individuals who enrolled in a PDP during the four year period between 2006 and 2010, 87% on average stayed in the same Part D plan even though the plans could change premiums, deductibles, cost-sharing amounts and the list of covered drugs each year. Health care costs are a central element to an individual's retirement plan. Prescription drugs can make up a sizable portion of those health care costs.

SUMMARY

Once you begin digging into the plans offered by the insurance carriers, the process can be overwhelming. There can be dozens of plans to sort through when looking at the various Medicare Advantage, Medicare Supplement and Medicare Prescription Drug plans. Health care options and choices are probably much more confusing to individuals than investment choices. It can lead to "choice overload". If you make a bad investment choice you see the results of that decision each day and can make necessary changes if you so choose. If you make a bad health care choice you may not know the consequences until well after the medical event has occurred, treatment has been rendered and you leave the hospital. When all the bills start coming in and you see what was not covered by your insurance policy; you then realize that your options are probably going to be very limited in what you can do. So what can you do?

Do your homework and plan ahead so you won't feel like you're being rushed into a decision when the Annual Enrollment Period begins during in fourth quarter. When you are looking at plan benefits, features and costs; fully understanding the following key points should assist you in arriving at the best purchase decision.

- Always read the sales material and documents. Don't go by what the agent says only. They may not know all the coverage details.
- What are copay dollar amounts?
- What are the coinsurance percentages?
- What are the deductibles and if there are any caps?
- Do you understand what procedures are covered and what type of facilities can be used?
- Are your existing physicians (PCP and specialists) covered in the plan?
- Does the plan cover the hospital you have procedures done at?
- Are your existing prescriptions covered?
- Don't make a snap decision. The terms of the plan won't change in a week if you want to take time and think it over.

If you trust your adult children make them part of the process. Don't be afraid to tell the insurance company or the independent agent you're working with that you need some time to think about it. If after the next day you feel like you still totally understand the above components of the policy, you're probably in a good position to make the right decision regarding what's best for you.

Though it may seem like a lot of information was presented, the surface was barely scratched. This chapter is designed for someone who wants a cursory overview of Medicare Advantage, Medicare Supplement/Medigap and Medicare Prescription Drug plans. The companion book I've written on Medicare goes into significantly more detail than this chapter did and is designed for someone who is either currently enrolled in Medicare and wants a comprehensive guide or for someone who will be turning age 65 and wants to investigate what their available options as a first time enrollee.

"General revenue - what taxpayers are willing to give government, what they think is fair to give government - is not going to grow at the same amount that the federal government basically forces us to spend on Medicaid."

Rick Scott
Republican
45th Governor of Florida
Businessman

CHAPTER THIRTEEN

THE MEDICAID PROGRAM

Medicaid is a welfare program which provides benefits for the indigent and impoverished; people and families with low incomes and resources. Medicaid was created by the *Social Security Amendments of 1965*, which added Title XIX to the *Social Security Act*. As with Medicare, the Medicaid program has changed through the years. In 1990, under the *Omnibus Budget Reconciliations Act (OBRA-90)*, the *Medicaid Drug Rebate* and the *Health Insurance Premium Payment* programs were created. The *OBRA-93* brought changes to the Medicaid Drug Rebate Program, as well as requiring states to implement a Medicaid estate recovery program to sue the estates of decedents for medical care costs paid by Medicaid. The *Balanced Budget Act of 1997* added the *Children's Health Insurance Program (CHIP)*. Then in 2010, the *Patient Protection and Affordability Care Act (PPACA or ACA)* expanded Medicaid eligibility starting in 2014. Currently, Medicaid provides health coverage to 11 million non-elderly low-income parents, other caretaker relatives, pregnant women, and other non-disabled adults.

Medicaid is separate from Medicare. Medicaid is a joint federal-state program. Each state administers its own Medicaid program which must conform to federal guidelines in order for the state to receive matching funds and grants from the federal government to provide health care coverage to low-income individuals, families and children and also the elderly and individuals with disabilities. The Centers for Medicare and Medicaid Services (CMS) monitors the state-run programs and establishes requirements for service delivery, quality, funding and eligibility standards. The Medicaid and CHIP programs provide free or low-cost health insurance coverage.

According to the CMS, in 2001 46 million Americans received their health care coverage through the Medicaid program. By 2010, nearly 60 million Americans received health care coverage through the Medicaid and CHIP programs. Medicaid provides health coverage to more than 4.6 million low-income seniors, nearly all of whom are also enrolled in Medicare. Medicaid also covers 3.7 million individuals with disabilities who are enrolled in Medicare. In total, 8.3 million individuals are "dual eligible" and enrolled in both Medicaid and Medicare composing more than 17% of all Medicaid enrollees. Medicaid payments currently assist nearly 60% of all nursing home residents. Medicaid plays a key role in child and maternal health, financing 40% of all births in the United States.

AFFORDABLE CARE ACT

The Affordable care Act (ACA) fills in current gaps in coverage for the poorest Americans by creating a minimum Medicaid income eligibility level across the country. Beginning in January 2014, individuals under 65 years of age with income below 133% of the federal poverty level (FPL) will be eligible for Medicaid. For the first time, low-income adults without children will be guaranteed coverage through Medicaid in every state without need for a waiver, and parents of children will be eligible at a uniform income level across all states. Medicaid and Children's Health Insurance Program (CHIP) eligibility and enrollment will be much simpler and will be coordinated with the newly created Health Insurance Marketplace.

The federal government currently pays about 57% of the cost of current Medicaid enrollees in each state. The authors of the ACA realized the federal government would need to provide an incentive for the state's to participate in what would likely be a significantly increase in "newly eligible" participants. Coverage for these newly eligible adults will be fully funded by the federal government at 100% for 2014, 2015 and 2016. It will then be phased down to 95% in 2017, 94% in 2018, 93% in 2019 and 90% in 2020 and all subsequent years.

Beginning in 2014, individuals with incomes of $15,000 or less will qualify for Medicaid in about half of all the states. The program is designed to be very affordable for every participant and cost-sharing is extremely limited. Every state's Medicaid and CHIP program is changing and improving. To easily see each state clink this link, www.medicaid.gov/Medicaid-CHIP-Program-information/By-State/By-State.html.

When individuals apply for health coverage through the Marketplace they are automatically screened for Medicaid eligibility. Depending on the state, the Marketplace will either assess or determine individuals' eligibility for Medicaid coverage. If individuals are assessed as eligible, they will be informed that their application will be sent to the state Medicaid agency for a final eligibility determination. If individuals are determined eligible for Medicaid, the Marketplace will notify consumers directly and the individual will then be given the option to enroll in a Medicaid plan.

The ACA also creates a new office within CMS, the Medicare-Medicaid Coordination Office, to coordinate care for individuals who are dual-eligible for both Medicaid and Medicare.

FEDERAL POVERTY LEVEL

The government's FPL guidelines are released each January and are based on the federal poverty threshold data for the previous year. Table 13.1 displays the annual guidelines established for the 48 contiguous states and the District of Columbia. Alaska and Hawaii (not shown) have their own FPL guidelines.

Table 13.1 Annual FPL Guidelines for 2014 for the 48 Contiguous States and Washington D.C.

Percent of Poverty Guidelines (in dollars rounded up)								
Family Size	1	2	3	4	5	6	7	8
100%	11,670	15,730	19,790	23,850	27,910	31,970	36,030	40,090
120%	14.004	18,876	23,748	28,620	33,492	38,364	43,236	48,108
133%	15,521	20,921	26,321	31,721	37,121	42,521	47,920	53,320
135%	15,755	21,236	26,717	32,198	37,679	43,160	48,641	54,122
150%	17,505	23,595	29,685	35,775	41,865	47,955	54,045	60,135
175%	20,423	27,528	34,633	41,738	48,843	55,948	63,053	70,158
185%	21,590	29,101	36,612	44,123	51,634	59,145	66,656	74,167
200%	23,340	31,460	39,580	47,700	55,820	63,940	72,060	80,180
250%	29,175	39,325	49,475	59,625	69,775	79,925	90,075	100,225

Courtesy: Medicaid

For family units of more than 8 members, add $4,060 for each additional member.

ELIGIBILITY

In order to participate in Medicaid, federal law requires states to cover certain population groups which are considered mandatory eligibility groups and gives the states the flexibility to cover other population groups which are called optional eligibility groups. For many eligibility groups, income is calculated in relation to a percentage of the FPL. Within each category there are requirements other than income that must be met. These other requirements include, but are not limited to; assets, age, pregnancy, disability, blindness, income and resources, and one's status as a U.S. citizen or a lawfully admitted immigrant. Medicaid is available to the following categories of individuals including:

- Pregnant Women

  o Pregnant women whose family income is at or below 133% FPL ($32,499 annually for a family of four, or $21,404 for a family of two in 2013). States have the option to extend this Medicaid coverage to or over 185% and most states have done so.
  o Once eligibility is established, pregnant women remain eligible for Medicaid until the end of the month, 60 days after the end of the pregnancy. This includes prenatal care through the pregnancy, labor, and delivery. The woman's child is eligible for the first year of life.

- Children

  o Most states have elected to provide Medicaid to children with family incomes above the minimum of 100% of the FPL. All states have expanded coverage to children with higher incomes through the Children's Health Insurance Program (CHIP).
  o Children who are recipients of adoption assistance and foster care under Title IV-E of the Social Security Act.

- Low-income Parents

  o Low-income parents and other relatives taking care of children under age 19 are covered in every state but the income limit for parents and caretaker relatives varies widely. In some states it's as low as

19% FPL (approximately $4,474 annually for a family of four, or $2,947 for a family of two). In other states, the income limit for parents and caretaker relatives is actually higher than for other adults and may be up to 150% of the FPL ($35,325 annually for a family of four, or $23,265 for a family of two). In states that expand Medicaid, low-income parent coverage will increase to 138% FPL.

Medicaid is also available to aged, blind, and consumers with disabilities who:

- Have limited income and resources.
- Are terminally ill and want to get hospice services.
- Live in a nursing home with limited income and resources.
- Need nursing home care or qualify for optional care at home with special community care services.
- Are eligible for Medicare and have limited income and resources (dual-eligible).

There are some optional groups that federal law doesn't require states to cover but that states may choose to cover.

- Adults with incomes up to 138% FPL.
- Recipients of Supplemental Security Income (SSI) payments.
- Consumers living in senior facilities if their income is up to 300% of the SSI federal benefit rate ($2,130 a month in 2013).
- Working consumers with disabilities.

Beginning January 2014, hospitals that provide Medicaid services can begin making presumptive eligibility decisions by giving temporary Medicaid coverage to children, pregnant women, parents, and qualifying adults in states which have expanded Medicaid coverage. Presumptive eligibility allows hospitals to make on-the-spot, temporary eligibility decisions based on an assessment of gross family income. Community-based organizations may temporarily enroll consumers, allowing their families to complete the application process later to keep their health coverage.

QUALIFICATIONS

To qualify for Medicaid consumers must also meet certain financial requirements. Under the ACA the formula for determining Medicaid eligibility will be streamlined and unified across states. The formula is based on modified adjusted gross income (MAGI). MAGI is a methodology for how income is counted and how household composition and family size are determined. Beginning October 1, 2013, MAGI must be used in most eligibility determinations for children and non-disabled adults under age 65, whether or not a state chooses to expand adult Medicaid coverage. MAGI is based on federal tax rules for determining adjusted gross income which include:

- Earned income (e.g., wages, salary, or any compensation for work).
- Self-employment income from a business or hobby.
- Social Security income, including Social Security Disability Insurance (SSDI) and retirement benefits.
- Unemployment benefits.
- Investment income, including interest, dividends, and capital gains.

Family size will now be defined using the tax filing definition. It will include those dependents that are reported and included when a family submits its federal income tax return. Applicants who do not file federal income tax returns and aren't claimed as dependents on someone else's federal tax return can base their household size on the immediate family members who live together.

There are some types of income that count under non-MAGI rules which aren't counted for MAGI determinations. This includes child support and veterans' benefits.

BENEFITS

Each state determines the type, amount, duration and scope of services they will provide within broad federal guidelines. However, some benefits which each state is required to cover are mandatory benefits while some states can choose to provide optional benefits through the Medicaid program. Medicaid does not pay benefits to individuals directly but sends benefit payments directly to the health care providers. Mandatory benefits include the following:

- Inpatient hospital services
- Outpatient hospital services
- Early and Periodic Screening, Diagnostic, and Treatment (EPSDT) services
- Nursing facility services
- Home health services
- Physician services
- Rural health clinic services
- Federally qualified health center services
- Laboratory and X-ray services
- Family planning services
- Nurse Midwife services
- Certified Pediatric and Family Nurse Practitioner services
- Freestanding Birth Center services (when licensed or otherwise recognized by the state)
- Transportation to medical care
- Tobacco cessation counseling for pregnant women
- Tobacco Cessation, http://www.governing.com/news/state/gov-Study-

Medicaid-Anti-Smoking-Programs-Lead-to-
Significant-Savings.html.

While optional benefits covered by each state could include:

- Prescription drugs
- Clinic services
- Physical therapy
- Occupational therapy
- Speech, hearing and language disorder services
- Respiratory care services
- Other diagnostic, screening, preventive and rehabilitative services
- Podiatry services
- Optometry services
- Dental services
- Dentures
- Prosthetics
- Eyeglasses
- Chiropractic services
- Other practitioner services
- Private duty nursing services
- Personal Care
- Hospice
- Case management
- Services for Individuals Age 65 or Older in an Institution for Mental Disease (IMD)
- Services in an intermediate care facility for the mentally retarded
- State Plan Home and Community Based Services
- Self-Directed Personal Assistance Services
- Community First Choice Option
- TB Related Services
- Inpatient psychiatric services for individuals under age 21
- Other services approved by the Secretary*

LOOK-BACK PROVISIONS

There was a time when financial planners engaged in Medicaid planning. The goal was to help middle-class clients become *artificially* impoverished by transferring assets so they became eligible for Medicaid. It is currently a misdemeanor for advisors/agents to assist clients in participating in Medicaid planning. To prevent this abuse in the program, Medicaid implemented a look-back period for assets that might have been transferred at less than fair value. The *Deficit Reduction Act of 2005 (DRA)* significantly changed the rules governing the treatment of asset transfers and homes of nursing home residents. The look-back period was changed from 3 years to 5 years. States are required to apply the DRA to their state programs because Medicaid is run by both the state and federal government.

INELIGIBILITY PERIOD

Asset transfers during the look-back period trigger the ineligibility period. The length of the ineligibility period is calculated by dividing the amount transferred by the average monthly cost of nursing home care in your area. The penalty period or ineligibility period for transferred assets is the date when the person applies for Medicaid - generally when the person enters a nursing home. That means that any transfers without fair market value (gifts of any kind) made by the Medicaid applicant during the preceding five years are penalized, dollar for dollar. All transfers made during the five-year look-back period are totaled, and the applicant is penalized that amount.

An example will help to put this in context. After Ted's death, Elizabeth gave her vacation home to her daughter Kimberly. The market value of the home was $200,000 and the monthly cost of nursing home care was $5,000 in Elizabeth's region. Elizabeth's ineligibility period is therefore 40 months ($200,000/$5,000 per month = 40 months). The ineligibility period begins to run when

Elizabeth applies for Medicaid and seeks long-term care assistance and expires 40 months from that date. However, if she gives the house to Kimberly **more than five years before her application date**, the look-back period would have expired no penalty period would be imposed.

Before the *DRA of 2005*, the ineligibility period would have started on the date that Elizabeth gave the vacation home to Kimberly. Now, the ineligibility period begins when Elizabeth applies for Medicaid, which is later than when she gave the home to Kimberly.

CHILDREN'S HEALTH INSURANCE PROGRAM

The Children's Health Insurance Program (CHIP) provides low-cost health coverage to children in families that earn too much money to qualify for Medicaid. In some states CHIP also covers parents and pregnant women. All states have a CHIP program and most programs are either combined with or closely coordinated with the state Medicaid program. States have broad discretion in setting their CHIP income eligibility standards and eligibility varies across states. Similar to Medicaid each state manages its own CHIP program, including eligibility requirements, scope of benefits, cost-sharing requirements and application and renewal procedures.

Eligibility

CHIP serves children up to age 19 in families with low incomes, but with incomes too high to qualify for Medicaid. Some states also require that children be uninsured for a period of time (up to 90 days) before they can enroll in CHIP. To be eligible for CHIP consumers must meet and provide proof of at least one of the following residency requirements including:

- United States (U.S.) citizenship.
- Residency for at least five years.

- Residency in a state that has elected to cover lawfully present immigrants regardless of when they entered the U.S.

Eligibility for CHIP is based on the child's immigration status, not the immigration status of the parents. States have the option to provide CHIP coverage to some low-income pregnant women. In some states, CHIP provides coverage from conception to birth. Infants born to women enrolled in Medicaid or CHIP are automatically eligible for Medicaid or CHIP up to one year of age. The ACA gives states the option to extend CHIP eligibility to state employees' children who were previously excluded from CHIP coverage.

Similar to Medicaid modified adjusted gross income (MAGI) will be used to calculate CHIP eligibility starting in 2014. Forty-six states and the District of Columbia cover children up to or above 200% of the FPL ($44,100 annually for a family of four, or $31,020 for a family of two in 2013). Twenty-four of these states offer coverage to children in families with income at 250% FPL ($55,125 annually for a family of four, or $38,775 for a family of two in 2013) or higher.

Some states charge small premiums and/or copayments for CHIP coverage. Families with children enrolled in CHIP aren't required to pay more than 5% of their annual income for CHIP coverage but most programs charge premiums that are far lower.

PRIVATIZING MEDICAID – THE FUTURE

In June 2013, federal officials gave final approval to Florida's Medicaid managed care program, essentially privatizing parts of Florida's Medicaid program. The state's Medicaid costs have been rising annually. For 2013-2014, Medicaid expenditures are projected to rise above $22 billion. Through this program Florida will move nearly 3 million Medicaid recipients from Medicaid's normal fee-for-service care into private HMOs by the beginning of 2014.

Florida's legislature first passed the initiative in 2011; then spent the next two years negotiating with Federal officials. As a result of those negotiations Florida also agreed to several regulations and consumer safeguards including:

- A rapid-cycle system for recipient complaints.
- Increased recipient participation in Florida Medical Care Advisory Committee.
- Continuation of current services for up to 60 days after enrollment.
- HMO validation by Florida's External Quality Assurance Organization.

It's expected this new program will help to curb future cost increases while improving the quality of care.

The most costly Medicaid patients to care for are those that are receiving long-term care benefits. The transition to the new program is going to begin with roughly 90,000 long-term care patients on Medicaid. They will have the choice of enrolling in one of seven available state-approved HMOs. Many have already enrolled and those that have not yet will have until December 1, 2013 to choose a plan. Under this program Medicaid funds will first be paid out to these select insurance carriers. Funds will be used to pay nursing homes, in-home caregivers and other elder care providers.

Florida is the first state to take this approach in hopes of creating greater efficiencies leading to cost savings. Nationwide, Medicaid payments assist nearly 60% of all nursing home residents. The retirement age population is growing larger every day. States will need to get creative in how they deal with the growing number of elderly who will probably qualify for Medicaid and ultimately need LTC.

One option is introducing legislation which would allow seniors to sell their life insurance policies; then designate the use of the proceeds to augment their LTC expenses.

Texas has already passed similar legislation to allow seniors this option. Their new law allows seniors to use the proceeds from their policies to pay for the LTC providers of their choosing. Florida introduced a bill earlier in 2013 but the bill did not get out of the sub-committee.

CONTACT YOUR STATE FOR MORE INFORMATION

State participation in Medicaid is voluntary; however, all states have participated since 1982 when Arizona formed its Arizona Health Care Cost Containment System (AHCCCS) program. Medicaid and CHIP program information is by state. Go to www.medicaid.gov, then choose your state profile. In some states Medicaid is subcontracted to private health insurance companies while other states pay health care providers such as physicians, clinics and hospitals directly.

Many attorneys specialize in Medicaid planning. If you hire an attorney these are some questions to ask.

- How does our state define assets? Are any of the transfers of property "exempt"?
- How do transfers of property between spouses affect eligibility?
- What's the maximum amount of assets a person can retain in my state and still qualify for Medicaid?

CHAPTER FOURTEEN

THE FUTURE OF HEALTH CARE

According to a research report from the Aite Group, a 65 year-old couple today is projected to need $230,000 to pay for medical expenses throughout their retirement, not including nursing home care or other types of long-term care. Think about what this number may look like for a 65 year-old couple twenty years from now.

The Kaiser Family Foundation, a non-profit, private operating foundation, is a leader in health policy analysis, health journalism and communication; dedicated to filling the need for trusted, independent information on the major health issues facing the nation and its people. Kaiser develops and runs its own research and communications programs, unlike a grant-making foundation. They have a number of papers addressing this subject.

During the managed care era of the late 1990s, health care inflation began to slow. After the public backlash against managed care caused many employers to drop that model, health care inflation rose sharply as the new millennium began. This sharp increase in health insurance premiums was coupled with declining inflation in household income. When health care reform policies are being debated by the U.S. Congress, as has historically been the case, the annual rate of inflation for health insurance premiums tends to slow down.

In the issue, *Annuals of Family Medicine, March/April 2012, Vol. 10 No. 2;* authors Richard A. Young, M.D. and Jennifer E. DeVoe, M.D.; D.Phil in their published article, *Who Will Have Health Insurance in the Future? An Updated Projection;* the authors update health insurance projections from an earlier published article, *Health Spending Projection Through 2019: The Recession's Impact Continues, Health Affairs, March 2010, Vol. 29, No. 3;* written by Christopher J. Truffer, Sean Keehan, Sheila Smith, Jonathan Cylus, Andrea Sisko, John A. Poisal, Joseph Lizonitz and M. Kent Clemens. The authors articulate a bleak scenario of what could happen if health insurance premiums remain on their current path over the next 20-25 years. Their hypothesis is that continuing to make incremental changes in U.S. health policy will likely not bend the cost curve, which has eluded policy makers for the past 50 years. Private health insurance will become increasingly unaffordable to low-to-middle–income Americans unless major changes are made in the U.S. health care system.

In Figure 14.1, on the next page, the graph plots the percentage change from the previous year for median household income and family health insurance premiums. The period from 2009 to 2010 slowed to the lowest level since the late 1990s. Even with this slowing, annual inflation rates still outpaced U.S. household earnings. As can be seen from this graph median household income stagnated from 2008 to 2011 and even included an absolute reduction in average household income from $50,300 in 2008 to $49,800 in 2009.

Figure 14.1 Percentage of Change in Median Household Income and Family Health Insurance

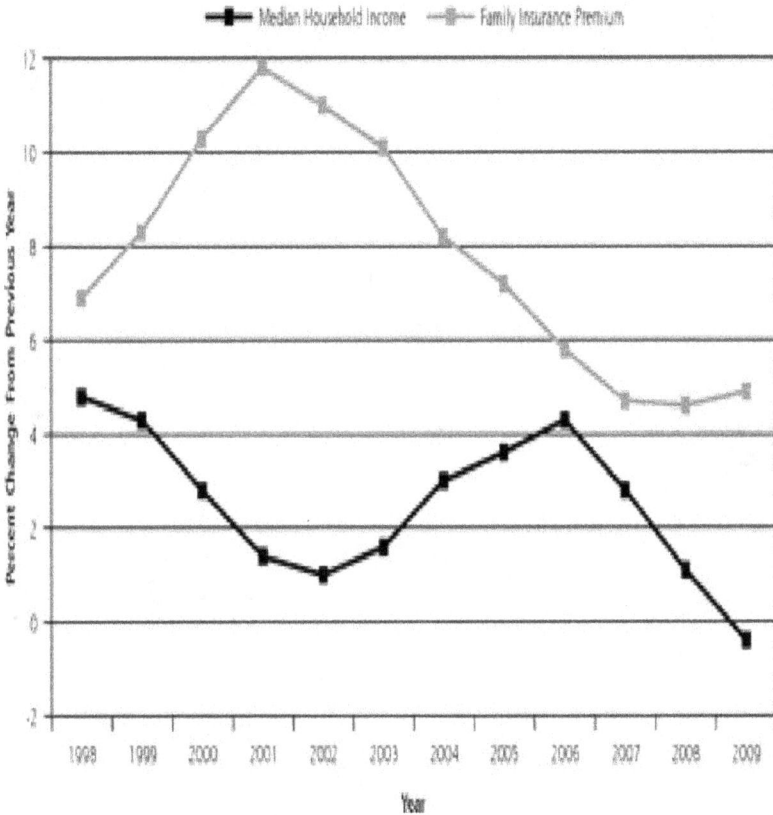

Courtesy: Annuals of Family Medicine, March/April 2012; Who Will Have Health Insurance in the Future? An Updated Projection

Using methods similar to those used by DeVoe, et al with data from the Medical Expenditure Panel Survey (MEPS) and the U.S. Census Bureau, the authors developed an updated model of insurance premium cost and household income projections. In Figure 14.2 on the next page the graph illustrates the projected annual family health insurance premium costs and average household income through 2035. The model presented in Figure 14.2 includes actual premiums and household income data from 2000 to 2009 and projected trends from 2010 to 2035.

Figure 14.2 Projected Annual Family Health Insurance Premium Cost and Average Household Income

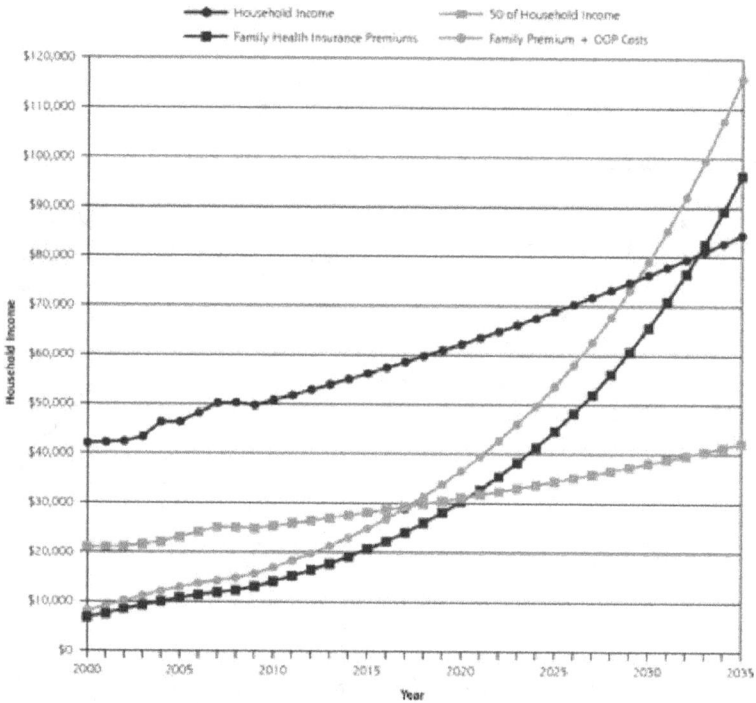

Courtesy: Annuals of Family Medicine, March/April 2012; Who Will Have Health Insurance in the Future? An Updated Projection

The average annual increase in insurance premiums was 8.0% while household incomes increased an average of 2.1% during the period from 2000 to 2009. The authors project that if health insurance premiums and national household wages continue to grow at recent rates and there are no major structural changes in the health care system, the average cost of a family health insurance premium will equal 50% of the household income by the year 2021 and surpass the average household income by the year 2033. If out-of-pocket (OOP) costs are added to the premium costs, the 50% threshold is crossed by 2018 and exceeds household income by 2030.

The authors felt it was important to include another projection; the total cost of health care for a family, as most workers do not currently pay the entire cost of their premiums. This is illustrated by the chart in Figure 14.3.

Figure 14.3 Projected Annual Family Health Care Costs

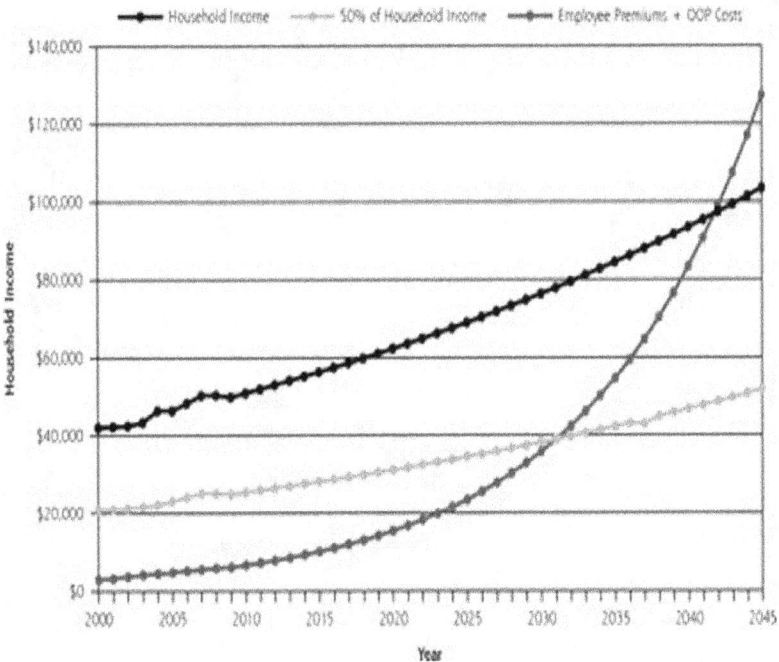

Courtesy: *Annuals of Family Medicine, March/April 2012; Who Will Have Health Insurance in the Future? An Updated Projection*

For this estimate they calculated the average amount an employee pays for a family health insurance premium plus out-of-pocket (OOP) family health care expenses. The MEPS database does not provide explicit OOP expense data for privately-insured families. These OOP expenses were obtained from the Milliman Medical Index. The authors conclude that without major structural changes in the US health care system, the employee contribution to a family premium plus out-of-pocket costs will comprise one-half the household income by 2031 and total income by 2042.

Figure 14.4 Family Health Insurance Premiums With and Without the ACA Assumptions of Cost Savings

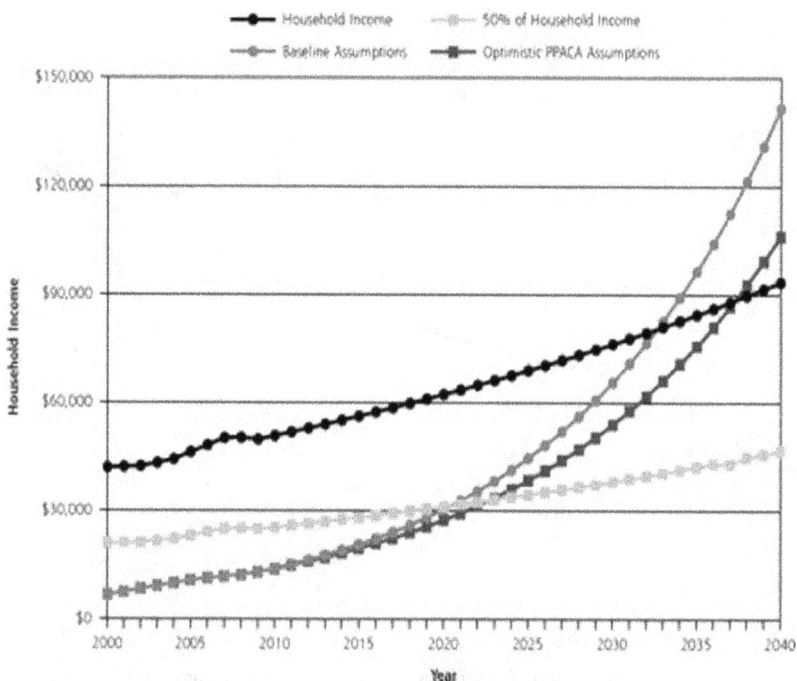

Courtesy: Annuals of Family Medicine, March/April 2012; Who Will Have Health Insurance in the Future? An Updated Projection

Figure 14.4, on the previous page, displays health insurance premiums with and without the ACA assumptions of cost savings. The first assumes no effect on the annual increase in health care insurance premium inflation compared with the experience of the last ten years (8.0%). The second model assumes a favorable impact of the ACA on reducing the growth rate in the cost of private health insurance (7.0%). Rising health care costs remain at the core of this unsustainable rise in insurance premiums.

Various elements of the Affordable Care Act have been enacted with more to be phased in during the coming years. There is no real consensus among health care experts as to whether ACA will raise private insurance costs, not have much of an effect or lower health insurance costs in the long run. The authors included two models on projected health care costs related to ACA.

In the previous article published in 2010, DeVoe et al estimated the cost of insurance premiums would surpass household income by 2025. The current author's new projection marginally moves the crossing point by eight years to 2033. This extension in the projection is due in part to the slowdown in the rate of premium increases from 2003 to 2009. During that same period, employee contributions to insurance premiums and out-of-pocket expenses grew faster than overall premium costs, suggesting that insurers have slowed the rate of growth in premiums by shifting more costs onto employees. Even though employee's no longer face double-digit increases in insurance premiums each year, they now pay higher deductibles and copays and receive fewer covered services.

The authors conclude if health care costs continue to rise at current unsustainable rates, it's doubtful affordable insurance coverage will be available for low- to middle-income Americans in the near future. They also noted their model did not include the taxes paid by American workers each year to finance Medicare and Medicaid. In 2009 this amounted to nearly $900 billion. This will increase with full implementation of the ACA. While being very complex the

U.S. health care system has been very adaptive. It may be possible other changes will occur which will avoid a complete meltdown of the health care system.

RETIREE HEALTH BENEFITS

Employer-provided health insurance for retirees has been declining for decades. According to Extend Health, a unit of the benefits consulting firm Towers Watson, 25% of employers who provide health insurance offer some type of financial assistance to retirees to help them with medical costs. This is down from more than 60% in the 1980s. Some companies are discontinuing their health plans for retirees and giving them a fixed amount of money to use towards their health expenses. With establishment of the Health Insurance Marketplace and with early retirees now having guaranteed access to health insurance coverage beginning in 2014, more large employers are likely to rethink their strategy for retired former employees under age 65. Many companies may now consider dropping their coverage altogether for this former employee segment.

Employees from the public sector are also not immune from these changes either. More municipalities which used to cover retiree health care expenses at 100% are now requiring formers workers to pay a monthly premium. While the premiums are usually modest, benefit coverage is also less than what it was. This trend will likely accelerate in the future with increasing premiums.

CONCIERGE MEDICINE

Think the USA television show *Royal Pains,* which is about a physician who leaves New York City and ends up in the Hamptons building a successful medical practice focused on concierge medicine is just for the wealthy and ultra-wealthy? Think again. This could be the wave of the future for many medical practices whose physicians focus on the primary care and family practice specialties of medicine.

Concierge medicine is a medical practice model based on a patient retainer or membership payment system. In this model, primary care and family practice physicians provide healthcare services in a more convenient, accessible and cost efficient manner to their patients. This type of practice model can go by several different names including:

- Membership Medicine
- Personal Care
- Direct Primary Care
- Direct Care
- Retainer-based Medicine
- Private Medicine
- Direct Practice

Patients pay a membership fee of between $600 and $1,800 per year. In some cases, the fee can be several thousand dollars higher. In exchange for paying this fee, concierge practices generally include:

- 24/7 access to a personal physicians' mobile number.
- Same-day appointments with no waiting.
- Personal coordination of care with specialists.
- Personal follow up when admitted to a hospital or emergency room.
- House calls.
- Consultations using video, email and/or phone.

Whereas a family practice physician could carry a patient load of 2,500 and more patients, a concierge physician may limit their practice to between 300 and 600 patients. While all concierge medical practices share similarities, they can vary considerably in their practice structure, payment requirements and form of operation. What differs is in the level of service provided and amount of the fee charged.

With what has been happening with health care reform over the last few years and now mandated health insurance coverage being enacted as the result of the ACA, the impact on primary care and family practice physicians in this field is beginning to create a bifurcation within the concierge medical practice model.

On one end is the high-end concierge practice where patients pay thousands of dollars a month for lavish celebrity-type treatment. These practices will typically bill the insurance carrier for medical services rendered on top of collecting its retainer fee from the patient.

At the other end is the pared-down practice which charges between $50 and $100 each month for basic primary care medicine, more accessible physicians and other money saving services. These practices usually don't accept insurance. They charge the patient directly for treatment along with the membership fee and many offer a menu-style pricing for services, requiring payment up-front. By focusing on simple services and eliminating insurance billing, these practices can cut their over-head expenses by 40%, enabling them to keep fees low.

With the health insurance marketplaces now operational and the ACA mandating every individual needs to have health care insurance coverage, will an indirect effect be to drive physicians to refuse to accept insurance. A clause exists within the ACA that allows direct primary care to count as ACA-compliant health insurance, as long as it is bundled with a wraparound catastrophic medical policy to cover emergencies.

According to Concierge Medicine Today, there are an estimated 5,500 concierge practices nationwide. About 66% of these practices charge less than $135 each month, on average, up from 49% three years ago. Inexpensive practices are adding offices at a rate of about 25% a year according to the American Academy of Private Physicians.

A PERSONAL STORY

If you have experienced a significant medical or life threatening event or know someone who has and you were involved with them through the process, you understand the emotional turmoil. You now have "prior experience."

My wife was diagnosed with cancer during the summer of 2011. It was a shocking experience for her. An experience she couldn't believe was happening to her. Her course of treatment included six weeks of radiation therapy; five days a week. This was coupled with a week of chemotherapy during the first week of radiation therapy and a week of chemo during the last week of her radiation treatments. In January 2012, she got a clean bill of health from her physicians, but will need periodic follow up visits and certain tests performed over the next couple of years as her physicians monitor her health. As anyone who has gone through this knows the side effects can be brutal. Hers' were bad during the last half of treatments. Mid-way through my wife's process, one of my son's experienced a cancer scare of his own. Fortunately, cancer was eventually ruled out six weeks later after monitoring and multiple ultrasounds.

Cancer is a catastrophic health care event for anyone who is diagnosed with it. There are only three outcomes.

1. Go through the radiation and chemo treatments and you're "cured".
2. The cancer goes into remission.
3. Go through all the treatment protocols and procedures and to no avail they don't work and you eventually succumb to the cancer.

Before all this happened in my immediate family, my niece had multiple forms of cancer, all in a period of five years. Some forms were quite rare. For a while she was fine. Unfortunately, her cancer reappeared in late 2012 and she passed away on January 1, 2013. She was only 49 years of age. My sister (her mother) was diagnosed with lung cancer (she smoked her entire adult life) in early January 2009. She underwent treatments but passed away within 2 months of her diagnosis in February 2009.

Having a family member experience cancer or any major medical event can be a financial nightmare if you do not have adequate health coverage. What can be the cost of a major medical event such as the cancer my wife had? During her ordeal she had medical procedures done at two different hospitals on multiple occasions and at one out-patient surgery facility. She was treated by three different medical specialists; gastrointestinal, radiation oncologist and chemotherapy oncologist. She had radiation therapy, had blood labs done constantly along with a few other procedures such as PET scans and colonoscopies. The aggregate costs she incurred as a result of her cancer are listed below.

- Total Health Care Costs Billed: $135,000
- Health Insurance Negotiated Adjustments: $49,000
- Payments Made by Her Insurance: $78,000
- Our Out of Pocket Expenses: $8,000

We only had one surprise regarding her health insurance coverage and billing. Copays and coinsurance expenses did not count towards the out-of-pocket maximum expenses. Those daily copays can add up quite quickly. If she didn't have health insurance, we would have been responsible for the entire billed amount. This medical event would have been catastrophic for our personal financial situation. In fact, health care expenses after a catastrophic medical event are a major reason why some individuals are forced to file for bankruptcy protection.

Choosing your health care options can be a challenging and time consuming process to go through. Thinking about the scope of services you've needed during the past year, how much you've spent and what you may need in the coming year is just too much effort for many of us to go through. My advice; sit down together and take the time to understand the health coverage you have and is it adequate for your current health? You just never know when a medical disaster will strike.

About the Author

Stephen J. Stellhorn is the founder of MSM Capital Management, LLC (MSM). His financial services career spans over twenty-five years in banking, investments and insurance. He has held positions in retail and institutional bond sales, fixed income portfolio management, U.S. Government bond trading, bank balance sheet management, brokerage branch sales management and insurance and financial planning.

The retirement model in the 21st century will be designed by collaborating with clients to assist them in developing a blueprint for understanding and efficiently utilizing their personal capital. When optimized, these capital sources; human, social and financial work synergistically to create a floor of income to offset "essential" expenses no matter what market conditions exist. This holistic approach to longevity planning is vastly different from traditional investment and retirement planning.

MSM's focus is personal capital management. Working together with clients, an assessment of their personal capital is established. From there, a plan is created for retirement income sustainability. This plan integrates both health care and social security planning. This approach ensures clients have an objective and unbiased assessment of where they are at and what action steps may need to be taken. As a solutions integrator, MSM provides Medicare health plans, health, dental, life, long-term care and final expense insurance along with annuities. For further information, visit www.msmcapital.net.

Stellhorn holds the Retirement Management Analyst (RMA℠) designation through the Retirement Income Industry Association® (RIIA®), of which he is an individual member. He has passed the FINRA securities exams for the Series 7, 8, 24, 4, 27, 55, 63 and 65, and also the MSRB securities exams for the Series 52 and 53. Stellhorn has also passed the State of Florida Life, Health & Variable Annuity 2-15 insurance exam. He is a Florida licensed insurance agent, appointed with a number of insurance carriers.

He has also completed the Retirement Management Analyst Program at Boston University's Center for Professional Education. He completed and received a Certificate in Financial Planning from Kaplan University. He is a graduate of The Florida State University; earning dual Bachelor of Science degrees in International Business and Biological Science. Stellhorn is a member of the fraternity of Phi Gamma Delta.

Past firms he has been associated with include Waddell & Reed Financial Advisors, AXA Advisors, LLC, Charles Schwab & Co., ABN AMRO North America, European American Bank (EAB), NCNB, Pan American Bank, Mabon Nugent & Co. and Southeast Bank.

He resides in Tampa, Florida with his lovely wife Linda, three boomeranging college students and his beloved Shih Tzu Jagger.

Index

www.ingramcontent.com/pod-product-compliance
Lightning Source LLC
Chambersburg PA
CBHW070759280326
41934CB00012B/2980